ON THE RACING ROAD

The Ultimate Journey to the Racecourses of the World

Nicholas Godfrey

A **RACING POST** COMPANY

To my Dad, who would have considered it the greatest book in the history of literature. He didn't read much.

KIRKLEES CULTURAL AND LEISURE SERVICES	
250 595 280	
Askews	28-Jan-2008
798.4	£15.99
TL	CUL44115

Cover photographs

Front: Birdsville, stuck in the middle of nowhere (© Jane Godfrey); Saint Liam wins Breeders' Cup Classic (© Racing Post/Edward Whitaker); Frankie Dettori surrounded by photographers after winning Japan Cup on Alkaased (©Jane Godfrey); racehorse trainer in Vietnam (© Jane Godfrey) Back: Racing at La Gavea, Rio (© Jane Godfrey); Deep Impact garlanded after winning Satsuki Sho (©Japan Racing Association); author ready for the road (© Racing Post).

Published in 2007 by Highdown
an imprint of Raceform Ltd
Compton, Newbury, Berkshire, RG20 6NL

A catalogue record for this book is available from the British Library.

ISBN 978-1-905156-31-3

Cover designed by Tracey Scarlett and Adrian Morrish

Interiors designed by Fiona Pike

Printed in Great Britain by Cromwell Press, Trowbridge

CONTENTS

You've always been searching for something

KEVIN ROWLAND

INTRODUCTION

DO not be misled. This, the first thing you are reading, was the last thing to be written.

My publishers requested an introduction to outline the motivation behind a trip that will probably be billed as an incredible journey or something like that. Such an explanation, it seems, is meant to imbue the text with a necessary human element. I am supposed to explain why someone with a senior job at the *Racing Post* would decide, after 16 years with Britain's racing daily, to step down from his position to spend more than eight months on a quixotic-sounding adventure travelling the world chasing after racehorses.

That's what they want. Ask me why and I'll spit in your eye, is what I feel like saying. Who *wouldn't* want to leave the mundanities of everyday life for an extended period experiencing different cultures and environments? If you really need to ask why, then it is unlikely you will be reading this book.

However, it seems that simply quoting Morrissey won't wash, and I delayed writing this introduction until it really could not be avoided any longer. The truth is I don't know specifically why, in March 2005, I set off around the world on an eight-month trip, accompanied by my wife Jane and her camera. At 37, I was still a tad on the youngish side for a midlife crisis. It was a dirty job, I suppose, but someone had to do it. Why me precisely? Well, at the risk of sounding a prosaic note, there was a fairly straightforward explanation: I like visiting other places and I like horse racing. Surely there could be few more enticing prospects than combining the two?

Still, though, that feels inadequate. There must have been more to it than that, and we are going to need some personal stuff here to articulate it a little better. Skip to the second part of this introduction if you don't fancy it.

OK, if you're still here, we had better get this straight from the start. I don't just like horse racing. I am passionate about it. My father was a betting-shop manager in Roehampton, near Putney in South London, for the last 25 years of his life, which probably explains how someone with no equine background whatsoever ended up as obsessed by horse racing and betting as he was by football, pop music and literature. Or, more specifically, Wimbledon FC, punk rock and its aftermath, US super-hero comics, and (a few years later) American beat writers.

Alongside Dons striker Alan Cork and the Green Arrow, my heroes were trainer Henry Cecil and jockey Geoff Lewis and, much more than any of the humans, Mill Reef, Tingle Creek and Monksfield. I visited racecourses like Brighton, Fontwell, Epsom and Sandown from a tender age, often with my nan, who figured among the fiercest critics of "that cowson Lester Piggott". My mum, on the other hand, was a betting-shop counterhand who disliked racing and actually used to sit reading a book in the car park for four hours while the rest of us enjoyed an afternoon at the track. Dad used to check on her midway through the card. I think.

Such antecedents might explain how I came to be hosting mock race meetings on the front-room carpet, using bits of paper fashioned from old show sheets brought home by my father for this specific purpose. These were the lists of runners on which betting-shop boardmen would ink current odds in marker pen back in the days when computerised betting screens and live pictures were just a twinkle in the eye of someone at Ladbrokes. I cut up these show sheets to leave slips of paper bearing the names of individual horses and framed my own races, propelling the names across the floor, one pace a furlong, for hours on end. For jumps, I threw these slips over felt-tip pens for hurdles, and books for fences; if they turned over, they were deemed to have fallen – and I ensured no-one missed the action by offering my own commentaries. As could probably go without saying, I was an only child, well used to finding solace in solitary pleasures, which came in handy in later years, particularly as a teenager when Debbie Harry was a regular on the TV!

I loved my dad's shop – and while he was the manager, not the owner, it was definitely *his* shop. I worked there under-age for years as a boardman before moving on to the counter; once I turned 18 I joined the Mecca bookmakers' 'pool', manning various outlets around West London, from the Goldhawk Road and Hammersmith, to Kingston and back home in Wimbledon.

Not allowed to bet in our own shop, we used to go to Glaswegian Alec's, the independent outlet around the corner. Sometimes this meant I ended up working for nothing unless it was a good day for Henry Cecil and Steve Cauthen, the brilliant American who revolutionised race-riding in Europe in the 1980s with his excellence in the realm of pace-making. As Cecil and Cauthen often had good days, work wasn't as financially unrewarding as might be imagined. It was in the cramped back room of the shop that I watched Slip Anchor win the Derby in 1985, and Dancing Brave lose it in 1986, on a tiny black-and-white television perched next to a mountain of betting slips waiting to be settled. It took Dad a bit longer the first time; on the second occasion, all he had to do was cross most of them out. Not that he was pleased at the ease of his labour. Thanks to my naïve conviction that Dancing Brave could never be beaten, we had both done our money at Alec's. "He's not gonna get there, Nick," winced my father at the telly, more upset for me than himself. I will never forget it.

I even remember the date of his death in racing terms. Having worked in the same shop from the early days of legalised off-course betting outlets, from the independent two-shop chain Joe Mack to Williams and Mecca, he never made it to William Hill. He died on the morning of Garrison Savannah's victory in the Cheltenham Gold Cup in March 1991. By then, I had been working at the *Racing Post* for a year and a half. It wasn't a lifelong ambition to be a racing journalist; I didn't have some epiphany when I was 12 or anything like that. In some respects it was a career choice totally lacking in imagination. If I had had my way, I would have been a racehorse trainer, but lack of any experience whatsoever in the field of equine husbandry seemed a hindrance. Jesus Christ would have better qualifications for that particular occupation. At least he was born in a stable.

Despite pole-axing personality deficiencies in certain crucial areas, I was an exam machine, having got into Oxford – evidently they were positively discriminating in favour of state-school applicants at the time – before eventually managing to obtain a military-medium 2:1 degree in English. It was a rude awakening to learn that simply getting into the university wasn't an end in itself and I was expected to find a job afterwards. The types of occupation that seemed to be offered to every

Oxbridge graduate in the 1980s weren't immediately attractive to a devotee of left-field literature and wonky independent rock music. Even if I had wanted to, I would never have cut the mustard in merchant banking and management consulting or advertising and marketing. And I didn't want to.

So I wrote to the *Racing Post*. It seemed obvious: I could just about string a sentence together, I had been president of the Oxford University Turf Society (in essence a punters' club, not to be confused wuth the hunt club) and I knew racing inside out, or thought I did. It worked out fine. I have never worked anywhere else since arriving at the paper as a trainee sub-editor directly from university in September 1989, the month the St Leger meeting at Doncaster was curtailed when horses started falling down drains. The salary was £10,000 a year – although it sounds poor, it beat hands down the £6,600 offered by Raceform.

While I might not host my own race meetings on the sitting-room carpet any more (well, not often), I remain worryingly obsessive about the sport – and I mean the sport itself, rather than any of the unfortunate social connotations that horse racing still engenders in certain quarters. Racing's traditional nickname may be historically accurate, for it most certainly was the 'Sport of Kings', but in the modern era it is little more than an anachronism, an unhelpful misnomer implying an air of snobbish social exclusion that offers little obvious benefit in image terms. Racing is the province of princes and paupers, pissheads and priests, while alliteration is the refuge of lazy writers.

I had various roles during my first decade and a half at the *Racing Post*, notably front-line reporting on some of the major events in racing's recent past, among them Frankie Dettori's 'Magnificent Seven', the postponed Grand National, Dubai Millennium's World Cup and a couple of Triple Crown derailings in the States courtesy of Funny Cide and Smarty Jones. At times this was a dream job, but it is also ancient history; for many years now I have been virtually office-bound, promoted into more organisational editorial roles when the paper merged with the *Sporting Life* in 1998.

It was around five years later that I hit upon the germ of an idea to seek out the sport in far-flung corners of the globe and find out how it compared to the original, British model. It seemed impossibly romantic. It wasn't. The hardest part was the initial decision to go – and there my hand was forced to an extent by certain practical considerations.

Both Jane and I were, and remain, keen to live and work abroad. Such opportunities do not make themselves available every day, however, and I am fairly choosy, having once turned down the chance to work as a racing reporter in Hong Kong. Fun to visit, I never fancied living there permanently, although I have friends who enjoyed themselves there and certainly gave the lie to the nasty old acronym about the territory's attracting only expatriate 'filth' ('Failed in London? Try Hong Kong').

Gradually, over several evenings and enough bottles of beer at a Ladbroke Grove bar, we arrived at the realisation that perhaps the best we could manage was a temporary period away, probably a few months. Push unexpectedly came to shove in the summer of 2004. Jane worked as personal assistant to the Tote chairman Peter Jones. The organisation closed its London office, a stone's throw from our Putney flat, to move lock, stock and barrel to its bigger base in Wigan. There was no way Jane was going with them, and she was entitled to a redundancy payment the following year when the relocation was due to go ahead.

For my part, commuting two hours a day standing up on the London underground to the confines of a Canary Wharf office building was beginning to lose its lustre, while the utter frustration of office politics had taken a hefty toll. Even newspapers employ people who use risible management-speak like 'blue-sky thinking' and 'brainstorming' without a trace of irony – and then exhort their workforce to think 'outside the box'. Obviously that sentiment doesn't apply to their vocabulary.

While these gripes were the same as those of a million other office workers, they played their role in our grasping the nettle. As, indeed, did a creeping sense of alienation from some of my colleagues. I always think a nickname is a sign of social inclusion. I had been called 'Einstein' or 'Alby' by nearly all those who had known me from my earliest days at the paper. Yet when I mentioned this to someone I hadn't known nearly as long, he said: "The thing is, Nick, I have never heard anyone call you that."

Plainly, it was time to get away. Instead of Jane's searching for another job, we decided it was now or never. Although saving has never been a vice of mine, I got together enough to make some sort of extended trip a viable proposition. It was late in 2004 that I hit upon the concept of combining work with pleasure and thankfully *Racing Post* editor Chris Smith, a close friend (who does occasionally call me 'Einst'), was enthusiastic, and pledged to ensure a job when I returned. This was just as well as I couldn't have afforded to resign, even if I had wanted to. A huge salary cut seemed a small price to pay for what was in store. I was going to write about whatever I found; Jane, who has no claims to being anything other than an amateur photographer, would take the pictures. I was to stay on the staff of the *Racing Post*, demoting myself from the role of deputy editor to weekly columnist, and the paper would pay me a salary equivalent to one day a week for an article of about 1,200 words from wherever we were.

The series would be called *On The Racing Road* as a nod to the Jack Kerouac novel that had influenced generations of impressionable readers. For some reason, the title mattered. I thought it explained everything. Maybe it does.

*

HORSE RACING, in one form or another, exists virtually everywhere. Admittedly, it is not always of the thoroughbred variety that dominates in major racing nations, but that particular breed is only a relatively recent construct. It dates back to the 17th and early 18th centuries, when three stallions – known as the Byerley Turk, the Darley Arabian, and the Godolphin Barb – were imported into Britain from the Middle East and North Africa. Breeding with British mares, they produced racehorses noted for their speed and endurance.

Although every modern thoroughbred horse can be traced back to one of those three stallions in the male line, organised horse racing as a whole is considerably older than the man-made thoroughbred. Chariot racing and bareback mounted races were both popular public entertainments for the Greeks and the Romans; horsemanship was highly developed in ancient civilizations like Persia and Arabia. Horse racing might have been exported alongside Britain's imperial ambitions to lay the foundations of the modern version of the sport in various corners of the globe, but its true origins were elsewhere.

While I am really only interested in thoroughbreds, I had no intention of being too choosy in that respect on the racing road. Other hybrids remain popular, like pure-bred Arab horses (small and slow compared to the thoroughbred), quarter horses (powerful types bred to race for just 440 yards) and trotters (a different breed who pull chariots in harness races). Pony racing is popular in Ireland and they race mounted mules at American county fairs. Every February at St Moritz, thoroughbreds pull skiers for a mile and three-quarters across a frozen lake in the Nordic sport of *skikjoring*, while 'heavy' horses drag along huge weights in Japan's *ban-ei* races. It would not surprise me to learn that there is a thriving zebra-racing community somewhere on the earth, where the field pulls along warthogs ridden by specially trained monkeys.

Mind you, I didn't find it. Perhaps it was located in one of the many countries I decided would not be featuring on my itinerary after regular visits to the Foreign and Commonwealth Office website in the six months preceding departure. At the time, the three strife-torn African nations that headed the FO's 'Don't Go There' list were Ivory Coast (terrorism, crime, political situation), Somalia (terrorism/security, crime, health) and Togo (political situation). Fortunately, none of them were renowned for their horse-racing community.

If danger was involved, rest assured, I had no intention of going there. War zones, extant or incipient, and terrorist hotspots would not be featuring, not even if there was a fair chance of running into the reincarnation of Phar Lap ridden by Lester Piggott.

Anywhere with excessive risk of crime to the person or severe health risks was also off-limits. Becoming a kidnap target had never been a particular ambition of mine, while I wasn't too struck on the idea of pestilence, plague or famine, either. There were no delusions: I felt like a holidaymaker on a self-indulgent busman's, not John Pilger.

For reasons of self-preservation, there were several nations where racing certainly exists that were definitely off the agenda. Colombia and Zimbabwe for a start, and Iraq, where Baghdad's Al-Amiryia racetrack was said to have been taken over by the local 'mafia' and become a target for Islamic fundamentalists opposed to gambling. It was a far cry from the old days, when it has been reported that Uday Hussein's uncle, having watched one of his horses narrowly beaten, snatched the reins of the winning horse and twisted them around the neck of its jockey, whom he dragged around the track and beat mercilessly.

I had a tip-off about the former Soviet republic of Kyrgyztan, where it appeared that Askar Akayev, the nation's long-time despotic ruler, had constructed a monument to himself in the form of a gilded racetrack on the outskirts of the city, where it was somewhat at odds with the surrounding area. Further research revealed that this (relatively) opulent hippodrome sometimes boasted some unusual equestrian attractions alongside the regular racing, like horseback wrestling, *kyz-kumay* ('kiss the girl', where, evidently, men gallop after women and get a slap if they fail to catch them, a kiss if they do) and *ulak tartysh* ('baby goat pulling' – two teams on horseback try to take possession of a goat carcass and score points by tossing it into a large container). The website that provided details of these and other Kyrgyz equine pastimes likened the goat-chucking to polo, but you really can't trust plenty of things that turn up on the internet – and since the autocratic Akayev was overthrown just before I left, putting the country on the brink of civil war, I had no plans to verify it.

Purely for logistical reasons, Mongolia was off the list as well, despite the fine efforts of their diplomatic envoy who visited the Cheltenham Festival in 2005 to support the novice chaser Ulaan Bataar, named after his nation's capital. He came out of the woodwork a little too late since, sadly, I was going nowhere near his horse-loving nation and its 20-mile Flat races. In late 2006, plans were announced for a more conventional racetrack close to Mongolia's central airport, so never say never.

By now, after this extensive list of racing nations to swerve, you could be forgiven for wondering exactly where beyond the exotic confines of Catterick Bridge and Cartmel I was planning to visit. There were plenty of places left: the racing road took me to four continents, where I was to attend some of the best-known races in the world at some of its finest racecourses. Plus a few that were a bit further off the beaten track, headed by Birdsville, miles away from anywhere in the middle of the Australian Outback. This once-a-year meeting provided the centrepiece for the entire trip after I noticed it figuring at number 36 in the *Rough Guide*'s '45 Things Not To Miss' in Australia. I had never even heard of this evidently celebrated racecourse, so it seemed like a good idea to find out.

Generally speaking, the trip was structured around certain major race meetings I hadn't seen live before, such as the Preakness Stakes at Pimlico in Baltimore in May, the one leg of the American Triple Crown I had yet to attend, and both Saratoga and Del Mar, the two best-loved of all US racecourses. The Nakayama Grand Jump was another race that had long since intrigued me, while the Breeders' Cup, still the world's most prestigious race meeting, provided a natural climax at Belmont Park in New York in early November, although I had been there a few times previously. Going to the Breeders' Cup meant missing the Melbourne Cup, with which it always clashes, but if finances held out, I intended to try to get to the Japan Cup four weeks later in Tokyo. Even this fairly short list of 'must-see' races demanded a circuitous route verging on the barmy, with three separate stints in the US and two in Japan. In the end, I travelled completely around the world three times – and even then missed out fantastic events that I had seen before, like the Dubai World Cup and the Kentucky Derby, arguably the best of them all.

The first four months or so were planned in meticulous fashion, with various non-racing excursions – a fortnight's tour in China here, ten days in Rajasthan there – scheduled to allow for visits to nearby race meetings. In this book, I have included only a few scene-setting details unrelated to horse racing: this is intended as a racing-based travelogue rather than a personal holiday diary. Anyone wanting details of how to book a trip to Machu Picchu shouldn't expect to find them here; they might, however, learn what it is like to go racing in Lima, with a bit of Peruvian racing history thrown in.

I also set myself another task. I wasn't foolish enough to think the trip might be subsidised by shrewd gambling, but I was determined to have a bet at every racecourse I visited. Just for research purposes. It is nice to have a sense of purpose.

A couple of weeks before I departed, a last-minute fillip was provided by the victories of horses like Hardy Eustace, Kicking King and especially Missed That at the Cheltenham Festival, prompting an upgrade in the quality of accommodation during the early part of the trip. A fortnight later, following months of flight-booking and visa-gathering, inoculations and stress-induced boils, I was ready to set out, with no higher purpose in mind than watching horse racing, and writing once a week about whatever equine-related matter I could find, wherever I found it.

My first piece appeared in the *Racing Post* in April 2005, underneath a suitable epigram from Oscar Wilde, who can always be relied upon on such occasions. "Some people cause happiness wherever they go, others whenever they go," it read. The piece was accompanied by a silly portrait of its author in clichéd traveller's garb of baseball cap, neckerchief and shorts, with a rucksack on my back.

I didn't see this photograph in the paper, though. By the time it was published, Jane and I were already in Bangkok. We had taken our first steps down the racing road.

A NOTE ON THE TEXT

Several of these chapters appeared, in vastly truncated form, in a series of articles in the Racing Post *in 2005.*

Most of the statistics at the beginning of each chapter come from figures supplied by member countries to the International Federation of Horseracing Authorities for the calendar year 2005 and are reproduced by permission. The exceptions are Thailand, for which information for 2004 was the most recent available, plus Vietnam, China, Trinidad, the Dominican Republic and the Philippines, where the figures were provided by local racing officials, hence their occasionally incomplete nature. Indeed, there were a few omissions in the IFHA statistics. Wherever possible, I have endeavoured to locate any missing data through inquiries to the nations concerned, although some figures can be regarded as only approximate.

Turnover and prize-money figures at the head of each chapter are converted to US dollars at the exchange rates used by international racing authorities for 2005. Each section is self-explanatory, with the possible exception of 'racehorses', which usually refers to the number of separate individual starters (i.e. different horses who ran at least once in the calendar year 2005).

Elsewhere in the written text I have offered sterling conversions where it felt appropriate to do so, given that this book is published in Britain. It seemed unnecessary to convert dollar amounts into sterling. Similarly, I have not religiously converted race distances, trusting the reader to know that 1,600 metres is an approximate metric mile. Generally I have employed the form of measurement favoured in the specific country I was visiting.

Although my wife Jane accompanied me almost everywhere, I have tended to use the first-person singular, preferring it to the royal 'we', which sounds rather twee. It is usually safe to assume, however, that Jane was there as well. She does, though, make more than the odd cameo appearance in the text in her role as photographer and was, of course, responsible for virtually all the pictures contained herein.

THAILAND

VITAL STATISTICS

RACING		FINANCE	
Racetracks	6	Total prize-money	$3.36m
Fixtures	52	Betting turnover	$66.75m
Races	480		
Racehorses	805		

All figures are for 2004; aside from number of racetracks, they refer to Bangkok only

BREEDING	
Stallions	45
Mares	489
Foals	189

CALL me old-fashioned if you like, but I have something of an aversion to dangerous firearms, which is why I really could have done without seeing that handgun.

OK, so there had been no suggestion of violence and the weapon wasn't pointed anywhere in my general direction. Yet in spite of these hopeful signs, the sudden, unexpected appearance of a heavy-duty pistol was about as reassuring as finding out that Gary Glitter had been left on playground duty.

Particularly when you consider that I was seated in the back of an armoured vehicle – a tank-like SUV complete with blacked-out windows, presumably bulletproof – wedged between a pair of sinister-looking Oriental heavies. Beefed-up and tooled-up, if they were not pissed-up as well, the same could certainly not be said of their boss, the mysterious leading player in this scenario, seated up front with his driver and my photographer as we crawled through the noxious traffic of a Central Bangkok evening en route to a drinking den somewhere in the bowels of the sleazy Patpong district.

This enigmatic figure directing operations had spent the previous few hours swallowing glass after glass of whisky at a Bangkok racecourse. Strong liquor can do funny things and it is not as if I had abstained, which may go some way to explaining how this suave, exceedingly generous racehorse owner seemed to have been transformed into a worryingly excitable Thai version of Mr. Big. In my mind, if nowhere else.

The man in charge, plainly used to getting his own way, was insistent when he suggested we headed downtown for further alcohol. It would have been rude to say no. But maybe if I had, then I wouldn't have had to ponder exactly how, barely four days into a round-the-world trip devoted to horse racing, I had unwittingly stumbled into a scene that would not have looked out of place in a Yakuza gangster movie.

*

THE Thais have a phrase for the hordes of unkempt westerners who visit Bangkok on a shoestring budget, making the place look untidy. *Farang kii nok*, they are called. Birdshit foreigners.

An extraordinarily diverse range of attractions ensures a glut of overseas visitors, birdshit or otherwise, to the sprawling, chaotic, compelling Thai capital. Culture junkies head for the ornate temples and corncob spires; the much-derided backpackers head for the cheap lodgings of Thanon Khao San, the 'Street of Uncooked Rice'; sex tourists still head for Patpong, spiritual home of the hoary anecdote and actual home of the 'Pussy Menu', on which a many and varied range of *à la carte* services is offered at reasonable prices for the discerning gentleman traveller.

It came as little surprise to discover that few of these visitors went racing. In general terms, the city is a young person's destination, and horse racing, certainly in Britain, is perceived as an old man's sport, its age demographic the stuff of a marketer's nightmare. Racing doesn't so much have an image as an image problem; its audience is less hip, more hip replacement.

I had never heard of anyone visiting Thailand for its horse racing and, given that the nation has never been close to achieving anything of note in the equine world, it probably wasn't the most obvious place to start, getting the nod on the basis of its long-held status as a mainstay on Asian itineraries. The country promised a gentle introduction, an environment alien enough to have made it interesting, but still offering a fairly comfortable prelude to anything potentially more challenging. And Thailand does have a well-established racing scene, which is how I came to find myself one of only a handful of non-Asian faces in a crowd of about 14,000 who endured the sweltering heat on a Sunday afternoon in late March 2005 at the Royal Turf Club's Nanglerng racecourse in the heart of Bangkok.

According to submissions made by the Bangkok racing authorities to the Asian Racing Conference – an annual meeting of representatives of the continent's main racing nations plus Australia, New Zealand and South Africa – racing in Thailand dates back to the closing years of the 19th century. Like it did in many other places, an organised version of the sport began as the result of British involvement. In 1892, an Englishman, one Franklin Hurst, was allowed to rent a piece of land for the purpose of hosting occasional horse races, alongside gymkhanas, cycle races and other pastimes.

Although Hurst's ground-breaking operation did not last long, it was only seven years before the next recorded instance of organised horse racing in Thailand, when a group of former European-based civil servants and students welcomed King Rama V back from a state visit with a race meeting in his honour. Carriage-pulling horses were used, and it seems the merry monarch enjoyed himself so much that he granted a request from a Mr A.E. Olaroffsky to establish a permanent club in Bangkok dedicated to the "improvement of the standard of horse breeding and race meetings".

In 1901, the royal charter was granted, and the Royal Bangkok Sports Club was born, situated where it stands today bang in the centre of the city at Pathumwan, visible from Ratchamdamri station on the Skytrain, the monorail system that dominates much of the Bangkok skyline. Although the Thai Derby takes place a couple of miles away at the Royal Turf Club, its older brother remains Thailand's premier horse racing venue, a venerable old country club whose members, according to the *Time Out City Guide*, "basically own or run the country".

The two tracks alternate in hosting ten-race cards nearly every weekend in Bangkok, and there are lesser circuits elsewhere, in places like the second city Chiang Mai and Khon Kaen in the north east. Other venues occasionally host more outlandish variations on a theme, like the once-a-year buffalo racing that takes place on the eastern seaboard at Chonburi as part of celebrations to mark the rice harvest. Evidently the lumbering beasts of burden race down a 110-metre track in groups of five or six, spurred on by riders wielding wooden sticks.

The Royal Turf Club, the track I visited, is located in the Dusit government district in the shadow of a flyover. It proved readily accessible, about a mile's walk from Ratchathewi Skytrain stop, though the ugliness of the clogged highways combined with the savage heat soon made me wish I had engaged a *tuktuk*, the classic three-wheeled, open-sided Thai conveyance, rather than playing chicken with the traffic.

Many of the regulars arrived on motorcycles, having threaded through the smog, while horses destined to race later in the day poked their heads out of primitive horseboxes, seemingly oblivious to the noise, fumes and exhausting midday temperatures.

Alongside some of Buddhism's most stunning architectural creations, Bangkok specialises in concrete monstrosities, among them the decaying Nanglerng grandstand. Although the entry fee was published at between 50 baht and 100 baht (the latter figure equated to about £1.35), the surcharge levied on foreigners pushed it up to 300 baht for a day pass to the equivalent of the members' enclosure, replete with air conditioning, restaurant and numerous TVs.

Thailand featured among the seven founder members of the Asian Racing Conference in Tokyo in 1960. However, despite its employing around 300,000 people, the standard of offerings is routinely dismal, a significant level or three beneath more obvious racing nations like Hong Kong, where racing is both hugely popular and a major contributor to the economy, or even Singapore, where the sport is properly organised and regulated, but seldom classy. In 2003, Thailand's most valuable race, the Thai Derby, was worth only around 1.88 million baht (at the time, approximately £25,000); on the day of my visit, the highlight was worth 400,000 baht (£5,300) in total. While that figure sounds derisory, I didn't have to visit many other countries to discover that it is by no means the worst in prize-money terms.

Little quality, then, and even less variety. The first race, scheduled to start at 12.20pm, was a 1,200-metre handicap – and so were each of the other nine on a card scheduled to end at 5.35pm, all of them beginning in the six-furlong chute on the far side of a tight, one-mile round turf circuit. Longer contests were seemingly few and far between once the hot, dry season hit Bangkok.

Not that this uniformity bothered the vociferous locals who inhabited the main stand, lured by one of the few opportunities for betting legally in Thailand, where only horse racing (on-course alone), *muay thai* (kick-boxing, the gruesome national sport) and the lottery were exempt from gambling bans.

In spite of legislative efforts to the contrary, however, betting remained a hit with the Thais, just as it is with huge swathes of Asia, and reports suggested the nation had a colossal black-market betting economy. A 1999 study estimated that around 70 per cent of Thai adults gambled regularly, betting a total of possibly over 200 billion baht a year. Though the accuracy of such an immense figure cannot be verified, it equates roughly to around $6 billion, nearly 100 times the amount bet legally on horses. Clearly, it was a fair amount. Warlords were said to own casinos operating on the Burmese side of the Mekong river, while both cockfighting and Premiership football were massively popular with the illegal bookmakers. They were even said to take bets on the buffalo when the mood took them.

Officially, though, the sole legal place to bet was the racecourse tote, at a minimum of 50 baht stake, simple win and place wagers only. It seemed this lack of choice would make for a tiny betting pool for the opening race, ahead of which I moved into the main stand to mix with the *hoi polloi*. It was a strange scene: the betting windows remained inactive until a couple of minutes before the appointed start-time, when the figures on the board started to move dramatically.

Hardly anyone had a bet until close to the off – and post-times, it soon emerged, were works of utter fiction. The polar icecap could have melted during the time horses were kept in the starting gate. Thoroughbred racehorses are often fractious animals and even the most placid might not necessarily have enjoyed being detained in the confined space of a starting stall for such an extended period. Such worries, though, meant nothing to the Thais. Later on, the field for one particular race was installed for upwards of 20 minutes – so long, indeed, that two jockeys took the chance to jump off and urinate in the trees next to the back straight.

Later, I was informed that the horses were deliberately held in the stalls until there was a worthwhile amount in the pool, which went a long way to explaining why the card was to finish 80 minutes late, under floodlights. Regardless of the illegal market, we were not talking peanuts: official figures published in 2002 suggested the average turnover for a day's racing was 70 million baht, which meant an average of roughly £95,000 per race.

Such ridiculous delays habitually resulted in ragged starts – maybe the participants nodded off – and it was by no means a rarity to see a furlong between first and last before the runners had reached even halfway. Race times, as shown in the racecard, differed markedly, from around 1min 13sec for the best to well over 1min 20sec – a huge difference in sprinting terms. This was unusual to someone used to better-quality racing in Europe, and not a little suspicious. Clearly, there were some seriously poor horses on show, but there may well have been a more unsavoury reason for the violent late betting moves, habitual delays and ragged races, given that Thai racing was reputed to be among the most corrupt in Asia.

According to an article published in *Newsweek International* in 2002, such dramatic late market moves were indicative of a racing system that was far from straight. "That is the telltale sign that owners, snug in their VIP boxes, have placed bets on certain horses, knowing in advance that the other jockeys have been instructed to lose," said the magazine, which alleged rampant backroom deals and lax drugs testing, particularly with regard to what it described as "drowsy, doped-up losers". If this was anywhere near accurate, even when the betting was straight, as in taxably legal rather than illegal, it was actually bent.

None of this seemed to concern the locals who, after a delay of only ten minutes ahead of the first contest, weren't slow to offer encouragement. Some, like their counterparts in Britain, huddled underneath TV screens; others started up a football-style chant almost as soon as the stalls opened, rising to a climax when the runners hit the furlong-and-a-half run-in. The result was popular, a victory for the heavily backed odds-on favourite.

Having found an English-language formcard ahead of the second race, it was time to start betting. The runners moved out onto the track as soon as the previous race was over, having been walked around the sand circle that acts as a rudimentary paddock for half an hour before that. Jockeys, declared only just before the race, therefore could not ride two in a row.

After many seconds' scrutiny of the fairly detailed form carried in *Siam Racing*, I plumped for a horse named Cheeseburger – well, it said Cheeseburger in *Siam Racing*; the translation in the Thai racecard suggested Cheese Baker – who was showing at 5-1 five minutes before the off. The tote teller, having accepted my money, said something that sounded worryingly close to "never mind". I could see why as Cheeseburger's odds lengthened quickly to 25-1. This drifter was unlikely to end up in any Thai punter's little red book. After such an unpromising market move, it was less than surprising to see Cheese Burger (or Baker) finish a hard-pushed sixth of ten. Ever get the feeling someone knows something you don't?

Shortly before my polo shirt melted in the heat, I returned to the more exclusive, air-conditioned members' enclosure, full of racehorse owners, many of them former army and police generals or members of the royal family. It was here, thanks to a helpful policeman midway through the marathon seven-hour card, that I was directed to the table of a well-fed, well-heeled character in his 40s who looked more Hawaiian than Thai. Let's just call him Michael. Offering his hand with a 'hail-fellow-well-met' gesture, my new friend revealed he was one of the top five owners in Thailand and, it soon transpired, a lover of England and all things English. Even journalists.

A fluent English speaker, Michael owned a house in St John's Wood that he rented out to an American banker. I inquired into his line of business. "You know, import/export," he replied. I didn't really know, but later he elucidated a little, saying he traded in Thai silk and cutlery. Michael's passion, though, besides the football team he described as "Chelski", was racehorses. "I am one of Thailand's biggest owner-breeders," he revealed. "I have about 50 horses – it costs me millions of baht a month."

At the time, there were about 70 baht to the pound, and Michael was clearly not short of them: his horses arrived at the track in the only thing we would recognise as a horsebox fit for transporting racehorses in Britain, emblazoned with his stable name 'VPP' on the side.

Despite Michael's friendliness, after ten minutes of chit-chat, often interrupted by the ring of his mobile phone, I was not entirely sure what I was getting myself into. As cheeses go, Michael was definitely among the big ones. Everyone within earshot deferred to him, and he was surrounded by a group of thickset, shifty-looking individuals, who seemed to do little other than take turns pouring his drinks. Michael, joviality itself, described them as his bodyguards. As I was puzzling over what it was that should make the silk trade so dangerous that it required so many minders to ensure the safety of a business magnate at a racetrack, Michael shifted one of his entourage to clear a space at his table for me. Now I was his guest: he ordered lunch and a Heineken for me, and lit up a cigar so huge it entered the realms of comedy. I was worried it might explode. Michael took more calls on his mobile, knocked back a big Scotch. Several passers-by were introduced, all of them generals, colonels, or, in one case, a superintendent. "I used to be a policeman," explained Michael, adding without any obvious sign of humility, "he was my boss; now I am his boss."

Many of Michael's associates had something to do with the racetrack but there was no doubt who was calling the shots. The boss's mobile phone rang non-stop ahead of one particular race, the seventh 1,200-metre handicap of the afternoon, in which he had a fancied runner named Porn Sopa. The champion jockey, Numsuk (a request for a first name received blank looks, which demonstrated the status of the role in Thai racing circles), was riding him, because Michael's regular rider had been sent up to the northern circuit to 'cool off' after some gambling problems.

Michael took control of the remote control to assess the betting screen, telling me to back his horse. "She won ten lengths on the sand last week in the north," he said, all but commanding me to have a bet. I didn't need telling twice. On a racecourse where I had no idea about the horses or the form, where the racing was allegedly a bigger stitch-up than Robert Maxwell's pension advice, and one of the nation's leading owners was telling me to have a bet on his horse? Yes sir, I think I can manage that.

Porn Sopa was favourite, a status depicted in red on the tote board. Let's not get carried away – money was going to be tight on this trip, so I parted with just 2,000 baht – nearly £30 – encouraged by an odds board that showed her to be strong favourite in a field of 14, five of whom were showing at the maximum 999-1. A slight drift before the off – 20 minutes late, as per Thai custom – meant that she started a 1-3 shot.

After the long wait, Porn Sopa virtually fell out of stall three (was the rider Numsuk or Numbnuts?), carried her head awkwardly high and ran greenly throughout. All was not lost, though, as Numsuk applied the whip liberally, and the partnership flew down the straight to cheers from our end of the enclosure. It was bear hugs all round from Michael as his green-and-orange silks flashed in front of us alongside another horse in a photo-finish. There was a bit of a snag, though. "I don't know what all the fuss is about," I whispered to my photographer, who had joined us. "She's obviously been beaten."

Porn Sopa's dilatory effort failed by a short head, yet the verdict did not dampen my host's enthusiasm. Indeed, he seemed more concerned that I had lost money on his horse than anything else, which might have had something to do with the huge wad of baht someone pressed into his hand just after the result was announced.

Unabashed, Michael told me to retrieve my losses in the final race on another of his horses, Lady Bangkok. "Confidence," he laughed, like many people in a nation that markets itself as the 'Land of Smiles'.

A 14-year-old boy arrived at our table: it was Sittidej, rider of Lady Bangkok, who was actually in his 20s. After another Scotch, an increasingly effusive Michael offered detailed instructions, mainly focusing on riding a strong finish – "bang, bang, bang", he repeatedly advised his rider, miming a passable whip action of his own.

The lights were switched on by the time we finally reached Lady Bangkok's race, scheduled for 5.35pm but off 80 minutes late. She was an 8-1 chance; I backed her win and place. Michael's mobile went mad and he slugged another shot of spirits.

Just like Numsuk, Sittidej also missed the break, but after a bit of bang, bang, bang – accompanied by a sustained two-furlong chant of "Lay-dee, Lay-dee" from our table – the filly snatched second. "If she had won, I could have bought a new yacht," said Michael, who, as always, looked pleased with the outcome. He said he had won a little – a little more than my 300 baht profit, I would imagine. That might just about have run to a rubber ring. Once a birdshit foreigner, always a birdshit foreigner, I suppose.

After the race, a man sat down at the adjacent table with a betting ledger

– an illegal bookmaker, Michael told me, though the guy wasn't exactly incognito. Like everybody else, he deferred to Michael, and he was still there half an hour after the last, hanging around among about 20 people, including Sittidej and the heavies but no Numsuk. "They are all waiting for me to leave – they all work for me," explained Michael, as he waved the illegal bookies away down the track.

Finally we left the Royal Turf Club, Michael having insisted we move on for further drinks in Central Bangkok. The scene as we headed off into the night was bizarre indeed: Nanglerng's swarthy potentate strode off in regal fashion followed by a not-inconsiderable retinue, bestowing bank notes on everybody who crossed his path, most of them in uniform.

We didn't have to wait long into our journey for the handgun to make its unwonted appearance, Michael passing it back from the front seat to one of his henchmen for safe-keeping in the backseat of the armoured jeep. With hindsight, it possibly wasn't that unusual for a high-ranking ex-government official to have bodyguards and weaponry, but I wasn't thinking clearly. I didn't know what I had got myself into, and though it was a relief not to see the firearm again, the fun and games were not yet quite over. As we entered an upscale drinking establishment in Patpong, Michael grabbed Sittidej's whip and smashed it down on a mobile phone sitting on a nearby table. Although the phone was sent flying across the room in a thousand pieces, its owner raised barely a murmur of dissent.

Michael, though, ever the gracious, observant host, noticed my own agitation, which was hardly mollified by this latest development. "Nick, I'm sorry, I have scared you," he said, with a degree of understatement. "Please don't worry, I didn't mean to frighten you, he is my friend. You are my friend."

As I made my excuses and left, citing an early-morning flight (from Paranoia to Cambodia?), it struck me that you probably wouldn't want him as your enemy.

VIETNAM

VITAL STATISTICS

RACING		BREEDING
Racetracks	1	*No stud farms*
Fixtures	100	
Races	about 800	FINANCE
Racehorses	40 (600 ponies)	*Unavailable*

Approximate figures for 2005

VIETNAM was next up, but only after a few days spent in Cambodia, which really had no place on any tour devoted to horse racing, as there isn't any there. Yet the first few weeks had been organised in meticulous fashion, which resulted in enough time for a brief interlude in a country safe again for foreigners. Give or take the odd landmine.

Cambodia has developed a growing reputation as a holiday destination, most obviously as home to the magnificent Angkor Wat, the ancient former capital celebrated for its fantastically ornate termite-mound towers and multitudinous galleried temples. But if this was a wondrous spectacle, the phrase 'culture shock' could almost have been invented for the current capital Phnom Penh, much of which was a shanty town. On the plus side, it was reputed to be a place where you could "shoot things cheap" according to Jonny, my ever-enthusiastic travel agent. Presumably he was thinking of the AK-47s that were said to be in common currency.

Edgy and primitive, Phnom Penh appeared to straddle an uncomfortable line between beauty and degradation. Guidebooks point visitors to its mainstream tourist attractions such as the golden spires of the Royal Palace or the Silver Pagoda and its emerald buddha. Certain travellers, though, are more beguiled by other unique features, such as Phnom Penh's notorious wooden-shack brothels, or restaurants where an extra-happy meal means your pizza comes with ganja thrown in.

Beset by a prevailing 'coffee-money' culture of corruption, this poverty-stricken nation was struggling to get on its feet after decades of civil war and the grotesque excesses of the Khmer Rouge; the startling number of amputees on the streets of Phnom Penh was testimony to the latter's derangement.

Racing was unlikely to figure there for the foreseeable future. Cambodia's people had rather more pressing matters to worry about. I hadn't, a thought that struck with a degree of force as I sat sipping cocktails in the privileged colonial confines of the Foreign Correspondents' Club at Phnom Penh's tourist-friendly Sisowath Quay on the banks of the majestic Mekong.

About the most pressing thing I had to think about was catching a plane to neighbouring Vietnam, where they do have horse racing – but not horse racing as we know it. Not much of it, anyway.

*

EXTENSIVE renovations in 2004 made a fair job of the facilities at Ho Chi Minh City's Phu Tho racetrack, but there was a huge shock in store when the runners and riders emerged into the parade ring just after midday for the first of an eight-race card.

Everything was in miniature, with minuscule jockeys aboard tiny horses. The riders, all aged between 13 and 17, sported rudimentary colours and crash helmets far too big for them, which from a distance made their heads look grossly malformed. Their horses were Vietnamese-bred, descended mainly from Mongolian ancestors, and no bigger than Shetland ponies. Put horse and fledgling rider together, and they might not have been out of place at the pony-club games, though they were probably not turned out quite smartly enough to join the well-groomed youngsters and manicured mounts who represent the Wylie Valley or the Eglinton at Wembley for the Horse of the Year show. This scene was more reminiscent of a Donkey Derby at Butlin's.

Nonetheless, these healthy-looking, pocket-sized horses and grinning pint-sized schoolboy riders managed to provide one of the limited opportunities for Vietnamese nationals to gamble legally. Vietnam has moved a long way from the hard line since the Americans were kicked out in 1975 and the Communist government outlawed betting as a bourgeois decadence, but embracing a market economy has still produced only a handful of ways to punt and stay within the law. On production of a passport, foreigners can play slot machines in five-star hotels at the major cities or visit a casino, but at the time of my visit the locals were restricted to various lotteries, a greyhound track at the seaside resort of Vung Tau, and the ponies – plus, it emerged, a handful of thoroughbreds – at Phu Tho, the nation's sole racetrack.

It wasn't always like that. The French army brought horse racing to Vietnam in the 19th century. When Phu Tho, which means 'prosperity', was constructed in 1930 in Saigon's Chinatown district, Cho Lon, it was merely one of many racecourses in the country alongside others in cities such as Da Nang, Da Lat and Hanoi in the north, where Ho Chi Minh's Communists seized power in 1945 after leading resistance against the Japanese occupation.

Although historical details are sketchy where racing is concerned, one account suggests the horses originally used by the French were a hybrid Indochinese breed, said to contain strains of thoroughbred blood intermingled with other locals. Whatever they were, it seems these animals failed to survive the Second World War. There are conflicting accounts of their fate, suggesting they were either taken back to Japan by occupying forces or eaten by a starving people during a war-induced famine in 1945.

Though it cannot have done the horses any favours, the latter was nowhere near the worst of the degradations visited upon the Vietnamese during that particular period, as the eating of horsemeat is generally considered taboo in only anglophone countries. Tender, sweet, low in fat and high in protein, horsemeat is more to the taste of other less squeamish palates, even if we consider it appropriate only for household pets and the Belgians. In some places it is even regarded as a delicacy; in the US alone in 2005, more than 90,000 horses were slaughtered, for overseas consumption as well as for carnivores in zoos. Ex-racehorses undoubtedly provide a significant proportion of those finding their way on to the menu, and it is not always the completely useless among them who meet such a grisly end. Exceller, who achieved racing history when he beat a pair of US Triple Crown winners, Seattle Slew and Affirmed, in the Jockey Club Gold Cup at Belmont was killed at a Swedish slaughterhouse in 1998 after flopping at stud. In another high-profile case, Ferdinand, the 1986 Kentucky Derby winner, is thought to have ended up as pet food in Japan.

Back to Vietnam, compared to which few other nations can have spent so large a proportion of the last century involved in conflict of one form or another. Peace and tranquillity did not follow the Second World War; instead came Hanoi's eight-year struggle against the French that ended in 1954 with the division of the country into two separate nations, North and South.

Racing continued at Phu Tho in the latter's capital, much to the disgust of the Communist government in the North. To them, gambling was a beyond-the-pale pursuit, the racetrack's very existence in Saigon seen as yet another example of the city's bankrupt morality. It is not as if such affronts were in short supply in a place with a healthy reputation for sex, drugs and whatever came before rock 'n' roll, as Associated Press writer Kathy Wilhelm pointed out in a report from the racecourse a couple of years before I got there. "Phu Tho," Wilhelm suggested, "was built by French colonialists and for decades was just one stop on a glittering circuit of casinos, baccarat clubs and other houses of fortune that made the city a Sodom on the Saigon River in the eyes of the Communists in Hanoi."

Regardless of such ideological significance, Phu Tho also became a major strategic target during the Vietnam War. As well as being the hub of many streets, the dusty red oval also offered a perfect landing zone for helicopters. It saw heavy action during the crucial Tet offensive, and was captured by the Viet Cong. After the fall of Saigon in 1975 and the ignominious American withdrawal, the city was renamed after the father of the nation; Phu Tho was turned into a sports college.

Saigon stayed Ho Chi Minh City, but the racecourse did not remain a sports college for long. It was reopened as a racetrack in 1989, thereby becoming the reunited Vietnam's only horse-racing venue, a status it retained 16 years later when I dropped in for a visit. A multi-million-dollar project in Hanoi had stalled, while rumours of small-scale regional horse racing could not be substantiated.

Cho Lon, which houses Phu Tho, was about three miles from the centre of the highly commercialised metropolis formerly known as Saigon – and still known as Saigon at the track, run by the Saigon Racing Club, a joint venture between the government and a development company. Allowing Ho's name to be attached to a betting venue would have been one step too far, even for a government more interested in revenue than principle.

Unless you wished to risk taking your life in your hands on a Honda Om among the motorcycle-taxi brigade that swarms around a frenetic city, the best option for getting there was a more conventional four-wheeler. With US currency preferred to Vietnamese dong (even people who couldn't speak English seemed to be overly familiar with the word "dollar"), this cost me around $3 from the War Remnants Museum, which featured an intriguing collection of grisly artefacts. Among its most memorable exhibits was a series of grim photographs documenting wartime atrocities –among them scenes of GIs grinning proudly as they displayed decapitated Viet Cong heads, others depicting soldiers mutilated in the fighting and the aftermath of a napalm strike – displayed alongside pickled foetuses, horribly disfigured, a pleasant after-effect of Agent Orange. All in all, it made a nice double after the Toul Sleng Museum of Genocidal Crime, housed in a former Khmer Rouge prison in Phnom Penh.

Be careful if you ever fancy going racing in Vietnam. There is a large grandstand-like building in the general vicinity of where the racecourse should be, and you might be tempted to get out of your taxi there, particularly if your driver nods vigorously (as well as saying "dollar") when you ask "Phu Tho?" with the necessary rising inflection to indicate a shade of doubt. This is indeed Phu Tho: the Phu Tho swimming centre. The racetrack, however, is about a mile away. You will know you've arrived, after the garbage dump, when you get to the car park and its serried ranks of thousands of virtually identical motorcycles.

Open for business every Saturday and Sunday, the racetrack averages crowds of around 4,000, packed into a yellow-and-green grandstand, the shell of which is a relic from bygone colonial days. Its renovation was just one feature of an extensive development programme also involving the installation of closed-circuit TV, starting stalls and new running rails.

Entry prices ranged from a mere 5,000 Vietnamese dong (around 16p at the time), up to 50,000 dong for VIP admission, and double that for what must have been VVIP admission. No time for messing about here, I thought, doling out the required VKD100,000 (£3.30) without a second's hesitation to join the cream of Ho Chi Minh City's racing society in unexpectedly civilised surroundings on the other side of the turnstile. There were computerised tote screens, art-deco stylings on some of the awnings, a nice floral display in front of the stands, perspex windows – and an important escape from the crushing midday heat under the ceiling fans in the VVIP suite, where patrons were treated to a piped timpani medley of 'classics' like *Cherry Pink and Apple-Blossom White, Ob-La-Di, Ob-La-Da* and *Guantanamera*. All day long.

Here, petite waitresses in neat navy-blue suits brought drinks to customers seated in wide leather armchairs in a distinctly Raffles-like environment. If this lounge was tailored entirely for tourists, the locals had plenty of choice elsewhere in the stand, peeling pastel parts of which exuded a fading grandeur redolent of a former era. Out front, women in wide conical hats wandered about selling the national staple, noodle soup (*pho*) and sticky rice, while sugar-cane juice, iced coffee and corn on the cob also seemed popular with a shorts-and-sandals crowd.

When racing started, they were three deep around the parade ring to watch the tiny, smiling riders get legged up, some of them looking more than a shade precarious, which was hardly surprising given their relative inexperience. Perhaps they could have done with adhesive Velcro-like strips, like those I had witnessed many years previously in Dubai to help child riders maintain their precarious balance on racing camels, prized examples of which, despite their lumbering gait, are worth a sheikh's ransom. Often, these animals seemed more in control than their partners, and it wasn't a vastly different scenario in Vietnam at times, particularly before the third race when a horse bolted, heading off into the electricity substation next to the back straight – but not until he had thrown his novice rider and followed up with a nasty kick. A replacement was taken down to the start on a motorbike, his seat on the back of the motorised conveyance not noticeably more secure than his predecessor's on horseback.

The dusty racetrack itself was a rutted dirt oval almost a mile in circumference. They raced right-handed, at trips ranging from 1,000 metres to 1,400m on the day I visited, but the standard was laughable. Of the eight races carded, the first seven were for the ponies, trained by their owners, some of whom pedalled bicycles down the highways to the racecourse, leading their charges behind them to the racecourse on a length of rope. I was told that some of them come from as far as 25 miles away in this fashion; later, when considering a bet, it struck me that it might have been useful to know exactly which ones.

Weights to be carried in these races went up to only 40 kilos, much lighter than would be carried by proper racehorses. Prize-money was determined by the size of the betting pools, about ten per cent of which goes to the first three home. With only the equivalent of £10,000 bet on an average race, this meant they were racing for first prizes that seldom made four figures in sterling terms.

The contests themselves were shoddy, wildly ragged affairs, presumably tainted by corruption. A proportion of the competitors showed less inclination to run than Inzamam-ul-Haq called for a quick single in a Twenty20 match, and whichever horse broke the best always seemed to win – but generally not until the rider had whipped his mount from start to finish, allowing him to veer across the track from left to right, and back to left. In one particular race, a horse finished at a virtual standstill nearly 40 seconds behind the remainder. Not bad going for a five-and-a-half-furlong event that even a moderate thoroughbred would cover in little more than 70 seconds. For all this engaging nonsense, it was the eighth and final race that offered a glimpse of what racecourse officials hoped would be the future for racing in Vietnam. This was the day's only thoroughbred race, with experienced adult jockeys flown in from other countries to ride 11 horses from the consignment of 40 shipped the previous September from Australia, where they were bought for a total cost of $359,000 by Thien Ma, the management company behind the joint venture with the government. They were also involved with the dog track at Vung Tao, where their nerve centre housed a computerised betting centre ready to service further venues in the future.

First, though, they had to make a success of Phu Tho, and they seemed to have started well enough when Vietnam's sports-loving prime minister Vo Van Kiet attended the opening meeting for thoroughbreds in November 2004. In the six months that followed, 20 of the original 40 thoroughbreds were purchased by local owners. Another 160 horses were expected later in the year, and a specialised breeding centre was set up about 100 miles away in the Central Highlands of Lam Dong province.

All this was explained by Hsu King Hoe, the Malaysian deputy director of Saigon Racing Club, who went to Phu Tho after years at the impressive Selangor racecourse in Kuala Lumpur. Outlining his ambitions for Phu Tho over a backing track of an even lighter-weight version of something by Herb Alpert and his Tijuana Brass, Hsu proved to be quite a straight talker. "The racing here is ridiculous really – I couldn't pretend otherwise to a racing man," he said. "The Vietnamese love to bet, but I wouldn't say this was attractive to a racing man. The horses aren't properly trained; we don't have proper jockeys. We are trying to teach them, but they ride only at the weekend, and at the moment they have a very short riding career – anyone over 17 or 18 is too big and they're finished.

"We hope to upgrade to an international standard in the long term, but we can't expect to change things overnight," he added. "In the shorter term, our ambition is to upgrade the racing to a standard acceptable to the region, but there are times when you have to realise that this is a Third World city. At least we have 40 thoroughbreds now, and there will be more – the train is on the track but we have a long way to go."

Still, even if much of what I had seen at Phu Tho appeared faintly ludicrous, it used to be worse, much worse. Before the November 2004 relaunch, the track was reputed to be a dangerous place to visit, full of pickpockets and other scumbags. "It was very different here then," said Hsu. "It wasn't a nice place for people to come. There was rubbish everywhere, the grass was overgrown, and the place was like a public toilet – men just used to stand there and pee."

There was no running rail, photo-finish or betting terminals; the only wager available was the exacta, with every combination returning the same 5-1 payout. Since all the tickets were pre-printed, only a limited number were available for each combination. "When they ran out of the favourite combinations, everyone went to the illegal bookmakers," explained Hsu.

In Phu Tho's former life, these illegal bookies did little to conceal their activities, probably because they didn't need to, money speaking many languages, including that of Vietnamese officialdom. Corruption was endemic, with jockeys bribed to throw races, horses routinely doped and not routinely dope-tested. Starters had been known to deliberately drop the flag when a certain well-backed horse was facing the wrong way; even certain racegoers did their best to influence the result, sometimes hurling stones at the field during races.

While such egregious examples of rigged races may have become less common, I didn't have to wait long to discover that the betting market here, as in Thailand, felt more than a little suspicious. The sixth race, for example, provided the vehicle for a devious piece of manipulation. The hot favourite here was a horse called Quang Thanh, who never showed at bigger than 1-5 before the race on the screens. After he duly won by ten lengths from the second favourite, a startling dividend of VKD52.50 to a VKD10 stake was declared, which represented a price of just over 4-1, much bigger than logic suggested it should have been.

The exacta, a bet requiring punters to forecast first and second in the correct order, paid only even money. I was bemused, until a fellow VIP revealed there had been a late plunge on the runner-up in the win pool, too late to register pre-race on the screens. As there was little liquidity in the racecourse betting pool, it took virtually nothing to manipulate the odds to make him the actual favourite in front of the eventual winner, whose price drifted as a result. While this was easy enough to understand, I couldn't work out what was in it for the punters who had plunged on the runner-up – until I was told that illegal bookmakers often paid out according to the dividend as it was declared in the legitimate on-course pool. So for a relatively small outlay on a horse that didn't win, they could force out the price of the other horse, the one who should really have been a long-odds-on shot. Then, of course, they could plunge on him with the illegal bookmakers, and get a hugely inflated payout when the horse won.

"They'll have been hit badly," grinned my informant, who seemed to know plenty about such chicanery. He added that number two would win the last, the race featuring the ex-Australian thoroughbreds and their imported professional jockeys, identified in the photocopied racecard by first names only, with 'Lauren' (Lauren Abbott from Townsville in

Queensland) and 'Popeye' (Malaysia's Abdul Faizal) joining Richard, Nicki and Alfie (full names unknown).

These riders were giants compared to the regulars, and the horses – a fairly nondescript bunch of four- and five-year-old mares and geldings – resembled equine titans compared to what had gone before. Crowding around the paddock, the locals were captivated, and, it seemed, a little anxious at the sight of such massive beasts. One horse shied, and a whole shrieking section of the crowd dived away from the rails as if a Chieftain tank was about to open fire.

Number two, my knowledgeable friend's selection, was a five-year-old grey mare named Bouclier who had made the frame on each of her last three outings, coming closest to winning on her most recent appearance a month previously. Sent off the even-money favourite, she missed the break by five lengths but still won comfortably, clocking a time 20 seconds faster than the fastest pony had managed. The margin of difference represented a superiority of about 120 lengths over the toy horses that had dominated Vietnamese racing for two decades.

I backed Bouclier to the tune of 50,000 dong, which meant I left the track 95 grand to the good following the odd success earlier in the afternoon, yet still 5,000 dong short of the entry fee. I had paid like a foreigner but gambled like a local, not parting with more than the equivalent of £2 in a single hit. If I was determined to mix it with the VIPs, I really ought to have learned how to bet like one.

JAPAN

VITAL STATISTICS

RACING			FINANCE	
Racetracks	32		Total prize-money	$953.51m
Fixtures	1,808		Betting turnover	$27,701.71m
Races	18,213			
Racehorses	26,420		All figures for 2005	

BREEDING	
Stallions	311
Mares	10,623
Foals	7,930

ETIQUETTE counts for a lot in Japan. It means never saying "no", never losing your temper, and most important of all, even for an ignorant *gaijin* visitor, never blowing your nose in public. On the other hand, while it is not exactly encouraged, it is relatively commonplace to see men urinating on the pavement. Perhaps this explains why Shomben Yokocho, one of the most infamous streets in the neon-clad Shinjuku district of Tokyo, is known as 'Piss Alley'.

At the heart of this neon-rampant, temple-strewn nation is a society governed by a bewildering set of rules, rituals and arcane manners. Consider, for example, the daunting social niceties of spending a couple of nights at a traditional family-run Japanese inn, or *ryokan*, as I did in the magically evocative city of Kyoto, the nation's capital for more than 1,000 years. To refer to the accommodation here as basic would have been to overstate the case. The barest of rooms housed a futon so uncomfortable that it was surely designed as an instrument of torture, plus a low table barely six inches off the ground that would have stretched even the most malleable of yoga experts if they had felt like serving tea, and the all-important rice-straw matting known as the *tatami*. The sole concession to the modern age was a tiny coin-operated black-and-white TV so ancient that it would have been no surprise to learn it was powered by a wind-up mechanism.

For some inexplicable reason, great significance was attached to the *tatami* – and woe betide anybody ignorant enough to place any sort of footwear on it. Outside shoes had to be surrendered at the front door to the superannuated widow who ran the place, after which guests were expected to change into one of the pairs of slippers lined up in rows for the use of patrons on their arrival. Having ascended the narrow staircase to the living quarters, these slippers had to be left on the floor the other side of the flimsy sliding screen that acted as a door between each room and the communal area. But if you had need of the toilet facilities, you had to put them on again to walk to the lavatory, then take them off once more and replace them with another separate pair provided especially for doing the necessary deed. After all that kerfuffle, is it any wonder some people favour the streets? At least they can keep their shoes on.

Japanese social convention also demands visitors make a point of complimenting their hosts, but this is by no means a chore when it comes to their horse racing. At least, not if the evidence of two days' racing at Nakayama featuring the Nakayama Grand Jump, billed as the world's richest international jumps race, is anything to go by.

Japan's massively lucrative industry cannot be far off racing nirvana. The sport is hugely popular in Japan, which boasts by far the highest betting turnover in the world, around twice that of the United States. At its zenith in the mid-1990s, the pari-mutuel betting handle on horse racing hit 4,000 billion yen. Put another way, that's four *trillion* yen, the equivalent of about £18 million, all of it generated by a wholly state-operated industry, which means the vast majority of the profits are re-invested in the sport, resulting in a famously richly endowed purse system. Admittedly, the numbers declined to around 3,328 billion yen (about £15 million) by 2004, but this was still a mind-boggling figure – dwarfing Britain, for example, which has more than double the number of operating racetracks. And the numbers were back on the way up in 2005.

Japan's breeding industry, based almost exclusively on the northern island of Hokkaido, is spoken of in awed tones by the rest of the world, and its poster boy, the late, great stallion Sunday Silence, is a bloodstock legend. Of the 8,536 thoroughbred foals registered in Japan in 2003, 94 per cent drew their first breath on Hokkaido. A figure around 600 below that two years later still ranked Japan fourth in global terms, exceeded only in the

US and Australia, both many times larger, and Ireland, where the breeding of racehorses is virtually the national pastime.

Not for nothing is Japan the envy of most other serious racing jurisdictions, as the *Racing Post*'s chief correspondent James Willoughby made plain in an essay in *Flat Horses of 2005*. The piece was ostensibly devoted to Cesario, the filly who confirmed Japan's status as a racing superpower when she became the first Japanese-trained horse to win a Grade 1 event in the US in the American Oaks at Hollywood Park in 2005. However, Willoughby took the opportunity to examine Japan's racing as a whole. "A state-funded racing industry unified towards the common good," he wrote. "The world's highest prize-money structure; a breeding industry committed to developing middle-distance horses. It sounds like Utopia, but it is actually Japan."

Horse racing in Japan can be traced back as far as the 8th century, when religious festivals featured popular *kurabeuma*, match races on dirt and sand between samurai at shrines and other sites a millennium before the introduction of western-style races in 1862 by foreign residents in Yokohama. Yet despite this long history, Japan has only recently gained admittance to racing's top table thanks mainly to the pulling power of the mighty yen, although the sport was popularised in the 1970s by the champion Haiseiko, a bronze statue of whom graces Nakayama racecourse in memory of a horse who graduated from local dirt racing to the nation's top races.

The real sea-change came about in the following decade, however, when almost unlimited financial muscle prompted an exodus of potential stallion talent from Europe to Japan. For a while it seemed as if no sooner had a Derby winner passed the post at Epsom than it was already on board a plane bound for the Far East.

But it was an American racehorse who proved the founding father of the nation's breeding dynasty, the 1989 Kentucky Derby winner Sunday Silence, celebrated for engendering a matchless blend of class, speed and agility in his offspring and responsible for scores of top-level winners in Japan, where he was untouched for several years as champion before his death in 2002 – and afterwards, while his offspring were still racing. The pedigrees of horses on Japanese racecards are dominated by Sunday Silence and his descendants, his standing with an enthusiastic public demonstrated by the fact that when I was there, three years after his death, you could still buy numerous souvenirs depicting the horse, who was regarded as a national treasure.

Given such tremendous levels of investment, it is easy to say with hindsight that it was only a matter of time before Japanese racehorses were recognised as a major force around the globe, but it wasn't long ago that their representatives abroad went largely unheeded, and usually were unsuccessful, on their rare sorties to foreign shores. An inward-looking dynamic at home did little to help their reputation, though criticism of such insularity must be set against the available prize-money, seldom as attractive in more difficult races elsewhere.

Less welcome, and suggestive of a national inferiority complex in matters equine, was a protectionist system that barred foreign-trained horses from all but a handful of Japanese races. As a result, the Japan Cup, a showpiece event in late November open to allcomers, became a high-profile anomaly – one that was habitually won by raiders from more established racing countries in its early years during the 1980s and '90s, lending credibility to the concept that Japanese racing, for all its finance, couldn't quite cut the mustard.

Such smug assumptions have been severely challenged, if not rendered completely ridiculous, since the mid-1990s, when Japanese racing started to become a more self-confident entity. An increasing number of Japanese races were opened up to outsiders – though still not a number of its most prestigious – and, more significantly, an ever-expanding number of representatives left their mark in top races around the world. In 1998, Seeking The Pearl and Taiki Shuttle became the first Japanese-trained horses to win at the top level in France, while a year later their compatriot El Condor Pasa came second to Montjeu in the Prix de l'Arc de Triomphe, Europe's most prestigious race. From only a still-limited number of runners, Japanese horses scored at the top level in Britain and Dubai, as well as the States, while closer to home a number of the major international races in Hong Kong went to Japan. More often than not, the Japan Cup also stayed at home.

Set against this backdrop, it looked like racing in Japan was ready for its golden age by the time I got there in April 2005. But even if it wasn't, going racing there after Bangkok and Ho Chi Minh City was like seeing a production at the RSC after a couple of embarrassing nights at the local amateur-dramatic society.

Racing in Japan is still divided into two spheres, 'national' and 'local'. The former features purely thoroughbred competition, both turf and dirt, at the nation's ten best-known racetracks operated by the Japan Racing Association, among them Tokyo racecourse itself, the home of the Japan Cup, and others like Kyoto and Hanshin.

Local racing, featuring lesser venues run by local governmental bodies, is the sphere in which Haiseiko originally shone, featuring only dirt racing with thoroughbreds sometimes joined by anglo-arabs. Evening meetings in this grade regularly attract 25,000 to Ohi racecourse in Tokyo; one track in Hokkaido has a capacity of only 800. At some venues, 'local' racing also features *ban-ei* races, in which draft horses pull a steel sleigh along a 200-metre track that has a couple of sleeping-policeman-style humps en route.

On the weekend I visited Nakayama racecourse, one of the country's finest, the Grand Jump provided one highlight of a major dual-purpose double-header at the track ahead of an even more valuable contest on the Sunday, the Satsuki Sho, Japan's version of the 2,000 Guineas and the first leg of the nation's triple crown. Having gone to Japan principally for the Grand Jump, an intriguing event that photographs suggested featured a brick wall among its many and varied obstacles, I had no idea that the latter race was to prove the more memorable.

Nakayama is situated about 40 minutes away from central Tokyo on the way to Narita international airport, itself around 60 miles outside the city, which is about as sensible as putting London's airport in Birmingham. Getting to the track looked easy enough on public transport, a ten-minute walk via an underground pedestrian concourse, including travelator, from Funibashi-hoten station on the JR Musashino railway line. However, here it must be admitted that your correspondent took an even easier option: a shuttle bus laid on by the racecourse that departed from the Tokyo Dome hotel, next to the city's massive baseball stadium, known colloquially as the 'Big Egg'.

Arriving at the track just after noon, the bus disgorged its occupants, among them the Australian, New Zealand and French contingents behind the trio of international big-race contenders. The meeting was already four races old. Evidently this was a matinee and afternoon meeting all in one, the Grand Jump (off at 3.35pm) merely the 11th of a 12-race card that had commenced at the ridiculous hour of 9.55am.

While I knew all about prize-money levels in Japan, the purses on offer for some of the more run-of-the-mill events were startling. Besides the £775,000 Grand Jump itself, the only steeplechase on the card, the main supporting event, the six-furlong Keiyo Stakes, was worth the equivalent of £250,000 – and it wasn't even important enough to merit Group-race status, the 1-2-3 ranking system by which the prestige of races in major countries is identified. Even the opening event, just after the crack of dawn, could still offer around £50,000 in total. On the same day, the Group 2 Yomiuri Milers' Cup at Hanshin was worth around £600,000, a figure that would put it in the top-ten races in Britain in prize-money terms.

After a couple of early races, it was tempting to see the racecourse experience as a microcosm of Japan in general, exemplifying certain national stereotypes. Everything seemed fastidiously punctual and precise. The track was perfectly ordered, scrupulously neat and tidy, from the well-manicured turf to the meticulously cultivated privet hedges that comprised the majority of the fences for the Grand Jump. A team of brightly clad cleaners was on constant patrol to ensure there was no litter; for all the huge levels of wagering, no discarded betting slips could be seen on the floor of the stand.

For a high-profile day's racing, the atmosphere seemed strangely subdued; a less charitable soul might say etherised. The majority of punters did not brave the great outdoors, preferring to sit behind the tinted windows of a five-storey, two-furlong-long stand that housed a vast media hall, an amphitheatre featuring betting windows and banks of seating in front of a massive screen.

Here, a recording of the Grand National produced one display of emotion, the sight of Aintree horses hurtling over the fearsome spruce fences, greenery flying everywhere, inducing a collective "oh" from the Nakayama enthusiasts. Unfortunately for them, their excitement was cut short when the coverage cut out at halfway to show the 1.55 race at Fukushima. They may never have found out about Hedgehunter's emphatic victory at Liverpool, but they certainly saw Mejiro Silhouette hold on from the fast-finishing Classic Rose.

Outside Europe, jump racing is usually regarded as little more than a curiosity and is practised on only a very limited scale. In 2005, in the rest of the world put together, there were barely 600 officially sanctioned jump races, 133 of them in Japan.

Nakayama appeared fairly deserted for the most valuable jumps race in the world, although that impression might have been illusory, since the official crowd figure was later put at 35,450. The following day, when I returned for the Guineas, it was standing room only among a crowd in excess of 85,000, which amply demonstrated the relative appreciation of the average Japanese racegoer for top-quality Flat racing compared to jumping. For all the yen attached to the Nakayama Grand Jump, it was treated as something of a novelty, to be rewarded with only polite applause at most, its status among the aficionados evidently akin to that of the cross-country chase at the Cheltenham Festival, where a mixed bag of horses negotiate a varied selection of obstacles at the steeplechasing mecca. Reactions to the latter range from mere tolerance to outright disdain among many a Festival diehard; at Nakayama, it almost appeared as if the jump race was thought of as a similar excrescence.

Anoraks may be interested to learn that in the end the Grand Jump was not the world's richest jumps race in either 2005 or 2006, when the Nakayama Daishogai, in the winter, was worth slightly more once owners' stake money was taken into account. A non-international event, it beat the Grand Jump by the equivalent of £50 in 2005. Despite the vast wealth on offer, there were no British- or Irish-trained horses contesting the Nakayama Grand Jump in 2005, and only a few had ever taken up this singular challenge. The third place achieved by the gelding The Outback Way for Hereford-based Venetia Williams in 2000, the first time the race was open to foreigners, represented by far the best effort from just a few representatives.

Perhaps there would be more British visitors were it not for the inconvenient timing of the race, which is scheduled just as the jumps season at home is reaching its climax with the Grand National meeting sandwiched between the major festivals in Britain and Ireland, Cheltenham and Punchestown.

The race's unusual attributes are another factor to consider for anyone who might be tempted, but at least I can explode one myth about the Nakayama Grand Jump: the field is not expected to straddle a five-foot wall. They used to jump something akin to that in the race's precursor, the Nakayami Daishogai, but now the obstacle is remembered only in an artificial brick effect at the bottom half of the race's best-known fence, the Grand Hedge.

This is a five-foot obstacle – but, as you might imagine, it is a hedge, a very well-tended hedge at that, and not a wall in any shape or form. Despite the absence of a brick wall, what the two-mile-five-furlong event lacked in cachet as far as the locals were concerned, it made up for in originality. Always run on firm ground, the Nakayama Grand Jump is started from a set of stalls, contrary to European practice, and features a weird and wonderful selection of obstacles, including a water jump, a variety of hedges, artificial brush hurdles, and a fence jumped from both sides.

While some of the fences looked stern enough, their box-like angularity was misleading, bark rather worse than bite. Though formidably sturdy in appearance, they were anything but solid, including the Grand Hedge itself (160cm tall and 205cm wide), and as much as six inches taller than British regulation fences, which are supposed to be built between 4ft 6½in and 4ft 7in. Horses tended simply to brush through the tops of these obstacles. It was closer to hurdling than steeplechasing, as is often the case with jump racing outside Europe – although even that proved too much for the Kiwi hope Fontera, who came to grief at the Grand Hedge approaching halfway, when he was in front.

This aside, the race seemed more of a speed test than a testing examination of jumping technique. Before his demise, Fontera vied with a couple of Japanese front-runners to set a generous pace, whirling around a tight, twisty circuit, which was largely enclosed within the turf and dirt tracks. Since the latter is less than a mile round, the jumps track would be tight enough if it was just one oval. But it isn't – the Grand Jump involves two ovals in a figure of eight, which cannot be more than a half a mile each in circumference. They cross the main tracks twice before rejoining the outside turf track for the last six furlongs.

Then there are the gradients. The race includes three dramatic, dangerous-looking dips, though crevasses might be a more appropriate term to describe these: a 5.3-metre incline downwards in a space of only 63 metres, followed by nearly the same climbing back up. It was like negotiating an inverse Hickstead-style bank. (By the way, if these figures seem overly precise, thank the organisers, who supplied them.)

While the New Zealander departed at the Grand Hedge, Australia's Karasi, trained by Eric Musgrave, enjoyed a faultless trip under his rider Brett Scott, who had been among the bus party on the way to the track. About half a mile out with three fences left to negotiate, he moved upsides the locally trained leader Laurel Royce in menacing fashion. After being kicked on, Karasi responded extremely well to fierce driving from Scott, windmilling his whip like Mick Channon in his former life at the Dell, to hold a powerful late rally from a Japanese horse, Cheers Shining.

While there was no direct British interest in this lucrative contest, there was an unexpected distant link to the winner. A ten-year-old gelding, Karasi was a son of the 1988 Epsom Derby winner Kahyasi; he was formerly owned by the Aga Khan and trained in Newmarket by Sir Michael Stoute. Horse racing everywhere is full of such connections – look at the pedigree of a field for a minor race in Outer Mongolia and the chances are you would find a recognisable name somewhere.

The victory involved a degree of poetic justice for Scott, who had missed out through injury on the ride on St Steven, the only previous overseas winner. That it meant a lot to him was suggested by the rider's flying dismount from Karasi after the race, and his enthusiasm during the post-race interviews, conducted on a hastily assembled victory dais in front of the winning post (called the 'goalpost' by the locals), where he stood garlanded alongside the winning owner and trainer.

"He's a very good horse with a big heart," Scott said. "He's a hard horse to ride – he made me work, and I had to ride him hard. But he jumped well

– we were a little concerned about the two bigger jumps but he handled them well for a small horse.

"I am overwhelmed to win this race," he added. "I've been coming for four years hoping to do it, so I am so happy to have done so."

The return journey to the Tokyo Dome was considerably noisier than the journey out, featuring full-throated versions of *The Wild Rover* and *The Wild Colonial Boy* from the back of the bus. Surprisingly, though, it wasn't the winner's connections belting out the classic singalongs, but the good-natured O'Leary clan associated with the luckless Fontera betraying their Irish roots, though they said they were Kiwis to a man and, clearly, good losers to boot.

As for the Aussies, most of them never made it back to the bus. And who could blame them? It isn't every day you win the best part of £400,000, is it?

*

THE following day, the Satsuki Sho offered chalk to the Grand Jump's cheese. This was Japan's first Classic race of the year, its equivalent to Newmarket's 2,000 Guineas in that it was the first top-level test for three-year-old colts, and it seemed to be treated as an altogether more serious business, attracting a mammoth crowd to Nakayama's colossal silver, grey and white grandstand.

Although there had been no shortage of vantage points the previous afternoon, it was a distinct struggle to locate a patch of bare earth in front of the stand, let alone a seat within it, thanks to the local habit of reserving a perch with a newspaper. Clearly the lure of a prestigious Group 1 race and a horse widely touted as a potential superstar in Deep Impact – a son of Sunday Silence, of course – ridden by Yutaka Take, the number-one jockey in Japan's racing history, was too much to resist for the nation's turf enthusiasts.

There was an unmistakeable buzz around Deep Impact, and it was purely a stroke of luck that I ran into him. Before I arrived in Tokyo, I had no idea the Satsuki Sho was taking place the same weekend as the Grand Jump. To be frank, I wouldn't even have known what the Satsuki Sho was, nor indeed the identity of a racehorse about to hold the whole of Japan in thrall before attempting to take on the world.

Deep Impact was unbeaten in three races, having been backed down to odds-on favourite for all of them. He won his first two in effortless fashion by a combined total of nine lengths, and while a neck verdict in his Satsuki Sho trial suggested he had been made to work somewhat harder, Deep Impact had been brought from a long way off the pace by his rider before being flung unhelpfully to the outside. Nevertheless, the colt had covered the final two furlongs of his most recent outing in just 34.1 seconds. If it was accurate, this time suggested a blistering turn of foot at the end of a mile-and-a-quarter event.

Ahead of the Satsuki Sho, Deep Impact's veteran 64-year-old trainer Yasuo Ikee, six times champion, told the media the colt was the "ideal thoroughbred", while his rider, many times Japanese champion and rider of 47 Group 1 winners at the time, made no secret of his admiration. "I know everyone is excited about this horse, but I'm the most excited," Take said.

I bought a copy of Tokyo's English-language newspaper the *Daily Yomiuri*, which did its best to set the scene. "There's good reason why runaway favourite Deep Impact has been generating unparalleled hype," it said. "Only a freak accident will prevent him from going under the wire first. If all goes right for this young superstar, the result could be embarrassing for the opposition."

He cannot have known it, but Deep Impact was carrying an immense burden of expectation on his young shoulders at Nakayama. Japan's racing public was ready to anoint a new king. The racecourse's cavernous betting halls were already full when I arrived at midday, in time for the fifth race on a 12-race card, and there were queues at many of the (literally) hundreds of automated betting outlets. Occasionally, a disembodied head poked through to aid some hapless punter who had hit the 'help' button as they tackled an array of wagering options, including exactas, trios, trifectas, quinellas (dual forecasts, selecting the first and second in either order), quinella places (two horses in the places) and bracketed quinellas, the latter involving a curious coupling of horses in up to eight separate groups denoted by their having the same cap colour.

Another testament to a vibrant mercantile spirit was the surfeit of fast-food outlets and the 'Turfy Shop', a well-populated boutique named after

Japan's racing mascot, a fluffy horse. Alongside DVDs and the like, the Turfy Shop offered every piece of twee souvenir racing-related tat you could conceivably require. Ever fancied a pillow featuring a photo of new female jockey pin-up Yukiko Makihora? Then you know where to go; they were a snip at 1,500Y (£7.30). And if that doesn't suit, there are always stickers, keyrings, T-shirts, posters, fridge magnets, lighters, biscuits, tissue-box holders decorated with a kitsch cartoon version of former star Air Groove, fully poseable Yutaka Take action figures (with accessories) and cuddly Sunday Silences. They even had face flannels embossed with a picture of Deep Impact.

The fascinating mix of the spiritual and the commercial that is intrinsic to Japan was exemplified in the scene behind the paddock, dominated by a vast totalisator board displaying the odds. Right in front of this bank of numbers was a shrine, but there was precious little devotional business going on as the horses arrived in the parade ring ahead of the main event, when photographers and punters clambered all over it to get a peek at the action.

Five floors of balconies overlooking the parade ring were crammed with racegoers craning their necks to see Deep Impact, the cynosure of all eyes. He was cheered into the paddock, applauded as he took his place out on the track, and cheered again as his name appeared on the big screen in front of the stand ahead of the race.

The crowd now was far from subdued; the atmosphere light years away from the previous day. Nakayama's main turf course is a mile oval, which means the Satsuki Sho start was just down from the stand at the turn into the home straight; as the starter made his way to the rostrum, he received a cheer as well, and there was yet another as the gates opened.

Although his rivals included the previous year's champion two-year-old Meiner Recolte and several other useful performers, Deep Impact was sent off 1-3 favourite for the mile-and-a-quarter event. But it nearly went wrong right at the start as he all but tripped on leaving the stalls. Slowly into stride as a result, Deep Impact was still 17th of the 18 runners as the field passed the stands after two furlongs, having ceded plenty of ground to his main rivals, who were all much more prominent at this stage.

What followed was astounding. At halfway, passing the last vestiges of Japan's transitory national bloom, the cherry blossom, on a clump of trees on the track's apron, Deep Impact's cocksure rider was still motionless, his mount buried deep in the field. At last Take started to ease him around the field, at least three horses wide. Although Deep Impact improved readily, he was still no better than tenth on turning for home. Take gave him a sharp crack of the whip, but a furlong and a half out he still had a handful of horses ahead of him, and now he was six or seven wide entering the straight.

It didn't matter. One more flash of the whip – the second and last – and Deep Impact demolished his rivals in the space of a few strides, having rounded the entire field. As the crowd roared, Deep Impact won going away from two more sons of the much-missed Sunday Silence, smashing the track record by well over half a second. It was an electrifying performance. "He was perfect," said Take. "He wasn't running, he was flying! Down the stretch, he was fantastic. I had a huge responsibility – it's a huge load off my shoulders."

While I could scarcely believe what I had seen, context is the key when attempting to assess the merit of any performance, and I could not pretend to any idea of the strength of the opposition. Visually, though, the impression could not have been more dazzling: Deep Impact looked like a wonderhorse.

I filed a report for the *Racing Post*, drawing analogies with two of the most celebrated displays of recent years by suggesting the performance had echoes of Arazi, with a bit of Dancing Brave thrown in at the end. Arazi entered the equine pantheon with his last-to-first effort circling the field at the 1991 Breeders' Cup in America, while Dancing Brave's victory in the 1986 Prix de l'Arc de Triomphe was unquestionably one of the most memorable of the modern era.

It may have sounded excessive, but Deep Impact's thrilling performance suggested that this deceptively unimposing colt merited keeping such exalted company. I did wonder, though, if maybe I had gone a little over the top. It soon became clear I needn't have worried.

*

DEEP IMPACT *went on to prove himself the most spectacular Classic performer anywhere in the world in 2005 with a string of extraordinary performances in which he treated his opponents with disdain. Having blitzed his rivals in the Tokyo Yushun, the Japanese Derby, he employed his signature late burst to telling effect in October at Kyoto to land the Kikuka Sho, the Japanese St Leger. With a career record of seven wins from seven starts at the time, Deep Impact was only the second unbeaten horse to secure Japan's triple crown after Symboli Rudolf in 1984, and the first of any kind to do so since Narita Brian ten years later.*

Having attained iconic status at home, where his presence attracted crowds of 160,000 to the racetrack, this phenomenon was on the verge of achieving the seemingly impossible in terms of Japanese racing: becoming more famous than his celebrated sire. "He's the best horse in the world today," claimed Yutaka Take after the Kikuka Sho victory. While the rider might not have been the most impartial of observers, that didn't necessarily mean he was mistaken.

In such a context, a defeat in the Arima Kinen, back at Nakayama on Christmas Day, was a bitter pill to swallow. Although it is restricted to domestic horses, this grand prix is Japan's biggest race, with the field determined by a public vote and habitually producing the highest betting turnover of any single race on the planet. Deep Impact looked a touch unlucky as his rider was caught out by a clever tactical effort from jockey Christophe Lemaire on top-class rival Heart's Cry. In those circumstances, amid much wailing and gnashing of teeth among his supporters, he suffered the first defeat of his life by a half-length.

Much worse, and much better, was to come in 2006 when, incidentally, Karasi won the Nakayama Grand Jump again. Deep Impact resumed winning ways and was untouchable at home before a summer break and a trip to Europe for the Prix de l'Arc de Triomphe. Anyone at Longchamp that day will never forget it as the superstar colt's travelling 'Barmy Army' of fans accompanied him from Japan, transforming Longchamp into a suburb of Tokyo.

In what was probably the most outrageous betting market in racing history, the weight of their yen sent Deep Impact off an odds-on favourite for Europe's most famous race, despite hugely talented rivals headed by the previous year's winner Hurricane Run. The race itself, though, was an anticlimax as Deep Impact attempted to make the running for the only time in his career, and his trademark acceleration went missing. He finished third behind Rail Link and Pride, beaten only a length.

While it was difficult to shake the impression that the real Deep Impact simply hadn't turned up in France, embarrassment was added to injury when he was disqualified for failing a post-race dope test. Although there was no suggestion of skulduggery – a legitimate medication hadn't cleared his system in time – it was as if a bomb had hit the Japanese racing world. It could have been worse. Imagine if he had won.

Deep Impact's team headed home to lick their wounds and prepare the colt for Japan's top races, the Japan Cup and the Arima Kinen. With his jockey Yutaka Take reverting to his usual style, settling the horse well off the pace, Deep Impact produced a pair of blistering performances, blowing away an international field in the Japan Cup before a contemptuous success over the best in Japan in the Arima Kinen. Handicappers rated the latter the best performance of an amazing career; it was also his last, his owner Makoto Kaneko having taken the unpopular decision to retire Deep Impact to stud on Hokkaido at the end of his four-year-old season in a syndication deal worth about $23m.

If it made financial sense, the decision left a little unfinished business. Deep Impact would never be allowed to atone for the debacle of the 2006 Arc, the only time he had been given the chance to display his fantastic ability on a foreign stage. He retired with only two defeats on his CV at a combined total of a length and a half, having won 12 of his 14 races, seven of those successes coming in Group 1 company. Remarkably, he had been an odds-on shot in every one of his races.

At the end of 2006, official international handicappers met to formulate the World Thoroughbred Racehorse Rankings, in effect a chart of the best horses in the world. Although the world champion was the dirt performer Invasor, the top-rated on turf was Deep Impact. They are welcome to their opinion, but to my mind Deep Impact was the best horse in the world in 2006 regardless of the surface.

I hadn't overdone the hyperbole at the Satsuki Sho. Deep Impact was probably the most audaciously talented racehorse I have seen since Dancing Brave. The pity is that Europe never saw him at his most stunning. I'm just glad I bumped into him at Nakayama.

The Nakayama Grand Jump winner Karasi wasn't too shabby either. Not only did he return to Japan to win the race in 2006, but he did it again a year later to complete the hat-trick.

SOUTH KOREA

VITAL STATISTICS

RACING

Racetracks	3	
Fixtures	185	
Races	1,238	
Racehorses	2,437	

FINANCE

Total prize-money	$78.90m
Betting turnover	$4,573.54m

All figures for 2005

BREEDING

Stallions	55
Mares	1,612
Foals	1,094

I DIDN'T really give Seoul much of a chance, just a three-day stopover between Japan and China, including a seven-hour stretch at the city's modern racetrack in the southern suburb of Kwachon (or perhaps Gwacheon, depending on which translation is preferred).

Even such a brief visit, however, was enough to see that the two halves of Korea were divided by rather more than the 38th parallel. Seoul, South Korea's populous capital, was only 68 kilometres away from the demilitarised zone, but they might as well have been living on another planet the other side of no-man's land in North Korea, where Kim Jong Il's Communist regime in Pyongyang presided over what is probably the most isolated nation on earth.

If these differences were derived from politics, they extended to virtually all aspects of everyday life. While I was there, English-language newspapers took great glee in mocking a series on North Korean state television called, snappily, *Let's Trim Our Hair In Accordance With The Socialist Lifestyle*. This improbably titled five-parter was devoted to exhorting young men to keep their locks shorn: although the 'dear leader' himself favoured a relatively bouffant hairdo, citizen wannabes in this conformist state were discouraged from emulating him. According to the *Guardian*, which picked up this curious story in Britain, the broadcast suggested long hair was unhealthy and prone to adversely affecting "human intelligence development". Shoulder-length hair was frowned upon in favour of officially sanctioned styles like the crew cut, although guidelines were not as strict for the over-50s, who were allowed a little more leeway as a means of hiding baldness.

While *Let's Trim Our Hair In Accordance With The Socialist Lifestyle* might have been a hit in Pyongyang – it wasn't as if they had much choice in the matter – you were more likely to encounter dubbed versions of *Friends* and *Sex And The City* in Seoul.

Despite abundant examples of such westernisation, parts of the city exuded a Cold War atmosphere, in particular the southern nightlife district of Itaewon, home to a strong, highly visible US military presence indicative of a stand-off between two ideologies, a painful discourse still keenly felt here – a situation that can only have been exacerbated in 2006 by news of the North's atomic-bomb tests. American Forces Network was available on TV in hotels in Seoul, where they practised regular emergency drills. Clear the street if the sirens start.

Seoul is home to just over a third of South Korea's population, around 15 million people from a total of 47.6m at the most recent count, and most of them live in the scores of ugly high-rises that flank the miles upon miles of traffic-choked highways clogging up the outwardly grey city centre. Yet although initial impressions were far from promising, the city proved slightly more attractive than it seemed at first glance, with acres of parks, lively streetlife, friendly people and a distinct air of prosperity, as might be expected of somewhere that had recently hosted one and a half of the world's most prestigious sporting events, the Olympics in 1988 and football's World Cup, alongside Japan, in 2002.

There is no great history of horse racing in Korea, either before or after the country's division. Cavalry horses were used for amateur versions of the sport at the turn of the century before betting was legalised in 1920, but while there were as many as nine separate racing clubs when the Sino-Japanese War started in 1939, only four were left in 1945 when 36 years of Japanese colonial rule came to an end. These remaining venues were not long for this world themselves, as the Korean War brought racing to an abrupt halt and tracks were used for military purposes. None of them survived, but the Korean Racing Association (KRA), in various guises the only body ever to have governed the sport, constructed a new track in the capital at Tsukseom. From 1954 until 1989, this was Korea's racing hub, a status it maintained when the sport was popularised in the 1980s with the advent of colour TV coverage and computerised pari-mutuel betting.

As popular as Tsukseom became, it was superseded in 1989. 'Seoul racecourse' stayed as an entity, but it was moved lock, stock and barrel to a bright, spanking modern development at Kwachon, originally built to host the Olympic equestrian events the previous year.

I visited Seoul racecourse at a boom time for Korean racing, with expansion and improvement the watchwords. Three weeks after my visit, Seoul hosted the biennial Asian Racing Conference; later in 2005, a new 32,000-capacity racecourse was due to open on the southern coast in Busan, as well as a new training centre at Jangsu. Total betting turnover in a state-run industry hovered around the £2.5 billion mark in 2004 and 2005, slightly down due to competition from the national lottery, but the number of off-course outlets was rising sharply. Attendance figures, too, were up to around 18 million, while the national breeding programme, based on the resort island of Jeju (or Cheju), produced more than 1,000 foals for the first time. Jeju itself was also home to the nation's second racetrack, where the native pony breed, designated as National Monument No. 347, raced around a sand track.

Seoul, Korea's premier track, was strictly thoroughbreds-only, open for business every Saturday and Sunday. It was a doddle to get to on the city's extensive underground network, with its own station on the Blue Line, about 30 minutes south of the downtown district, Myong Dong.

The local delicacies still had to be negotiated, however. Leaving the station via a noisy underpass, the smell coming from the street vendors was close to overpowering, an especially rancid whiff coming from one particular bowl. Closer inspection revealed a Korean favourite – silkworm pupae, admirably pungent when boiled. Despite her one-dish speciality being noted for rich vitamin content, the vendor wasn't doing a roaring trade.

On arrival, it was evident this was not a racetrack to deal in understatement. After negotiating a phalanx of form-guide salesmen displaying an intimidating array of form guides, you enter the racecourse itself through a grandiose walkway and gigantic horseshoe-shaped arch.

Half an hour before the first at 11am, there were already thousands of people inside, hardly surprising when the average gate was reported to be 30,000. Entry to the track, with access virtually everywhere, cost a mere 800 Korean won. That was the equivalent of just 42p – and it was well worth paying, because the racecourse, not unlike the city that housed it, was a pleasant surprise, ringed by mountains on three sides, with distant city skyscrapers visible on the other. It followed the Japanese model, with precise ornamental gardens, artificial waterfalls and statuary inside, cherry blossoms on the infield, and a five-tier grandstand the length of the straight.

It was really two separate buildings joined in the middle: one, a modern silver-grey construction, came complete with faux temple-style entrance and high-tech, capsule-style windowed elevators. This was 'Happy Ville', while 'Lucky Ville', older and less well-maintained, looked out over the winning post and a wonderful sunken parade ring in which jockeys formed a line ahead of every race, like a football team about to meet the visiting dignitary, and bowed to the crowd before mounting. Between them, Happy Ville and Lucky Ville had a capacity in excess of 70,000; the twee nomenclature was echoed in cartoon mosaics on the floor of the stand, and the KRA's slogans, like 'Live and Love with KRA' and 'Joyful Race Lovely KRA' could be seen all over the place. Perhaps something was lost in translation.

The shabbier of the two stands seemed the more popular with the locals, many of whom could be seen crouching over unfathomable papers – presumably form and tips – spread across the floor. None of this for me, though, for a degree of segregation was in operation and I took a pew in the purpose-built 130-seater 'Foreigner Lounge' on the fourth floor, with a view across the track and English-speaking betting assistants (and Chinese- and Japanese-speaking betting assistants), and English-language form guides (and Chinese- and Japanese-language form guides). Whether Korean nationals were prohibited was unclear – in theory, a passport or some other form of identification was required, but I was asked no questions.

This Seoul meeting was yet another extended card of the type with which I had become familiar in Asia – 11 races, starting at 11.30am and ending at 6pm. Indeed, it seemed 11 were not nearly enough, for the early part of the programme also involved a simulcast of two races beamed from Jeju given their own slot in the racecard. They took the place of a race at Seoul, which meant the gaps between the second and third live contests was an hour, rather than half an hour. Not that you noticed, since the lively local punters paid as much attention to the two races on the big screen as they did the corporeal equines in front of them.

Every race at Seoul had between eight and 12 runners over trips ranging from 1,000 metres up to 2,000 metres on either of two sand ovals, one inside the other, both also used for training purposes. In order to protect the national breed, only unraced horses could be imported from abroad and some races were restricted to home-breds, but Korean owners had not been slow to try their luck elsewhere, and the card featured horses bred in the US, Australia, New Zealand and Japan.

Serious efforts were also being made to improve the local stock: stallions imported to the Jeju breeding station by the KRA included Commendable, a winner of the Belmont Stakes, the third leg of America's Triple Crown, and Exploit, a son of Storm Cat, the world's most expensive stallion. Neither would have been near Korea if they had been anything like successful in an established arena.

The racing at Seoul appeared only slightly less questionable than certain other venues I had visited in the previous few weeks, with the betting yet again habitually revolving around just a smattering of horses in each race. The first nine races involved an odds-on favourite, while an inordinate proportion of runners were sent off at more than 100-1.

The evidence of one day also suggested that front-runners were very likely to stay in front, and jockeys were wont to make full use of the whip from the stalls in a bid to secure a prominent position, like Woo Chang Ku, whose performance on fourth-race favourite Pinocchio was anything but wooden. He administered six cracks before the end of the first furlong, achieved the lead and never saw another horse. Sophisticated it wasn't, which probably accounted for the KRA's bringing in three Australian jockeys later that year to educate the locals. It was partially successful; although two of them didn't complete their six-month tour of duty, the third, Gary Baker, rode plenty of winners.

South Korea's most valuable races were the Derby and Grand Prix, held in May and December respectively and both worth 200 million won (about £104,000). I had to make do with just the Chairman's Cup, designated a Grade 3 event on the Korean scale. Worth rather less, this 2,000-metre handicap was the highlight of a four-race TV broadcast that began midway through the afternoon and featured a pair of pundits whose gigantic talking heads eerily filled the big screens in front of the stands before and after the last few races.

By now it was clear that the starter was also determined to be one of the stars of the show. In crimson tonic-suit, white gloves and what looked in the distance like a porkpie hat, he could have passed for an Asian version of Chas Smash from Madness. Sadly, though, he disappointed his public by declining the opportunity to 'nutty dance' his way to his mobile rostrum, although he certainly wielded his blue flag with an almighty flourish for the cameras.

After the embarrassment of wagering the equivalent of half a can of Tizer so far, I upped the ante in Seoul to lose around £25 before the big race, the legacy of a few thousand Korean won on a 1-3 favourite who missed the break, and various quinella places on horses who didn't place.

Fortunately, help was on hand ahead of the day's main event. As the jockeys lined up in customary fashion ahead of the race to bow to the crowd, Korean TV's answer to Britain's Zoey Bird – a smart, smiley racing presenter blessed with quite a following among certain male viewers – moved down the line with her microphone. She started with Park Soo Hong, rider of market leader Subsidy, a five-year-old American-bred gelding, number one on the racecard. A cheery, flirtatious-looking exchange ensued. I recalled that inveterate horse player Charles Bukowski and an adolescent baseball opponent who, the writer suggests, "couldn't keep his pecker-mind off of snatch-thoughts". Subsidy was ruled out for betting purposes.

Korean Zoey moved on quickly to the riders of horses four, five and six, but left Shih Seung Tae crestfallen by heartlessly missing him out on her way to number nine, the top-weight Tempest West. According to the form guide, this US-bred six-year-old had recorded the fastest time in the book, scoring twice in his last four starts, and he was ridden by Cho Kyoung Ho, no stranger to victory with 128 career wins beside his name.

Cho did enough in his brief exchange with 'Zoey' to convince me – it wasn't so much what he said, it was the way he said it. It was time to get serious: 40,000 big ones (or big wons) on Tempest West. It was all looking good as Subsidy drifted to odds against in the last few seconds before the off, with Tempest West a solid second choice at 5-1.

A last run-through of the runners and riders appeared on the big screen as the field went down to the start, to the accompaniment of the sort of uplifting music often used in black-and-white war films to accompany footage of soldiers marching to war, assuring us they're all bloody good chaps as they go to get their heads shot off in some foreign field that is forever England.

The jaunty number ended and Chas Smash flourished his flag. Subsidy broke well from the inside berth, Park Soo Hong liberal with his whip before establishing a five-length lead that none of his rivals looked overly inclined to make up. The favourite won unchallenged after what greyhound aficionados would recognise as a solo effort. Tempest West stayed on for a poor fifth of the 11 runners, and they seldom pay out on that.

Still, where there's life, there's hope. And while I had all but run out of Korean currency playing on horses about which I knew absolutely nothing, at least I knew I could get a nutritious meal on the way home. Anyone fancy a nice bag of bugs?

*

THE Asian Racing Conference went ahead without a hitch in Seoul in April 2005, while South Korea's third racecourse, in Busan, opened a few months behind schedule in September with around 1,000 horses on site. There are plans for an international invitation race at Seoul racecourse in 2008, when they will be hoping for a better outcome than the only time the track made international headlines in 2006. Then, the nation's principal raceday in December turned into a complete farce when the abandonment of the Seoul Grand Prix due to heavy snow prompted irate racegoers to burn down a ticket booth. They also had a snowball fight. The day ended with 18 people arrested for alleged assault on racecourse staff.

CHINA

VITAL STATISTICS

RACING		FINANCE	
Racetracks	1	Total prize-money	*unknown*
Fixtures	21	Betting turnover	*nil*
Races	168		
Racehorses	800	All figures for 2005 for Beijing only; tracks in Hong Kong and Macau are excluded	

BREEDING	
Stallions	24
Mares	700
Foals	420

IF this wasn't horse racing's final frontier, it will do until one comes along. Fly halfway around the world, then turn right at the backend of beyond, and you just might have been able to locate Beijing racecourse.

There, possibly the biggest gamble in horse-racing history was taking place in a nation where betting had been illegal for more than half a century. Approximately $100 million had been spent in constructing a fully functioning horse-racing and bloodstock-breeding centre in the most unlikely of settings: the capital of the People's Republic of China, where gambling was outlawed when Chairman Mao took power in 1949. In effect, it was a colossal bet that the Chinese government would rescind its ban on betting, leaving those behind the Beijing operation in pole position to exploit a huge, untapped market within the world's fastest-growing economy, with a population of 1.3 billion, one-fifth of the global total.

Way out to the north east of the city on land that just five years previously had been little more than a patch of scrub, a 3,000-acre site housed the facilities of the Beijing Tongzhou Jockey Club, a joint venture between a deep-pocketed Hong Kong-based entrepreneur and a body with state interests, which operated an international-standard racetrack plus state-of-the-art training and stud facilities.

Race meetings were held every other Saturday featuring professional trainers and jockeys and proper thoroughbreds racing on a turf surface manicured and tended to rival any in Britain. Around 1,000 racehorses, many of them bred on site from the centre's 24 stallions and 700 mares, were housed in huge, purpose-built training barns. These horses were tended by a workforce of 1,000 employees, ridden by homegrown jockeys taught by experts at the facility and prepared by a training community featuring several expatriates from racing jurisdictions around the world.

There was just one problem when I finally found this impressive operation. The whole thing was living on borrowed time.

*

CHINA has not always been a stranger to betting. According to some historians, a form of lottery was used by the Tang Dynasty (618-907) to help finance the building of the Great Wall, while at the time of the British possession of Hong Kong in 1841, at least 25 racetracks were in operation. Although this was an amateur sport run by expatriate westerners, it was popular with the Chinese themselves. Using native ponies, the original Peking racecourse drew crowds of 80,000-plus in the mid-1860s.

Horse racing was still a major sport in China until the Second World War, with the mercantile centre of Shanghai taking over with the showpiece venue in the interwar years. A thriving concern reputed to house the largest grandstand in the world at the time, the racecourse's patrons are known to have included Henry Morriss, whose Manna won the 2,000 Guineas and Derby in 1925.

Racing was suspended in 1941, never to resume after the Communist revolution eight years later anywhere other than Hong Kong and Macau, the British and Portuguese colonies where the vigour of the locals at the betting windows paid ample testimony to the enthusiasm for gambling among the indigenous population.

Elsewhere, though, betting was forbidden by Chairman Mao. He might have been famous for his little red ledger, but he wasn't going to have anyone else making a book. And even allowing for the radical free-market changes of the last two decades of the 20th century, the issue remained sensitive, and the government wary.

That the appetite for betting persisted in China was not open to question, however. Estimates published in 2004 struggled to put a cap on the level of underground activity, reckoned to account for the equivalent of billions of dollars a year, but any such figures might as well have been plucked from the ether, as it is next to impossible to quantify the level of small-scale private gambling among individuals on pastimes like mah-jongg, the four-person tiles game popular throughout the country seldom played without betting money.

After reverting to Chinese ownership in 1997 and 1999 respectively, Hong Kong and Macau retained their status as renowned hotbeds of gambling, allowed to continue there by the government under its 'one country, two systems' policy with regard to that pair of capitalist former colonies.

When racing restarted in Beijing in August 2002, the gambling ban was circumvented via what was labelled a 'guessing' game, a semantic dodge that somehow, despite its title, portrayed the practice of making money from finding winners as a test of skill. Racegoers purchased a voucher for a certain value, named their selection and an amount, which was then deducted from their ticket. Games were operated on a win, place and forecast basis; each resultant pool was divided between the winning vouchers – the same as those used in Macau and Hong Kong – which were then cashed in by the punter. Sorry, 'guesser'.

If this sounds suspiciously like the pari-mutuel tote system in operation in most other racing arenas, there's a good reason for that. It was virtually identical. It beggars reason that China's rulers could have considered this as anything other than betting, which suggests they were minded to turn a blind eye and pocket their rake-off from crowds of up to 5,000.

All of this must have seemed encouraging to Yun Pung Cheng, a toy-manufacturing tycoon with extensive equine interests in Australia, known to all and sundry, on the Beijing racing scene at least, as 'The Boss'. Cheng was the businessman behind the project, pumping in millions to develop from scratch a fully functional thoroughbred racing and breeding centre in a joint venture with a government quango in a bid to be first in line when it came to milking a legal Chinese betting market.

Reputed to be mainland China's sole licensed racecourse, the Beijing track was billed on its informative website as "one of the biggest international standard horse racing clubs in Asia" promising fully furnished VIP rooms with CCTV and "hundreds of audiences" (sic) in attendance every weekend. Information about runners and riders would be published in the *Beijing Star*, it promised, while four races a week were shown on Beijing TV's Channel 6.

That was then, but this is now. In May 2005, when I visited the track, racing Beijing-style had hit a severe bump in the road, an appropriate analogy for an inaccessible racecourse and equine centre reached only via rutted dirt tracks after a 75-minute taxi journey from central Beijing.

"It's as if someone has put a pin into a balloon and just let all the air out of it," South African-born trainer John Gorton told me, alluding to a racecourse almost devoid of atmosphere, and crowd. Gorton rode Sleeping Partner to win the Oaks at Epsom in 1969 as part of a five-year stint retained by Lord Rosebery in Britain. Alongside an unlikely UK representative in the minor-league jumps trainer Nigel Smith and assorted Australians, New Zealanders, French and Irish, he was one of a wild bunch of pioneering expatriate trainers making a living before the forecast goldrush.

Except that many of them doubted the goldrush would ever arrive. At the end of 2004, racing had been temporarily halted yet again as the state launched an investigation into illegal gambling elsewhere in China. The inquiry was in no way connected to the racecourse, but when racing resumed, it returned only in neutered form as a stunted, massively scaled-down version of the previous year's ambitious model. Cheng decided to keep a tighter grip on the cash register until something positive happened, not doing anything in the meantime to frighten the government.

What this meant was that by the time I reached Beijing, the number of fixtures had been halved to only two Saturdays a month, alongside drastic cuts in prize-money. Not that you would have been aware of even this limited existence, for there was no advertising, no television and no mention in the listings paper.

Public transport was non-existent – a railway was due to be built, should gambling have become legal. I had a map and the destination in writing – Chinese writing at that, copied down by a helpful hotel employee from the local yellow pages. Yet it still required that tortuously extended taxi ride to get there, the most worrying moment of which involved the driver negotiating seven lines of traffic to ask directions from an itinerant salesman on a rusty bicycle on the inside lane.

This was miles off the tourist track, outside the capital's sixth outer ring road about 35 miles from central Beijing's best-known landmarks like Tiananmen Square, the immense showpiece plaza where local guides will offer you chapter and verse on anything except the thing you know most about, the student massacre of 1989, and the Forbidden City, draped in scaffolding as it was spruced up ahead of the 2008 Olympics.

A new town – signposted Tongzhou, praise be – and another quarter of an hour in densely forested countryside, a few turns down pitted dirt tracks, and we finally ended up facing the blue-and-white barns of the Beijing training centre. Half a mile down the road, a potholed single-track dirt effort, and the taxi dropped me outside the gate, half an hour before the first race of an eight-race card that lasted only three hours in total, with 25 minutes between each contest. You didn't need time for a bet, after all.

After paying the entry fee of just ten yuan (70p) and five more for an A5 racecard printed in both English and Chinese, another couple of negatives immediately emerged. Something was missing, and it was something major. There was no stand. A series of rudimentary, temporary-looking single-storey concrete-based huts did the job. Most were padlocked, as they were surplus to requirements for this most meagre of crowds. At a generous estimate, maybe 150 people turned up, a few of them standing on the concrete steps, most sheltered under TV terminals.

A handful of westerners were picnicking on the grass. It was lucky they brought their own scoff – on-site refreshments were provided by a lone woman selling cans of lukewarm Coke and Sprite, and no food. Even the director of racing, the smart-suited, silver-haired Irishman Kevin Connolly, had cheese-and-tomato sarnies brought in by his wife.

Connolly had been in Beijing since July 1999 overseeing the development for Cheng, for whom he used to train. He explained the rationale behind the $100 million punt in straightforward terms. "The Chinese like to get involved with any sort of lottery or betting, any game of chance," said Connolly. "Betting isn't legal, but maybe in years to come it will be. Of course the aim is legal betting at the end of it, and I know people have called it a huge gamble – it's a huge gamble that we'll get in first."

The Beijing operation was not alone in banking on the Chinese government's allowing the prospect of huge betting-tax revenues to overcome ideological concerns. Others were waiting in the wings. Although precise details were hard to come by, there were reports of facilities either part-built or ready to roll in the northern coastal city of Dalian, as well as Ningbo and Wuhan further south. Ningbo, in the prosperous south east near Shanghai, hosted a few meetings with no betting in 2001 plus the odd endurance horse race afterwards, while in Wuhan, the capital of Hubei province on the Yangtze, racing was said to be a significant part of the Orient Lucky City project also due to feature a five-star hotel, shopping mall and residential apartments.

Other developments had already failed in the modern era, notably a bold enterprise in Guangzhou, the former Canton, which hosted regular racing for eight years between 1991 and 1999 with crowds of up to 40,000 drawn by a 'guessing' game similar to Beijing. After key figures became involved in a corruption scandal, the track was shut down. It was now said to resemble a "parking lot", according to Connolly.

I suggested to him that Beijing wasn't in too great a shape itself, given that the track's website led you to expect a vibrant, well-populated racecourse, not a virtually deserted line of tin shacks. "OK, we're in the doldrums a bit right now," Connolly admitted. "But we've just got to sit back and wait until things change. Last year, when the government launched their big investigation into illegal gambling, we were the only gambling-based activity that wasn't entirely shut down."

Yet while nowhere else hosted regular organised racing, Wuhan held its third annual International Horse Racing Festival later in 2005, a four-day affair featuring pageantry and other equine pursuits alongside a presumably amateur form of racing.

Connolly wasn't overly interested in potential rival operations elsewhere. "We're the only legal, licensed racetrack in mainland China, and this track is as good as anywhere in the world," he added. "Our credibility is very, very high. There are no half-measures here. We've come a very long way since we started racing in August 2002; everything's here that you need for a proper racing and breeding industry. And we know we can do it – we've already proved that last year, and the plans are in place. We're just carrying on softly for now until things change – we can be ready at the flick of a switch.

"This is a whole racing industry, from breeding to selling to racing – we're very proud of what we've achieved in a reasonably short time. In five or six years, I'd like to think we'd have the infrastructure and the horses to allow us to compete abroad – Hong Kong and Macau to begin with, and then farther afield."

Such ambitions sounded a little far-fetched set against the scene outside: where Hong Kong attracted racegoers in their tens of thousands twice a week, Beijing struggled to get tens of tens twice a month. However, there was a startling dichotomy between the spartan customer facilities and the racing side of the project, where it was obvious little expense had been spared.

The racetrack itself looked beautiful – three circuits, two lush turf tracks outside a sand training track, and a showjumping circuit inside that – and the style of racing that emerged later in the afternoon was as close to European-style action as I encountered on the Asian leg of my trip. Here I did not see horses tailed off suspiciously after a furlong; it seemed possible to win from both front and back on an 11-furlong circuit configured like Ascot. Later research also revealed spacious stables, professional stockmen, top-class veterinary teams and all mod cons in the training department. State-of-the-art laser photo-finish equipment determined the results, four horses per race were dope-tested, extensive stipendiary stewards' reports were carried in the racecard.

The horses themselves were the offspring of reputable sires, most of them bred at the centre's on-site stud farm, where stallions included Bigstone, once a winner of Glorious Goodwood's most prestigious event, the Sussex Stakes. There were also Australian-bred runners by the likes of Kentucky Derby winner Thunder Gulch and top-class French sprinter Dolphin Street, and the Japan Cup third Bubble Gum Fellow.

Jockeys, many of them highly competent, emerged for the opener in single-colour silks corresponding to their racecard number, to be greeted by trainers decked out in jacket and tie as if they were at a much swankier venue. Connolly explained the dress code by saying that they didn't want to let standards drop, despite the slowdown.

The eight races on the card were worth up to 70,000 yuan (just under £5,000) each, much less than the previous season, when the most prestigious race, the China Cup, carried a purse of around three million yuan (about £250,000). All taking place on the lush turf track, they ranged from between four and a half furlongs and a mile, though at other times a more varied programme was offered. There were even a couple of five-mile races at one time, in deference to the Chinese tradition for endurance races, but they did not prove popular with Beijing-based trainers.

While everything in equine terms was first class, in itself an enormous achievement in such a short time, the atmosphere was wholly surreal. Tote screens were illuminated next to the closed 'guessing' terminals, but they didn't move from race to race other than to record the result.

One of the picnicking westerners, an Australian student, told me he had visited the track in 2004 and found a vastly different beast. "You could use your vouchers and there was a real atmosphere – lots of Chinese having a bet, probably well over 1,000 people here," he said. "This isn't much cop now, is it? There doesn't seem any point."

After a security guard upbraided him for walking around with no shoes, just before the field left the stalls for the second race accompanied by a sandstorm blowing in from the Gobi desert, he and his friends gave up and left. There were only about a dozen of them, but their departure diminished the crowd at a stroke by around 20 per cent.

*

LOOK down the 700-metre Beijing straight and not at the paucity of spectators, and it could almost have been Ascot. An array of national flags were buffeted by the ever-increasing winds high above the course to identify the multicultural identity of the training community, over half of which comprised salaried expatriates existing on interpreters, golf, karaoke and only eight races a fortnight.

Among the newest arrivals was Nigel Smith, giddy with enthusiasm since becoming Britain's only representative on horse racing's final frontier only four months previously, a far-from-obvious career development for the burly 49-year-old.

I collared Smith for a chat between races. "You can call me a struggling jumps trainer, because that's what I was," he said, recalling 20 years' labour on the family farm at the village of Upper Snodsbury, 20 minutes from Worcester, where his best horses were the durable sprinter Petraco and hurdlers City Index and Holt Place, none of them exactly household names.

Smith admitted to not being the most adventurous type, yet here he was, a small-time jumps trainer handling a team of Flat racers in the most alien of environments, thousands of miles away from his safe European home. It was incongruous, so how exactly had he got there?

"This is virtually the first time I've ever been out of Worcestershire," he admitted. "I came home pissed from the pub one night and saw an advert in the *Racing Post*. I wrote back saying that if it's got four legs, two ears and eats grass, then I can train it. For some reason they replied wanting to know more – and somehow I ended up getting the job from 56 applications!"

Far from being a fish out of water, Smith took to his new challenge like a Peking duck to plum sauce. Although this was only the third meeting of the season, he saddled his third winner from just a handful of runners with a three-year-old filly named Dependable.

"I really am chuffed to bits with the way it has started," said Smith. "When I trained the first two-year-old winner here with the Union Jack flying, I was that proud, I tell you it brought a tear to my eye."

A garrulous type, Smith carried with him the air of a man who could not quite believe what was happening to him. Union Jack badge pinned proudly to his lapel, he admitted as much. "This is a bit of a trainer's dream," he gushed. "There's one all-weather track for training and two grass tracks to race on that would stand up to anywhere in the world. Then there's trotting tracks, horse walkers, swimming pools, labs, a whole team of vets. Everything you could ask for – and where else could I get a good salary and have accommodation, a driver and an interpreter?"

Smith picked up the racecard and examined the final race. "These horses are very well-bred, superb really. I'm running a horse this afternoon by a winner of the Japan Cup – at home they wouldn't even have let me lead her up! The most horses I've ever had before was 27 – and then I came here and they said, 'here's 56 horses!' Some of them would definitely be able to win races in Britain. As soon as gambling is made legal, you'll be shaking trainers off with a stick."

I suggested to him that this was a case of 'if' rather than 'when' – and that racing was untenable in the longer term without betting. Typically, Smith preferred to accentuate the positive.

"Soon after I arrived, they said the government hadn't made its mind up about gambling," he explained. "Yes, it is a worry, but while I am sure it will go ahead, if it does not then I will still have had a life-changing experience and will be a better trainer because of it. I fully intend to be the best I can be out here and I've budgeted to be champion trainer out here in three or four years.

"I know I can train and I feel I've now been given a chance. There are some class horses here and I would give my right arm to train them from an early age, and then show the racing world that the boss has the horsepower to make them all go a bit, to make them realise that this set-up is able to compete with anyone, anywhere, at any time."

Smith came prepared for a massive dose of culture shock when he arrived in January 2005. "It was minus 20 with a horrendous wind-chill," he said. "You needed full face mask and goggles, and I was kitted out like the SAS – I was prepared for anything. I had enough food for two weeks and arctic gear, but while I have never been so cold, I thought that if other people can come here and put up with it, so can I.

"I had an open mind about what I'd find, but even though I expected to live on biscuits and cheese, I like the food and the people – I actually find the Chinese very open and extremely friendly. They are warm-hearted people – they'd feed you before themselves."

Language, too, was not proving an insurmountable barrier. "It is a problem but I have an interpreter who tries his best, but the staff know what I expect because I show them," he said. "And if the jockeys make a nuts of the riding then 'you are a pillock' is the same in any country!"

Smith set out his stall as soon as he arrived, keen to foster a team ethos among his staff, to whom he supplied blue-and-yellow polo shirts with the stable's name embossed. "I think possibly a lot of Chinese treat other Chinese pretty rough but I think man-management is important," he said. "We can go out together to a piss-up or a karaoke – I just wanted to show them I'm a normal bloke."

This easy camaraderie extended to the other expat trainers, albeit imbued with a competitive edge. Beijing's leading overseas trainer at the time of my visit was the Australian Brian Lawrence, who offered some helpful advice.

"Are you going to take a picture of this fella?" he asked. "If you do, make sure he's got his mouth open. If he hasn't, it won't be a natural shot! We call him 'Soapy', you know – because he never has a shower."

Winners during the afternoon were shared out between a range of trainers, including John Gorton, Claude Piccioni, who used to ride for French legend François Boutin before moving to Macau en route to Beijing, and the Irishman John Murphy, who netted a double. Lawrence, a former teacher and small-scale trainer from Wagga Wagga, also got his name on the scoresheet to keep up the pressure on the 2004 champion, H.K. Cheong, who had the advantage of the pick of Cheng's better horses.

Lawrence was in his third year in Beijing. "It's easy being a trainer," he said. "Anyone could do it – then again, I'm a liar." I was unsure whether to believe him.

He was talking to me as we watched the racing with other trainers gathered around a table in front of the CCTV in one of the huts, where the talk was ribald and the atmosphere one of excitable competition, the volume switched up several notches, and the expletive level similarly amplified, as push came to shove in the final couple of furlongs.

Smith, by no means the calmest, became particularly animated when his representative went clear in the second race, making more noise than everyone else at the track put together. He went out to greet his winner, and posed for the ubiquitous post-race photo. No-one was watching, though this was partly owing to a specific climate variable, as every race other than the opener took place in a vicious sandstorm.

There was no appreciative crowd and no owners. As 95 per cent of the equine competitors were still owned by the company behind the joint venture, the whole thing had the feeling of phoney war, a private competition between the trainers chasing their percentage. It was utterly bizarre: excellent facilities, talented horses, able horsemen but, without the betting, a circle jerk, existing only for itself. This was Stepford-synthetic horse racing. Nearly all the parts were in the right place, but still there was no life. It felt like a practice match.

Lawrence agreed. "It's like we're holding a series of full-scale barrier trials," he said. "Without betting there's no buzz. It's like taking a shower with your raincoat on."

Talk turned to the standard of jockeyship. "They'd ridden mainly oxen and donkeys before, so they've come in among thoroughbreds with no knowledge of them, but also no fear of them," said Lawrence. "The horses pick this up and as a result are nice and relaxed – we've got a couple of stallions who I've been kicked by, but the Chinese bloke leads them around like they're pet dogs."

He also admitted to the odd language problem. "Once I asked him to tell a jockey to give his horse a nice pat," he said. "The message obviously got mixed up. The kid hopped off and gave it a kick in the guts."

It seemed the English-speaking trainers had their own system for identifying individual riders as well. Two of the better ones were 'Michael The Fucker' and 'Brownie Little Cunt'.

As racing drew to a close, Lawrence presented Gorton with a bottle of homemade kumquat grog, passed around to universal disapproval. That was when things started to go a bit astray for me among the somewhat stir-crazy expatriates. First stop was the trainers' bar. "You'll have to borrow a proper pair of shoes," warned Lawrence, always ready for a potential wind-up. "Those sneakers might lower the tone."

Such a change of footwear might have been somewhat excessive, as it turned out. The so-called trainers' bar was a tiny shack on the corner opposite the training centre that the wind whipped through, blowing beers everywhere. Seated on rickety wooden stalls, the multinational team knocked back tinnies, hiding as best we could from the sand, while the jockeys did the same inside, seated with the proprietor behind a flyscreen.

Half an hour later, Smith took me, via a small, impoverished settlement, to an establishment he referred to as the 'International Railway Hotel', a fleapit in a disused railway building that serviced the racing accommodation block, set alongside what looked like a garbage dump, waste paper strewn everywhere by gale-force winds. After ten days in a tour group being frogmarched between tourist-trap restaurants, at last this was a local bar for local people, albeit one peopled by representatives of at least six nations during the three hours I spent there.

Smith ordered chicken and beef, manfully overcoming his language deficiencies with a couple of moos and flapping his wings; Lawrence showed up, alongside fellow Aussie Geoffrey Barton, a former Darwin-based jockey, horse-breaker extraordinaire and racecourse starter to boot. The latter arrived astride a Harley-Davidson in classic outlaw pose at one of racing's last outposts. Sanjay from the stallion yard, Karen from the equestrian centre and Margaret the interpreter joined us as the beer flowed, a bottle at a time, divided between everyone's shot glasses Chinese-style. There is no way of knowing what you are consuming. The food, by the way, was wonderful and as we prepared to move on, I learned the crucial difference between a 'fasty' and a 'snappy'. Here's a hint for future visitors. There isn't one.

I thought I recognised Michael The Fucker among a group of jockeys who arrived at the next-door table, although it could have been Brownie Little Cunt; one last snappy preceded one last fasty; Smith launched into a tale of the day his family landed a touch at Cheltenham with 50-1 chance Holt Place. A mock brawl ensued as Lawrence tried to shut him up, two of China's top trainers left rolling around the restaurant floor. "Will this bloke ever find the off button?" asked the Aussie, understandably.

Later details are necessarily sketchy, but karaoke was involved – I think my *Rhinestone Cowboy* beat Smith's *Dancing Queen* – and so was a car journey involving seven people jammed inside a bashed-up Nissan or perhaps a Volkswagen Polo, or maybe a Citroen. Our driver, with his thick horn-rimmed specs, hadn't had a drop, although behind the wheel he certainly managed a fine impression of Mr Shaky Hands Man from Channel 4's cult TV programme *Banzai*.

With the early hours beckoning, Barton escorted me back into town to the Goose And Duck pub. I have no recollection of where it was, but it was definitely in Beijing. I made my excuses and left, thus ending a day that I won't forget in a hurry. The parts I can remember, that is.

※

IT was fortunate that I got to Beijing racecourse when I did, because it didn't last long. With no sign of any relaxation in gambling legislation, racing at the purpose-built equine centre was suddenly halted without any warning at the beginning of October 2005. On the eve of the richest meeting of the season, Cheng ran out of patience and the operation was almost entirely shut down.

It came as a complete shock to the trainers, who expressed bitterness at how they had been treated. "I was in the car with my parents who had come to see the racing when I was texted about it and I was simply astounded," said Nigel Smith, who was told to take an extended holiday.

Although visas were renewed until December 2006, the majority were sceptical and immediately looked to find employment elsewhere, while their Chinese staff, which included the vast majority of jockeys employed at the track, seemed likely to be left out in the cold. "It left a very sick taste in the mouth," said Smith, who trained four winners and 29 placed horses in his one season in China. "It's a very sad story – I was happy and was settling to training a large team and had moulded a good staff to my way. We were told we might restart in 18 months and would be offered our old jobs back but it was still a good kick in the nuts – all the horses I had got used to and the staff, all gone.

"My staff clubbed together and took me for a last dinner, which was very sad all round," he added. "I gave presents to them all and wished them luck. It was a very sad occasion. My ideal job went wrong – and for once, it wasn't my fault."

Brian Lawrence, Wagga Wagga's finest, was still leading overseas trainer in Beijing when racing was stopped, and second overall behind H.K. Cheung. "We can find another job but the local people will have difficulty I would imagine," he said. "It is also very sad for the big boss after such a huge investment."

Lawrence went back to Australia, while Smith, never short of an idea, trained a few showjumpers and gave golf lessons to the locals in central Beijing before joining his New Zealand colleague Leigh McKenzie in a business venture selling equine supplies worldwide via the internet.

However, while the ending of racing in Beijing was bad enough for the human workforce, it was worse for a significant proportion of the horses. I was told that as many as 600 thoroughbreds were slaughtered following the abrupt decision to cease operations, around 400 racehorses and 200 mares put down in humane fashion by lethal injection.

Although the culling of aged and infirm racehorses is a fact of life in the racing world, it was the level of the alleged Beijing cull that sparked concern, as it featured a quarter of the entire equine population there. "It is an open secret here," said one source, who did not wish to be named.

Kevin Connolly admitted a cull had taken place but denied both its significance and its magnitude. "It's not a secret, open or otherwise," he said in an email. "We normally cull at the end of each season, retired and injured horses, mares that have not conceived for a number of seasons etc, the same as most places."

He took issue with claims that as many as 600 horses had been slaughtered almost as soon as the decision to stop racing had been reached. "We did cull horses," said Connolly.

"We do it every year, the same as other racing jurisdictions. It is just that this year it coincided with the staff being let go, so they were upset about it. I know some of the locals were upset because they saw us doing it and the staff are losing their jobs, which is upsetting for them. But we are an open book here – we may cull some more horses, it is certainly a possibility. I planned to cull 500. Should racing start again, we will have more than enough horses to race."

Nigel Smith confirmed that hundreds of horses had been put down. "I think the ones that were culled were the lucky ones," he said, in an article published in the Racing Post in June 2007. "When I had to go back to the racing centre to collect a piece of paper saying I no longer worked for the Jockey Club, I was greeted by the pathetic sight of thin, undernourished horses basically just surviving. The sight of these remaining horses made me sick to my stomach. I could not get away from there fast enough."

In comparison with certain other racing operations, Beijing was a busted flush in 2006 when, not for the first time, there was talk of government-approved horse racing being introduced as an experiment in the rich south-eastern province of Jiangsu. An all-weather track was installed at the capital Nanjing, while Wuhan again hosted its annual equine festival in 2006. An aerial map of the latter revealed a sand oval, while photographs of the festival showed an impressive-looking stand full of people.

By the end of 2006, the possibility of limited legalised gambling was mooted yet again after research involving government lottery officials, who were said to be examining the possibility of a racing-based game. Although it sounded promising, I can think of a few people who wouldn't have been holding their breath.

MEXICO

VITAL STATISTICS

RACING		FINANCE	
Racetracks	1	Total prize-money	$9.22m
Fixtures	150	Betting turnover	$20.98m
Races	1,500		
Racehorses	1,353	All figures for 2005	

BREEDING	
Stallions	68
Mares	599
Foals	421

ACCORDING to the acclaimed writer Michael Bywater, in the pages of *The Observer*, the arrogant old conjugation used to be: I am an explorer, you are a traveller, they are tourists.

While I was away for more than eight months in one stint, I felt I never really graduated to even the lesser rank of 'traveller', itself a superior being, accorded infinitely more respect than the humble vacationer by the rucksack cognoscenti. I just had a number of holidays one after the other, that was all. Maybe I should have grown a beard and visited an ashram in Kathmandu. Instead, I grew nervous and went to a racecourse in Mexico City.

That's not to say the round-the-world ticket didn't allow for some ludicrous journeys, including the one that came after China. Across the international dateline from Beijing to San Francisco, then a change of flight to Mexico City and an overnight stay in an airport hotel before yet another flight, early morning, to Cancun. The journey concluded with two hours in a group taxi, or *colectivo*, to Tulum, a stronghold of the ancient Mayans on the Yucatan peninsula south of the fabled Chichen Itza (a fantastic place hidden in the jungle, by the way, especially memorable surrounded by the morning mist).

So a fortnight in China was followed by a fortnight in Mexico, which was to prove a favourite, although it wasn't without its more challenging moments. You seldom suffer from altitude sickness in Fulham, where it would be highly unusual to encounter a scorpion ascending the walls of your flat. The latter episode probably sounds scarier than it actually was, as the venomous creature in question was tiny and no sooner did it crawl into my beach hut in Tulum than it left by another window.

Of greater concern was the gang of five youths who relieved Jane and me of a few dollars in Mexico City, an extraordinary capital but possibly not the safest. Yet while it was distinctly unsettling to see another gun, pointed at us this time, they weren't the most frightening bunch of hoods you are ever likely to see. The weapon looked so phoney that I was reminded of Woody Allen's 1969 film *Take The Money And Run*, in which the director plays an incompetent crook who tries to pull off a mugging with a fake pistol fashioned in soap. The hold-up fails when it rains, and the gun starts foaming up over his hands. No such luck with our assailants, though it was tempting to ask if their mothers knew they were out.

Guidebooks tell you never to resist in such circumstances and, as we had stupidly disregarded their advice not to walk around after dark in the first place, it was probably sensible just to cough up the 'street tax'. Even to a bunch of pre-teens. Although it certainly shook us up, neither of us was carrying anything of value and, frankly, it was our own fault. For the record, though, you would be more likely to run into Sir Mark Prescott at a rave than find me out again on the streets of Mexico City after nightfall.

*

MEXICO fitted in nicely before a month-long stay in the United States scheduled to begin at the Preakness Stakes, the second leg of the American Triple Crown. This was one of the handful of major races around which I had specifically framed the trip; the same cannot be said of a Sunday meeting at the grandly titled Hipodromo de las Americas, the 'Racecourse of the Americas' in Mexico City.

Racing in Mexico, where the Jockey Club was founded in 1881, has fallen a long way since the salad days of the 1930s and '40s when the celebrated Agua Caliente track was a magnet for Hollywood's glitterati in the border city of Tijuana, a playground for the rich and famous during the Prohibition era. Not to be denied their debauch, the licentious movie-industry set found a home from home, gambling all day and drinking all night. The racetrack, built when the original Tijuana racecourse 400 metres inside the Mexican border was levelled by a flood in 1915, was merely the best-known among a range of attractions at the Agua Caliente resort alongside an exclusive casino and nightclub, a bullring and greyhound racing.

In its heyday, when gambling was illegal in California and there were restrictions on Sunday racing owing to rest-day laws, the track became a popular outcrop of the nascent West Coast racing scene, the parvenu upstart that rivalled the old-money East Coast circuit focused on New York. Only half an hour's drive south from Del Mar racetrack near San Diego, Agua Caliente attracted many of the biggest names in US racing, among them legendary jockeys like Bill Shoemaker, Eddie Arcaro, John Longden and George Woolf, and trainer Charlie Whittingham. These were among the sport's dominant figures – and the Mexican track didn't miss out on equine superstars either.

Among those who won the rich Caliente Handicap were two of the century's most famous horses, Phar Lap and Seabiscuit, a pair who were both destined to become celluloid heroes themselves. The former, the greatest horse in Australian racing history, scored his only North American success at Caliente, while Seabiscuit, whose rags-to-riches story became a surprise hit when Laura Hillenbrand's book was made into a feel-good movie, was another shipped south of the border down Mexico way to score in 1938.

As late as 1958, when Caliente's star was fading, the great Round Table, a US Horse of the Year and three times turf champion, topped the $1 million mark in career earnings with a victory there. When he retired, he was the world's leading prize-money winner.

Given such a storied history, the racecourse deserves its own book, and it has one: *The Agua Caliente Story, Remembering Mexico's Legendary Racetrack*, by David Jimenez Beltran, a Tijuana native and regular racegoer. Much of the information here was gleaned from that labour of love.

As well as offering regular $100,000 events before they were customary across the US itself, Agua Caliente also played a pivotal role in the development of US thoroughbred horse racing as a testing ground for many innovations that were subsequently introduced across its more powerful northern neighbour. These included live racecourse commentaries via public address, exotic wagers like the Pick 6 and the daily double, and jockeys' safety helmets. The last-named were introduced in April 1956 after the young rider LeRoy Nelson had been trampled to death in a spill the previous December. Tijuana's innovations weren't restricted to the racecourse, either. The Caesar salad was also invented during this period, reputedly at the Hotel Cesar on the Avenida Revolution, while the actress Rita Hayworth was discovered in a show at one of the city's playhouses.

For all its glamour, though, Agua Caliente struggled to break even. The casino and greyhound racing were better earners than its beloved horse track and when betting was legalised again in California and Sunday racing returned, the latter lost its *raison d'être*. The original venue was already a light of former years by the time it burned down in 1971, and yet another rebuilt facility closed once and for all in 1992 – but not before Tijuana-born jockey David Flores, destined to become a top-flight rider on the southern California tracks, had ridden his first winner there in 1984.

The name 'Caliente' survived only in the casino and spa, as well as in a chain of off-course bookmakers – another less celebrated track in Ciudad Juarez, on the Texan border at El Paso, was also closed down – to leave Mexico City's Hipodromo de las Americas, founded in 1943, as the only racetrack on a hugely diminished racing scene where well-heeled visitors dropping in from California were notable only for their absence. For a three-year spell in the 1990s, there was no racing whatsoever after the government, unimpressed with the racecourse administration, closed down even this final track, where top US-based jockey Victor Espinoza, rider of 2002 Kentucky Derby winner War Emblem, cut his teeth.

In 2005, more than 1,500 races were staged at the sole remaining racecourse, where the racetrack training centre housed stabling for 1,240 horses in pioneering two-storey barns ascending the backstretch hillside. Yet although they raced three times every weekend, Friday night, Saturday and Sunday, horse racing appeared a long way down the list of priorities to the average sports-mad Mexican, well behind football, bullfighting and, of all things, masked wrestling. When I was there, the biggest cheer of the day was elicited from local football club America's scoring the goal that took them to a Mexican Cup semi-final derby with Cruz Azul, while the Cuatro Caminos metro station – at the end of the dirt-cheap underground system, reputed to be the cheapest subway in the world at two pesos (10p) anywhere – was overrun with *colectivos* ferrying fans to the nearby *toreo* dome. In case you are planning a visit, I found out later that a better route is to take any bus marked 'Hipodromo' from the Reforma, the capital's central thoroughfare, or use the metro stops at Chapultepec or Auditorio.

As for the wrestling, *lucha libre* – literally, 'free fight' – retains an improbable hold on the popular consciousness as the spiritual descendants of Jackie Pallo and Mick McManus perform highly choreographed moves, all the time donning brightly coloured costumes like comic-book superheroes. Their bouts are regularly televised, while the wrestlers' lives – or those of their alter egos – are recounted in photo magazines and films. Bizarrely, some wrestlers have emerged as unlikely political figures. One particular lucha, 'Superbarrio' ('Superneighbourhood'), exists only outside the ring, where he has become part of the mainstream opposition, campaigning on various populist issues and lambasting leaders for corruption, at times challenging government officials to take them on over two falls or a submission. Think George Galloway in a cowl.

These bouts have to be seen to be believed. The top performers are found at the Coliseo in central Mexico City, where I witnessed the unlikely spectacle of a wrestler named Viper, sporting combat gear and a swastika mask, strutting around the ring offering Nazi salutes to the crowd. Perhaps he, too, was preparing for a future in the political arena. But a word of warning for would-be fight fans: their nickname is a trifle unfortunate in translation. These are the 'Heroes of the Ring'.

My visit to Mexico City's racecourse to find the heroes of the track revealed an outwardly unlovely venue, all multi-storey car parks, metal detectors and armed security presence. A pictorial warning at the ticket booth told me that guns were not allowed, alongside such other threatening objects like soft-drink cartons and hamburgers.

Moving inside revealed a sand circuit, seven furlongs round with a pleasant enough landscaped infield, somewhat spoiled by the featureless grey wall of the Banamex Conference Centre that overshadowed the back straight, book-ended by another pair of car parks. This was directly opposite the grandstand, a four-floor building of separate enclosures, or *tribunas*, all of them draped with huge advertising banners offering Coca-Cola, Bacardi, Corona beer and the like.

A capacity crowd in excess of 10,000 was expected a week later at the Handicap de las Americas, the biggest race of the year worth $1 million pesos (just under £50,000); about half as many turned up to this run-of-the-mill meeting, including a high proportion of women and children. Families were huddled around TV monitors glued to the football, eating nachos and cheesy fries, candyfloss and toffee apples. Given that there was a petting zoo-type theme park at one end of the track, it had the air of a Sunday family fun-day rather than a hard-nosed betting environment.

All that was missing was Keith Chegwin and the bouncy castle, though the segue of anodyne 1980s chart hits that provided a non-stop aural backdrop to the day's proceedings might have been enough on its own to suggest you had just entered the ninth circle of Dante's inferno. If Vietnam had its ceaseless timpani repertoire, here we were treated to *Addicted To Love*, *White Wedding*, *We Built This City* and *Never Gonna Give You Up* piped out in an interminable medley. To enter the Hipodromo de las Americas was to encounter a parallel world where it was always 1987, you couldn't turn off the radio, and the playlist had been compiled by Bruno Brookes and Gary Davies.

Fortunately, there was a degree of variety on the track, with a mixed card of seven thoroughbred races – mainly claimers at trips up to a mile, none of them worth more than about £1,700 – and three events for quarter horses, the equine variant bred specifically to race over two furlongs.

Owner-trainer Fausto Gutierrez, introduced to me in the minuscule media centre, said the thoroughbreds here were a "very particular" type of horse, used to racing so far above sea level. A trip to Puerto Rico, where purses were more worthwhile, was the best for which they could realistically hope, and the better among them could hold their own there. In December 2004, for example, Casty, the four-year-old who was to win the Handicap de las Americas a week after my visit, had finished second in the Clasico del Caribe (Caribbean Classic), an annual event featuring native-bred three-year-old thoroughbreds from member nations of the Caribbean Racing Confederation – Colombia, the Dominican Republic,

Ecuador, Jamaica, Mexico, Panama, Puerto Rico, Trinidad & Tobago and Venezuela. Staged at various venues in the Caribbean since the inaugural running in 1966, the nine-furlong dirt event, known colloquially as the 'Caribbean Derby', now has a permanent home in Puerto Rico, where it is run every December. Although Mexico has won its share in the past, the nation's most recent winner was as long ago as 1995, when a horse called Locochon took the spoils.

Generally, though, Mexico City racing was low-grade stuff. Gutierrez, who was to saddle Yack Lider to finish fifth in the 2005 Clasico the following December, blamed competition from off-track betting sites such as Caliente that he said returned nothing to the sport. "This is not really a gambling crowd here and our average betting turnover per day is only between two and three million pesos," he explained. That upper limit was about £150,000.

It could have been worse, though. Gutierrez recalled the day the police arrived to shut the place down. "They came down to the training centre in the morning with guns," he said. "We thought we'd be open again the next day and it took nearly three years!"

A good ploy betting-wise would have been simply to follow current leading rider Isaias Cardenas, who rode a four-timer, but it was time for something completely different. Race eight, a 330-yard heat half a furlong short of the full quarter, looked just the antidote to anything requiring ascetic dedication to the form book. I decided on a horse called Show Me The Money, winner of his last two starts with the fastest time in the race. He always seemed to win when drawn one, and he was drawn one in that particular race – it was plain to see his rivals wouldn't get close enough to whistle up his arsehole, yet he was 7-4 against.

Suffice it to say that, after the stetsonned gauchos had loaded them up ahead of just 15 seconds of competitive action, a visit to the payout windows was necessary to collect the equivalent of £17.50. If memory serves, this was my biggest win for two months, although it wasn't as if I had been anywhere that I could have pretended to know what I was doing.

As twilight descended, so did the ninth-race highlight, the Quarterhorse Breeders' Association Stakes, worth 407,000 pesos (just over £20,000). This one was a full quarter-mile in duration, so I left it alone for betting purposes. I didn't like those marathon events, unsure how the form would stand up over such an extended trip.

The field emerged on to the track for their short amble down to the stalls, in a chute at the foot of the straight. Presumably not the highest-calibre bunch of quarter horses ever assembled, their latent power was obvious; the closest comparison that came to mind were those Australian sprinters like Royal Ascot winners Choisir and Takeover Target, noted for their massive strength behind the saddle. These quarter horses possessed mighty hindquarters – big bums to the layman – ready to propel them from the gate like a shot from a cannon for their brutal task, over in 20 seconds.

The race provided a brief, exhilarating spectacle. The favourite, She Dashing, was in a different league to her rivals, exploding from the stalls and never being headed as her rider deftly switched his whip from hand to hand to keep her in a straight line. Earlier races had demonstrated how far a horse could veer diagonally in such a short stretch of ground.

She Dashing's rider barely touched her with the stick, an example the jockey on 31-1 shot Miss Darling Kiss might have done well to consider. This particular filly must have been a lazy type, as her jockey felt it necessary to hit her 24 times in the first furlong before being forced to restrain himself as his mount became the meat in a sandwich between two of her opponents. Still, all was not lost, The slow-motion replay revealed there was still time for half a dozen more cracks before the line. Miss Darling Kiss finished eighth of nine. Let's hope it was worth the effort.

USA

VITAL STATISTICS

RACING

		FINANCE	
Racetracks	176	Total prize-money	$1,085.01m
Fixtures	6,323	Betting turnover	$14,561.23m
Races	52,257		
Racehorses	66,903	All figures for 2005	

BREEDING

Stallions	3,535
Mares	58,808
Foals	34,070

IF AMERICAN racing isn't necessarily better, it is certainly bigger most of the time. There are more racecourses in Australia, and around twice as much is gambled annually in Japan, but otherwise the USA tops the world's list in almost every area.

The world's most powerful nation hosts more races than anywhere else – more than 52,000 took place in 2005, for example, compared to Australia, the next highest with just under 20,000 – and vastly more racehorses. There were nearly 67,000 individual starters in the US in 2005, where around 34,000 registered thoroughbred foals are dropped on an annual basis. The total number of starts was a whopping 428,000. A total of 176 racecourses are dotted around more than 30 US states, with anything up to 25 separate tracks operating at the same time of the year, nearly every day. Christmas Day is the only day on which there is a total blank. With bookmaking illegal outside the Las Vegas 'future books', the aggregate betting handle on the pari-mutuel is about $15 billion a year, while aggregate purses top the $1 billion mark.

These are some pretty big numbers – and they reflect only thoroughbred racing, which exists alongside hybrids like harness racing and quarter horses, serviced by industries of their own. Further variants, like mule racing, are popular on the county fair circuits that thrive in places like northern California, Texas, Oregon and Washington State. They usually manage to find room for a few thoroughbred races as well.

Despite its vast range, offering scope for everything from the mundane to the magnificent, US racing is often disdained by jingoistic English types, contemptuous of its apparent lack of diversity compared to the wonderful variety on offer in major European racing nations. While it is possible this argument is reflective of a more deeply entrenched anti-Americanism, US racing is certainly more homogenous in nature than its European counterpart. There isn't much steeplechasing for a start, and the gigantic Flat programme takes place on invariably oval circuits, all of them left-handed and usually a mile in circumference, with the majority offering only low-level dirt-track claimers featuring single-figure fields – at the same track for weeks on end.

Detractors deride it unfairly as dog racing, with punters interested only in numbers rather than horses. The accusation might have something to do with the intimidating mass of figures provided in papers like the *Daily Racing Form* for form students, known as 'handicappers', in a nation where the stopwatch is king. While these are virtually impenetrable to the neophyte, or indeed anyone used to more verbal British-style representations of form, they contain a welter of information for punters trying to identify a likely winner – so much, in fact, that American visitors have been known to mutter darkly about the inadequacies of the European model. I guess it's a case of different strokes for different folks, but getting to grips with the US form, quite an intellectual challenge in itself, is crucial to any understanding of the sport in the country.

Meetings in the States generally last for several weeks, with separate racing communities based at a single track for a couple of months before moving on to the next venue. Daily life is concentrated on the 'backside', among vast training barns on the backstretch training centre, usually situated alongside the back straight or sometimes to the side. Here, horses are prepared for their morning routines, being walked along the 'shedrow' to warm them up before a gallop out on the track itself in front of workwatchers who clock their every move, and then being hosed down and returned to their boxes. If they are due to race that day, they will be led around the track in the afternoon to the saddling boxes behind the main grandstand, race, and then go back home. Only the better horses travel between racecourses, and only the very best cross the country.

A notable feature of such backstretch racecourse communities is their ethnicity. American racing has come to depend on immigrant labour for much of its workforce and at many tracks you could be forgiven for thinking that every second person is of Hispanic descent. I am talking specifically about the men; backstretch females are more likely to be WASPs.

Presumably, a mixture of economic, social and physical factors are at play here. Working with horses is a specialist skill, often poorly rewarded at the lowest level; perhaps a significant proportion of the native population are both unwilling, and unqualified, for the role. Then again, they might just be too well-nourished for the job. You don't see many fat blokes riding trackwork in the morning.

Although it is rare to find a top-level Hispanic trainer, which probably says something about status levels, Latin Americans dominate the riding scene in a manner that exceeds levels of Irish influence in Britain. If the US jockey colony is a melting pot, many of the main ingredients have been imported from abroad, including some of the very biggest names, riding legends like Laffit Pincay (Panama) and Angel Cordero (Puerto Rico), and others like Alydar's rider Jorge Velasquez and Jacinto Vasquez, rider of the great filly Ruffian. Both of them were from Panama.

At the end of 2005, only three of the top ten riders in prize-money terms were Americans, the soon-to-retire Jerry Bailey, Garrett Gomez and Pat Valenzuela. The others were from Puerto Rico (the champion John Velazquez), Peru (Edgar Prado, Rafael Bejarano), Venezuela (Javier Castellano, Ramon Dominguez), Mexico (Victor Espinoza) and Panama (Cornelio Velasquez). Not far behind were Eibar Coa (Venezuela) and Alex Solis (Panama), while Jose Santos (Chile), partner of 2003 Kentucky Derby winner Funny Cide, was still active in New York. Fernando Jara, who partnered Invasor to win America's richest race, the $5 million Breeders' Cup Classic in 2006 at the age of 18, is another Panamanian.

If there's a degree of diversity among the racing community, the racetracks themselves are hardly identical either. In New York, for example, the racing calendar moves between blue-collar Aqueduct, a functional winter venue near JFK airport, to historic Belmont Park, a more wooded track housed in a slice of Long Island suburbia. For six weeks in the summer, though, the New York racing scene moves upstate to the wonderful Saratoga, the nation's oldest racecourse located in a genteel spa town between the Catskills and the Adirondacks and a byword for racing elegance.

Far from any stultifying uniformity, all nuances and shades exist. Beautiful Santa Anita in Arcadia, California, rests in the shadow of the San Gabriel mountains; at the other end of the scale, Hawthorne in Chicago sits in the middle of an industrial estate 25 minutes north of the city centre and rejoices in the colloquial title of 'Refinery Downs'. A number of eastern venues host jump racing, albeit often resembling amateur point-to-points, while Santa Anita has a downhill turf sprint course and the fairs circuit features tight bullring tracks, half a mile in circumference. Other venues, like Colonial Downs in Virginia, concentrate atypically on grass rather than dirt.

Nevertheless, day after day at track after track, the menu is often the same and the chances are that if you drop into an American racetrack in midweek, you'll be greeted by an eight- or nine-race card featuring races of the lowest quality at a severely restricted range of trips, seldom more than a mile.

The better-class races are mainly concentrated on the circuits in New York, southern California and Kentucky, with only a handful of the very top events, the valuable Grade 1s, held elsewhere in places like Florida, Chicago and the mid-Atlantic states. The trend towards speed also means that any race beyond a mile is regarded as a middle-distance event, and races over the Epsom Derby trip of a mile and a half are regarded as marathons. Such races are few and far between. In some quarters, the mile-and-a-half Belmont Stakes, final leg of the Triple Crown, is considered an anachronism.

Another oft-rehearsed criticism of US racing concerns its evident reliance on drugs, in particular two forms of medication banned in most other racing jurisdictions – the painkiller Butazolidin, better known as just Bute, and Furosemide, usually referred to by the trade name Lasix or Salix. The latter is used to prevent racehorses breaking blood vessels during a race, a common problem when they are exerting themselves. A host of formerly European-based 'bleeders' have gone on to thrive in the US once they have been given the treatment.

Critics argue, perhaps justifiably, that the systemic use of such legal medication, a consequence of the industry's relentless commercial drive as it serves to keep horses on the go, must have an adverse effect on the thoroughbred breed. Internal ailments and frailties may remain hidden in horses running through the pain barrier; severe, possibly life-threatening injury may be just a run away, as a horse feeling no pain will not transmit any telltale warning signs indicating a deeper pathology, perhaps until it is too late. Longer term, in weakening the immune system, it could be to the detriment of the breed's general soundness as a whole, sacrificed on the altar of commerciality to service the never-ending diet of low-level racing on easy-to-maintain, unforgiving dirt tracks, using 'em up and wearing 'em out.

In 2003, respected *Lexington Herald-Leader* journalist Maryjean Wall suggested legal medication had turned the American thoroughbred into a drug-dependent breed of "china dolls". Offering the prohibition of all such medication in graded stakes as a potential solution, Wall also quoted Andy Beyer, the originator of the speed figures that are treated almost as scripture by many American punters. "When I was in Australia ten years ago, there were no drugs," said Beyer. "These horses were like iron … everyone else manages to get along without this stuff."

In 2005, however, US racing was bracing itself for a sea change, with the installation of synthetic surfaces like Polytrack at certain high-profile racecourses like *chi-chi* Keeneland threatening a racing revolution. Though US racing is all about speed in the modern era, artificial surfaces are generally slower than the natural dirt base – and less punishing to the horse. That's the theory, anyway.

Even more contentious are suspicions surrounding the alleged use of illegal medication. Doping, in short. At certain tracks, cynical punters suggest the identity of the trainer's vet is the most important consideration in attempting to find a winner. Such innuendo sometimes reaches even the highest echelons of the sport, though not always supported by any firm evidence. One particular leading practitioner, whose attentions have wrought a remarkable transformation in the fortunes of certain barns, is nicknamed 'Dr Someday' by the satirical backstretch journal *Indian Charlie* – because someday we'll be told how he does it.

In 2005, my *Racing Post* colleague Paul Haigh wrote an award-winning investigation on the subject, examining the cult of the so-called supertrainer, handlers who suddenly begin firing in the winners at an unprecedented strike-rate. Haigh quoted Richard Bomze, president of the New York Horsemen's Association. "The playing field isn't even," Bomze said. "The racing game is amazing. It's the only game in the world where a mediocre trainer, a run-of-the-mill guy with a ten per cent or lower win rate, all of a sudden can't lose. He claims a loser by 20 lengths, moves it up in class and it romps by ten... Come on, give me a break. You don't become a Michael Jordan, Kobe Bryant, Sammy Sosa or Wayne Gretzky overnight. Only in racing do guys become superstars at the snap of a finger. It ain't talent, baby – it's chemicals and painkillers, and we all know who the bums are."

However, this is to focus unduly on the perceived negatives, which is unreasonable given that several of my personal racing heroes, both human and equine, are American, notably Steve Cauthen, rider of 1978 Triple Crown winner Affirmed, who turned jockeyship in Britain on its head when he crossed the Atlantic, and equine legends like Secretariat and Cigar, christened "the unconquerable, the invincible, the unbeatable Cigar" by Belmont track-caller Tom Durkin when the horse won the 1995 Breeders' Cup Classic under Jerry Bailey. A framed photograph of Secretariat's 31-length Belmont romp in 1973 is on my wall, while Cigar's courageous victory in the inaugural Dubai World Cup in 1996 during a run of 16 consecutive wins remains one of the most exhilarating performances I have ever seen in the flesh. That's why I got Bailey to sign my racecard like some starstruck fan.

Then there are the head-to-head battles, the fierce stretch duels that US racing habitually seems to produce, like Affirmed and Alydar, Easy Goer and Sunday Silence, Ferdinand and Alysheba – or those involving European-trained horses at the Breeders' Cup, such as those titanic clashes between Tiznow and both Giant's Causeway and Sakhee. I defy any horse-racing enthusiast to visit a major meeting in the States and not be utterly enthralled by the athletic spectacle. It was Haigh who best articulated to me the intoxicating nature of its appeal on one of my first visits to an American racetrack, a couple of days before the Breeders' Cup in 1997 at Hollywood

Park. Huddled over the *Daily Racing Form*, spectacles perched professorially on his nose as he tried to 'dope out' a winner, Haigh watched a minor race. "The thing is, Nick," he said, still aghast after a couple of decades visiting American racetracks, "they go so fucking fast!"

He wasn't wrong. I still love racing at home, but, for all its alleged shortcomings, this was a compellingly different beast. I was hooked.

*

ALTHOUGH records are incomplete, American racing probably started in some form in the mid-17th century, when gentlemen plantation owners in the south raced their horses against each other. In the north, the first formal racecourse is thought to have been laid out in 1665 on the Hempstead Plain on Long Island, near the site of the modern Belmont Park.

Stallions descended from the three Arabian forefathers of the Stud Book in England arrived in the colonies by 1730, and by the time of the American War of Independence, when racing stopped for a spell, their numbers were into three figures. Four Derby winners were in the States by the end of the century, among them Diomed, winner of the first Derby in 1780.

US racing had become organised even earlier than that through a network of state jockey clubs, the first of which may have been in South Carolina, founded in 1732. There is no longer any racing in that state, but Maryland, which came next with the formation of its own club in Annapolis in 1743, is home to Pimlico and Laurel. George Washington was a regular at early meetings in the state, while his brother Charles was an administrator. Both Charles Town and its racecourse are named after the latter.

The oldest stakes race in the country is the Phoenix Stakes, first run in 1831 at the old Lexington racecourse in Kentucky and now run every October as the Phoenix Breeders' Cup Stakes, still in Lexington at Keeneland racecourse. Kentucky's picture-perfect pastureland meant it rapidly became the country's bloodstock heartland, home to numerous horse farms and, eventually, the nation's most beloved race, the Kentucky Derby. Incidentally, while it is known as the Bluegrass state, the grass isn't really blue. It is a trick of the eye derived from buds that lend its fields a bluish-purple tinge in the spring. The rest of the time, the grass remains a disappointingly conventional green.

Despite Kentucky's status as the centre of the American breeding scene, the powerhouse of US racing was the monied New York circuit, home to Saratoga, founded in 1864. The Belmont Stakes, which started in 1867, is the oldest leg of the Triple Crown, six years ahead of the Preakness (1873) and eight in front of the Kentucky Derby (1875).

Put the three races together and you have the heart and soul of American racing, its Holy Grail. Although the term originated in England with West Australian's victory in the 2,000 Guineas, Derby and St Leger of 1853, our Triple Crown has become almost an obsolete concept in the modern era, although Nijinsky managed the feat in 1970. Few horses even race in all three British Classics, let alone win them all. In the States, the Triple Crown is very much alive, although it has become a source of national rancour that no horse has completed the sweep since Affirmed in 1978, despite many having tried.

Beginning with the Kentucky Derby on the first Saturday in May and stretching over only a five-week period, it is the sternest of tests for any racehorse. The Derby alone represents a new frontier, its mile-and-a-quarter trip the first time any of the three-year-olds involved will have gone as far as that – and this in front of a screaming six-figure crowd in a big field that can be guaranteed to go a hell-for-leather pace. It is a race unlike any other. Pimlico's Preakness Stakes a fortnight later is actually run over a distance half a furlong shorter, before the Belmont in early June, over an extended trip that often, amid much consternation, sees the undoing of Triple Crown aspirants.

Sir Barton was the first horse to complete the Triple Crown in 1919, although the races weren't linked until Omaha emulated him in 1935. The 11 horses who have done it represent a hall of fame on their own, featuring some of the most celebrated names in US racing history like the legendary Citation (1948) and Secretariat (1973), considered by many the best ever.

Although memorable visits to the Kentucky Derby and the Belmont featured among many racing trips to the States before I hit the racing road in 2005, a notable omission was the Preakness – pronounced 'Preak-nus', with the emphasis on the first syllable and named after the colt who won a stakes race at the inaugural meeting at Pimlico racecourse in 1870. It was here that the US leg of my trip started, and after the Mexican trauma it was a joy to go there and meet up again with my good friend Dan Farley, the *Racing Post*'s US correspondent, who took us to a crabshack where he taught me how to crack open the local speciality crustacean on the eve of the race.

The Preakness was quite a contest. In the recent past, the Classic had been little more than a lap of honour for Kentucky Derby winners like the people's favourites Funny Cide and Smarty Jones. No-one expected it to be the same way for Giacomo, the most unheralded Derby winner in living memory after scoring two weeks previously at Churchill Downs. "One-hit wonder?" asked a vaguely insulting headline on the front page of the *Daily Racing Form* about a horse owned by former record-company executive Jerry Moss, who named him for the son of his friend Sting.

Seldom can a Derby winner have been accorded less reverence. I had been in China when the race took place, but watching reruns of the race, it was easy to see why Giacomo's 50-1 victory was being dismissed as a fluke. A suicidal early pace left the race open to a late-closing type, and Giacomo, trained in California by John Shirreffs and ridden by the veteran Mike Smith, duly chugged home to win from an even bigger outsider, the 72-1 chance Closing Argument.

Two weeks later, the Preakness offered Giacomo the chance to silence the doubters, but it wasn't to be, although he wasn't entirely disgraced in third, around ten lengths behind the winner Afleet Alex, who had done best of the fancied horses in Kentucky. The bare facts fail to tell the real story, however, for this was an astonishing race featuring a fantastic display of acrobatics from Jeremy Rose, a second-division rider based mainly at mid-Atlantic tracks who had faced criticism for his Derby efforts. If I'd been looking for a rodeo act, I might have gone to Wyoming. I certainly did not expect it full tilt on the home turn in one of the world's most prestigious horse races, yet this was where Rose grabbed Afleet Alex's mane for dear life, the talented colt having been on his knees after being impeded by a rival.

It was a brilliant display of jockeyship. Afleet Alex, the Preakness favourite with millions of dollars riding on him after his Derby third, rushed up in menacing fashion to challenge the leader Scrappy T. This apparent no-hoper outran his odds, but he also came close to notoriety of a less welcome nature as he started to tire and veered violently outwards away from his rider Ramon Dominguez's whip, swerving into the path of the market leader. To gasps from a record crowd of 115,318, Afleet Alex clipped Scrappy T's off-hind heel and stumbled badly, face almost in the dirt. Rose would have done well simply to stay on; for him to transform near-disaster into emphatic success was little short of astounding.

"I was scared," said the 26-year-old rider. "I just held on and his nose got a little dirty out there. The thought process was I was going to get run over, but the instinct was to hold on and get my balance back.

"It wasn't my athleticism, but Alex's," he added. "He could easily have gone down and we'd have been run over by the entire field."

Delaware-based trainer Tom Ritchey, 53, was elated after the biggest win of his career. "In over 30 years of racing, I've seen horses take bad steps and win," he said. "I've never seen a horse take a bad step like that in a Grade 1 stakes and win."

Such a dramatic victory added an unlikely episode to the history of a racecourse not short on them already. Yet there were those worried that the chapter might have been the epilogue as far as Pimlico, a track redolent of American racing's past, was concerned.

One of the strangest sights on Preakness day occurs as soon as the horses have crossed the line, when a painter is lifted up on a hydraulic lift to a weather vane shaped like a horse and rider above a dome on the track's infield. There, he proceeds to paint in the colours of the winning silks on the jockey and number the horse's saddlecloth, an admirable effort destined to last a year in deference to a tradition dating back to 1909. Such devotion to times past was everywhere at Pimlico, the second-oldest track in the United States behind Saratoga. The Maryland Jockey Club claims to be the nation's oldest sporting association.

The weather vane was a replica of one that stood atop the track's Old Clubhouse, a Victorian building that stood at the foot of the home stretch and was considered the height of racing elegance until it was consumed by fire in 1966. Several of the other buildings at Pimlico had survived, lending the track the distinct patina of age. The rickety wooden viewing facility farthest from the winning post, for example, resembled the sort that used to act as main stand at football grounds in the old Division 4.

On Preakness day, with the stands full to capacity, the tumbledown surroundings were imbued with a certain old-fashioned charm evocative of the pre-war era, when Pimlico led the States in terms of purse distribution. Standing close to the running rail, the track seemed unusually narrow: seldom can you get so close to such top-class performers when they are racing. It took no immense leap of imagination to envisage Seabiscuit taking on War Admiral in that famous match race in 1938 for the Pimlico Special, in latter years the highlight of the Friday card the day before the Preakness, won in the past by Triple Crown winners like Whirlaway and the great Citation – both in a walk-over – and, more recently, superstars such as Cigar, Skip Away and Mineshaft.

It was doubtful whether Eddington's decisive victory in May 2005 added much lustre to the roll of honour after a contest in which Kentucky Derby winner Funny Cide finished only fourth, his own glory days probably behind him. The worry was that the same was being said about Pimlico. The track probably would not have seemed so quaint on other, less densely populated racing days, which meant every other afternoon of the year. Situated in an unlovely, borderline dangerous suburb 20 minutes from the centre of Baltimore, the whole place seemed in need of a coat of paint, not just the weather vane.

Make no mistake, this was a racecourse with a glorious past that faced trouble in the present. Maryland's government could not agree to the introduction of slot-machine gambling in the state – and, without it, there were those who believed the days of Pimlico, for all its rich history, were numbered.

A report in *USA Today* ahead of the Preakness suggested it was the only day of the year on which the racecourse made a profit. Nearby tracks like Charles Town and Delaware Park in neighbouring states were formerly considered minor league in comparison; now they often boasted better purses, thanks to the introduction of one-armed bandits, the installation of which subsidised horse racing at numerous venues. For a large proportion of the patrons at certain tracks, horse racing has been reduced to a mere backdrop for a day at the fruit machines, profits from which – as the tail wags the dog – are channelled back into purses.

Not so in Maryland, where state governor Robert Ehrlich vowed not to allow Baltimore to lose its premier horse race, an event of extraordinary local importance to a city that lost its NFL franchise when the Colts were moved to Indianapolis in 1984. "I will not stand for another Colts-type episode on my watch," he said.

Slots offered a potential saviour, but they weren't needed on Preakness day to entertain a record crowd at a track known colloquially as Old Hilltop, a nickname that time has turned into a misnomer, since it refers to a small rise on the infield, long since levelled, that used to be popular with trainers and racegoers. Like everything else at Pimlico, the tradition was remembered. Around 60,000 revellers flocked to the infield, which resembled one gigantic fraternity party as a vast cross-section of humanity fought for space to guzzle beers or black-eyed susans, the official drink of the Preakness featuring a yellowish concoction of rum, Cointreau and vodka, plus mixers.

The infield was not a place for the antisocial as thousands of T-shirted and bikini-topped specimens of humanity (most of them) pressed up against each other like rush hour on the underground, in increasing states of inebriation. It was a raucous occasion: cheap strings of beads offered for a glimpse of breast, as is customary on such occasions.

You entered the infield via a tunnel under the track. On the back of the T-shirt of the guy in front of me I read the legend: "Suck me, shuck me, eat me raw." I was relieved to see he was advertising a clamhouse on the front. Another character proffered a piece of cardboard with holes cut out; further investigation revealed it as a 'breastometer', designed to measure various sizes. Inexplicably, two females standing on cooling boxes appeared keen to oblige him. He was no shrinking violet himself. Lifting up his coattails, our bosom professor revealed a tuberous inflatable cock and balls. One group of internet entrepreneurs appeared sporting identical navy blue T-shirts. They were representatives of www.partiers.com, it seems, motto: "You bare it, we share it!" It was nice of them to think of those who couldn't make it to Baltimore.

With viewing restricted at best, many of those indulging in this orgy of drinking and shouting were possibly unaware that a race meeting was taking place around them, though this didn't stop their enjoying a mass drunken rendition of *Maryland, My Maryland* before the big race.

It was a pity they couldn't really see the Preakness, though. They missed something special. And who knows? They might not have many more chances at Pimlico.

*

I EXPECTED to see Afleet Alex three weeks later in the Belmont Stakes. In the interim, I crossed the country to a less-celebrated racecourse in the Pacific Northwest, in Washington State to be precise. Emerald Downs, Seattle: here we are now, entertain us.

Apologies for that. Seattle may be home to Amazon, Microsoft and Starbucks, but it was entirely predictable, given my obsession for pop-culture allusions, that some lame Kurt Cobain reference would appear in a section of this book involving the city in which that iconic figure made his name, although he was actually from the depressingly backwoods redneck town of Aberdeen. In any event, the Cobain analogy is far from appropriate, as Emerald Downs, while not exactly nirvana, was anything but grungy, and smelled more like candyfloss and popcorn than anything else, teen spirit or otherwise.

While the racecourse is named after Seattle, known as the 'Emerald City', it was about 30 minutes' drive south down Interstate I-5, near Tacoma, which provides the 'Tac' half of Sea-Tac airport, the international facility that services the area and lies dead centre between the two cities, which between them form a not-quite-conurbation alongside the beautiful Puget Sound.

Emerald Downs is located just outside the town of Auburn, and on arrival it felt strangely rural. This was odd because, while there was greenery around, a large industrial park sat next to the far side of the track, and the racing surface itself was an asphalt grey mile oval, with no turf track. A grey-green corrugated grandstand sat above a vast car-parking facility with signs saying 'lot full', testament to a crowd of around 5,000; this, despite my having chosen a nondescript Sunday with the most moderate of cards. Highlight of the day was a poor $20,000 claimer; nine out of ten were such contests.

Entry cost only $4 for five levels of grandstand – the sixth-floor clubhouse was only $2.50 more – and inside, it was almost as if you have entered a horse-racing theme park. Candy-coloured signage dominated, everywhere emblazoned with the Emerald Downs logo. A pantomime-horse mascot bounded around on a playground scooter. It was all very welcoming: trackside deli, espresso bar, ice-cream parlour, gift shop, all smart and spotlessly clean. If it seemed a little artificial, a touch 'Disneyfied', that was probably just a function of American taste.

Emerald Downs opened for business in June 1996, rising from the ashes of Washington's premier track, Longacres, from whom it inherited its only Graded race, the $250,000 Longacres Mile. It is the central track on a distinct northwest circuit, a sort of regional division compared to the premierships of New York and Los Angeles. A fair comparison in Britain is possibly a track like Ayr, discounting the latter's jumping programme: off the beaten track, with a few decent races, but not in the top flight. Mind you, the Emerald Downs betting handle still averaged over $1.2 million a day – not bad for the minor leagues – and a strongish purse structure, bolstered by a partnership with the local Muckleshoot Indian tribe, which operates casinos in the vicinity.

The season at Emerald Downs, scheduled to dovetail with Oregon's Portland Meadows, is six months in duration, from April to October. The track's racing community seemed a curious cross between the welcomingly inclusive and incestuously parochial at the same time. Among riders in action on the day I visited were jockeys from Panama, Australia, Mexico, Trinidad and the Virgin Islands, yet nearly everyone else seemed to have some connection with the Baze family.

The prolific Russell Baze, whose father Joe was a successful rider at Longacres before he became a trainer, started out in Washington in the formative years of what was to be a record-breaking career. Baze moved to the northern California circuit in 1979, soon becoming the dominant force, and hasn't been a regular visitor to Emerald Downs since. On the other hand, his cousin Gary, the state's all-time leading rider, was still based at the track when I went there, as was Debbie Hoonan, who returned after a 12-year hiatus to partner 52 winners in 2004. She made a victorious return on a horse owned by her cousin, Lisa Baze.

I knew all about these people because I had done my research after some unprofitable days' betting in many and varied racing environments. I knew the riders and was watching for the top two in the jockeys' list. Kevin Krigger was one of the few black riders operating at anything approaching a decent level in the States, while his rival Ricky Frazier was a part-time stuntman who, besides *Seabiscuit*, also got involved again alongside actor Tobey Maguire in *Spiderman 2*, caught in a fight between the eponymous webslinger and Doc Ock, his multitentacled nemesis.

I knew the trainers, I'd studied the Beyer speed figures and I knew there was a significant speed bias – a week previously, the track claimed a six-and-a-half-furlong world record for former Longacres Mile winner Sabertooth.

In short, after hours of 'handicapping', I had the day's sure thing. Voile Soir in the fifth. Scratched minutes before the off. No matter. Krigger was on the favourite in the next, Ben's Quest. Hooked up in a speed duel, he lost lengths on the turn, and just failed to get back up as his rival's stamina faltered.

In the next, Tropical River looked certain to step up from a recent effort and, unusually, all four *Daily Racing Form* pundits selected him. He was showing at a generous 5-1 in a ten-runner event. I should have smelled a rat. Instead, I had a win single and various exactas involving other possibles, among them Datzig, from the dangerous Dan Markle barn. Tropical River led until past halfway before falling into a heap; Datzig, a 9-1 chance, won easily, from an unconsidered outsider. Unconsidered by me, that was.

Time for the main event, in which, according to the *Form*'s front page, trainer Joe Toye had shipped in a pair of fillies who had done well at Arizona's Turf Paradise. I went for Darling Silver over Bobbie Wagner. Naturally, Toye won it – with Bobbie Wagner, ridden by Frazier, who had a treble. So did Krigger. I backed none of them.

Oh well, whatever, never mind; it is better to burn out than to fade away.

Or so one tragically tormented soul once suggested. Just before he loaded the shotgun.

*

NEXT up was a fantastic 24-hour train journey south on Amtrak's Coast Starlight via Portland, Oregon, to San Francisco, the idiosyncratic city that, in conjunction with New York, gave birth to the Beat Generation, those self-proclaimed "angel-headed hipsters" and "crazy dumbsaints of the mind", without whom it is likely no-one would ever have pulled on a rucksack. I probably wouldn't have done, anyway.

Fifty years after Jack Kerouac, Allen Ginsberg and their comrades launched their full-frontal assault on American social mores, 40 years after the flower children, and 30 years after the queer heyday of the Castro, this idiosyncratic city remains a magnet for non-conformists and wannabe non-conformists of many and varied hues.

Any of them searching for "eyeball kicks", to borrow the argot of one Beat icon, ought to try a visit to Golden Gate Fields. If the racetrack's very name sounded impossibly romantic, its setting more than lived up to the billing, offering a prospect that was nothing short of spectacular.

Situated just across the bay from San Francisco itself close to the university town of Berkeley, spiritual home of American dissent, the racetrack is the only thing that sits between a stretch of freeway and the water at Point Fleming, formerly the site of a dynamite manufacturer. The view from the car park beside the grandstand was unforgettable, worth the trek on its own. Dump your vehicle and turn left away from the track instead of right and you will be greeted by the wide red span of the Golden Gate, often obscured around town, in its full glory directly ahead across a couple of miles of San Francisco Bay. To its left are the towering structures of the city's compact financial district; further left still is the huge, Meccano-like Bay Bridge that links to Oakland, its blue-collar engine room.

The standard of horse racing at Golden Gate Fields never quite matches its magnificent position, rating a sharp level below the premier US tracks. Although it hosts a few Graded races, alongside its neighbour Bay Meadows, the pair represent a lesser northern Californian circuit, far removed from the likes of Hollywood Park and Santa Anita in Los Angeles.

Golden Gate did boast a phenomenon in riding terms, mind you, in the shape of the incredible Russell Baze, who had recently moved past the 9,000-mark in terms of winners when I caught up with him, still about 500 adrift of world-record holder Laffit Pincay jnr, the legendary Panamanian having retired on the 9,530-mark in 2003. At the time, he was about to catch the Brazilian Jorge Ricardo, who had also ridden more than 9,000 winners. The pair were destined to compete against each other for some time.

While he has never ridden regularly at the most prestigious tracks, Baze's efforts in northern California are amazing. Consider the statistics. Born in 1958 in Vancouver, Canada to American parents, Baze rode his first winner in 1974 at Yakima Meadows in Washington. At the end of 2005, he led the nation in terms of races won for the eighth time, although a total of 375 meant he missed the 400-mark for only the third time in 14 seasons. Injury intervened on the other three occasions – but no-one else has managed it more than three times. Inducted into American racing's Hall of Fame in 1999, Baze has won over 60 single-meeting riding titles at either Golden Gate or Bay Meadows, which is known locally as 'Baze Meadows' in his honour.

"Catching Laffit is obviously the next goal," the rider said. "I appreciate the significance of it. There's only room for one guy at the top and it would be very gratifying to be that guy. Hopefully I can win enough races where it's going to be my name at the top for a good long time. If I can catch Laffit, I'd like to ride 10,000."

Baze's remarkable achievements have been crabbed in some quarters as he has spent only a short time during his career at a major racing centre, preferring to stay away from the bright lights. In a 30-year-plus career, he had ridden only twice in the Kentucky Derby, for example, while his name has appeared on the jockeys' list in three Breeders' Cup races, without any sniff of victory. He did ride in the vastly more competitive arena of southern California for a spell between 1989 and 1991, winning a few Grade 1s, before returning north to his adopted home.

"People have said to me, 'Don't you wish you would have stayed down south," Baze explained. "I could have stayed down there and done all right and I might have taken off and done real well. By the same token, coming back here was definitely not a mistake – I've achieved great success since I've been up here. I don't think I've made any real serious mistakes in my career."

I was intrigued by exactly how many of the Baze family were involved in horse racing. "It starts with my grandfather's generation," he said. "My grandfather was Burt and his brother was Bob. Both of them had large families of boys and all of them were in the horse-racing business. Both Burt and Bob trained horses and they ran on the minor circuits. I think they called it the Blue Mountain circuit up there in Washington, Idaho and Oregon. My grandmother rode my grandad's horses in the match races. All the boys got into the business in one area or another – trainers or riders or horse-shoers. I don't think we've had any veterinarians yet – we're not smart enough to be vets, I guess."

The day-to-day realities of American racing, wherever you go, are exemplified in a morning down the 'backside' among the training barns, situated next to the track, sometimes at the backstretch, sometimes to one side, as was the case at Golden Gate. Here's where you encounter the reality of Stateside racing as its racing community goes about its daily business, Baze among them; where horses are conditioned on the track in timed workouts that are there for all to see, producing a set of times that are published soon afterwards.

I made the effort to visit, for the purpose dragging myself out of my San Francisco hotel – in the North Beach district, at an establishment where Ginsberg, author of the revolutionary poem *Howl*, used to stay, "naturally enough," according to *Time Out*, "in a small queen". Boom boom.

Over at Golden Gate, there were horses everywhere, poking heads over barn doors, loosening up on circular walkers, being ponied to the track ready for action, putting in 'bullet' workouts, hosed down afterwards. Horses just being horses; jockeys and work-riders, some in yellow-and-black leather-tasselled cowboy chaps, milling about with trainers and owners; Hispanic stablehands shooting everywhere on pushbikes, zipping among the straw bales under telegraph wires down the central thoroughfare known as Main Street; others mucking out and sweeping up around huge barns with names like Buddy Lee, Dan Franko and Chuck

Perry on the side; everyone moving to the track canteen for breakfast.

Enthralling to watch as it was to the newcomer, it was also more than a little bewildering. OK, let's be upfront about this – I really hadn't a clue what was going on. At 8.15am, as things seemed to be slowing down and the track was deserted, I began to move towards the exit. A moustachioed fellow on a tricycle shouted at me. "Hey man, aren't you going to see the big horse?"

"Of course I am," I lied, entirely ignorant. It turned out to be a sprint sensation named Lost In The Fog – with hindsight, perhaps the baseball caps sported by a few of those round about might have been a giveaway – who had won six out of six by an average of nearly eight lengths at four different tracks. Trained by Greg Gilchrist at Golden Gate, the colt had broken the track record on his previous start. Someone else took pity on the hapless limey visitor, informing me that Lost In The Fog was the dark bay with the white blaze, jogging around under Baze, who, incidentally, is much respected for his dedication and work ethic.

Lost In The Fog then breezed five furlongs; everyone seemed pleased and I watched him being hosed down. A few days later, he recorded win number seven in Grade 2 company across the continent at Belmont. Sadly, though, Baze was missing, as he broke his collarbone a couple of days after my visit.

Baze was not yet *hors de combat* on the preceding Saturday afternoon at a track marketed as 'where the bay comes to play'. It exuded a welcoming, laid-back atmosphere, with a mixed-ethnicity crowd that seemed to be there for the punting rather than any other fripperies, few of which were on offer anyway.

Golden Gate, despite an elegant clubhouse enclosure, felt like a proper horseplayers' track. Sparsely attended, a couple of thousand indulged themselves, betting at home and away on simulcasts from all over the States and farther afield, including Fort Erie and Woodbine in Canada and Maronas in Uruguay. Apparently the time zones were wrong from Timbuktu, or doubtless that would have been shown as well, if they could have squeezed it into a racecard already featuring 70 contests.

Only nine of them were held at Golden Gate, on a fairly typical card, dominated by single-figure fields, among them a four-and-a-half-furlong juvenile race – and, inevitably, resulting in a hatful for the remorseless Baze. Four times he visited the 'Shoemaker winners' circle' – named in honour of the riding legend who recorded the first success of his career at the track in 1949 – but he had to settle for second in the four-runner feature on turf, the $100,000 Rolling Green Handicap, which went to Capitano under Jon Court, himself completing a lucrative week after a couple of stakes wins at Lone Star Park in Texas.

I had reason to thank the ubiquitous Baze and leading trainer Jerry Hollendorfer, who combined to win a decent two-year-old race – a six-furlong event, better class than the shorter juvenile contest – with a debutant called Sabi Sand. The colt was sent off a 3-1 chance, and Baze amply demonstrated where those thousands of winners came from by stealing first run on the home turn as the favourite got snarled up behind horses.

This manoeuvre meant that I had to ask someone how to redeem a profit on my voucher from the automated machine. Remarkably, after a series of deplorable excuses for gambling elsewhere, and thanks mainly to other Baze-centric tickles – plus Capitano, sent off 9-5 third favourite – I somehow managed to exhaust betting opportunities at Golden Gate with a decent profit.

Russell Baze, I love you.

*

TRIPLE CROWN winners became almost commonplace in the 1970s, when Secretariat (1973), Seattle Slew (1977) and Affirmed (1978) were almost joined by a fourth in Spectacular Bid, "the greatest horse ever to look through a bridle," according to his trainer, Bud Delp. 'Bid' missed out in the final leg in unfortunate circumstances after a safety pin became lodged in a hoof the night before the race. The colt would have been a worthy addition to the elect. The following season, he went unbeaten in nine races as a four-year-old, setting seven track records.

The Belmont Stakes continued to produce memorable contests throughout the 1980s, when trainer Woody Stephens achieved the outstanding feat of saddling five consecutive winners between 1982 and 1986. Stephens' exploits are remembered in a display featuring a large painting and several trophies situated under a large arch as you enter the main stand. It is known as 'Woody's Corner'.

Stephens never trained a Triple Crown winner, and America's oldest Classic developed a reputation as a breaker of hearts after Spectacular Bid's defeat set a trend for a series of contenders who failed at the final step in the race known as the 'Test of the Champion' – sometimes in the most unfortunate of circumstances, such as when Charismatic broke a leg when leading in the final furlong in 1999. The two previous seasons had also seen near-misses involving the California-based Andy Warhol lookalike Bob Baffert. First the trainer's famously gritty iron-grey battler Silver Charm missed the Belmont by three-quarters of a length when Touch Gold crept up on the blind side, then stablemate Real Quiet was touched off by a nose by Victory Gallop.

The air of expectation is tangible at Belmont Park, one of the most cherished venues in the nation, when the ultimate prize is on the line – and the sense of anticlimax when the dreams are shattered, as they have been ever since Affirmed, is palpable. I experienced this in person in 2003 and 2004, when both Funny Cide, the humble New York-bred gelding, and 'America's horse' Smarty Jones fell at the final hurdle.

There was no potential Triple Crown winner when I returned in June 2005, which certainly made it easier to get a seat on the racetrack special out to the track from Penn Station to a grandstand nowhere near as full as in the previous two years. Then again, we were talking about a huge, ivy-clad behemoth that runs the length of the home stretch of the 'Big Sandy', nickname for the widest oval among major American tracks. A crowd of 62,274 wasn't too shabby.

Thoughts of the Triple Crown still managed to dominate matters after Afleet Alex repeated his Preakness dose, pulverising his Belmont rivals with a second blistering display. The extra distance, the undoing of so many in the past, proved no impediment whatsoever to a horse who looked a true champion. Therein was the problem: this was a case of what might have been.

Such was the overwhelming nature of Afleet Alex's Belmont superiority – albeit over a moderate bunch – in a race that has unhinged so many others that the impression of what was lost when he was beaten a mere length by

Giacomo in the Kentucky Derby was never far from the surface, even amid joyous scenes after such an energising victory.

Jeremy Rose admitted as much. "He should have been a Triple Crown winner but I messed up," said Rose. "I say I messed up because I had the best horse. You can't blame Tom and you can't blame Afleet Alex. So, if you have to blame someone, blame me!" Whatever the merits or otherwise of his efforts in the Derby, Rose had performed wonders since, his Preakness acrobatics being followed by a Belmont display that was coolness personified.

Though many experts questioned Afleet Alex's stamina credentials for the USA's only mile-and-a-half Grade 1 event, the colt was sent off hot favourite as the day turned to dusk for the 11th race of a 13-race card, more than six hours after the opener. The crowd found enough reserves of stamina to produce a spirited rendition of the Belmont 'hymn', the *Theme From New York, New York* ten minutes before the off; after the gates opened, Afleet Alex had the staying power to come up with a more memorable performance.

Giacomo, thought likely to appreciate the trip, hit the front unexpectedly early as the pace-setters crumbled over three furlongs out. Rose, clearly possessed of confidence and sangfroid in abundance, had settled Afleet Alex well towards the rear of the main body of the field. After a ground-saving trip, he sent his mount through the field and, three wide, passed his main rival as if he were standing still. On entering the Belmont stretch, he shot five clear and went on to post the fastest closing quarter-mile since 1969 to win with complete authority, going away by seven lengths from outsider Andromeda's Hero. The hapless Giacomo faded to finish a sad seventh.

Rose modestly played down his role in events. "I had the best horse, and I knew I had the fastest quarter-mile when I needed it," he said. "The only thing that could get him beat was me, so I stayed out of his way. I don't want to hear any more criticism of this horse. Knock me, but don't knock him. He's one of the best we'll see for a long time."

Afleet Alex may not have enjoyed the public profile of a Funny Cide or a Smarty Jones, but it wouldn't have been America if someone hadn't unearthed a human-interest story to go with the horse. This one was a tearjerker. Two days before her first birthday, a little girl named Alexandra 'Alex' Scott was diagnosed with malignant cancer. She died when she was eight, but not before she had started a lemonade stand in July 2000 to raise money for cancer research and her hospital. By the time of the 2005 Belmont, the Alex's Lemonade Stand cause had raised $1.6 million. Such stands were selling lemonade at the racetrack and among those to have hooked up with a cause that touched a nation's hearts was the Cash Is King partnership that owned Afleet Alex. Though the colt's name was unrelated to little Alex Scott, his owners, moved by her story, donated a proportion of their purse earnings to the cause.

In a TV interview before the Belmont, Rose suggested the reason the partnership had stayed intact in the Preakness was because they had an angel watching over them, a sickly line allocated a predictably large amount of airplay by the New York media as they covered the feel-good side of the Afleet Alex story.

Sadly, the racing angle wasn't destined to run and run. Afleet Alex suffered a foot injury later in the summer and never raced again.

*

AFTER *he returned from injury, Russell Baze rode Lost In The Fog to a rare Grade 1 victory in August 2005 at Saratoga during a ten-race winning streak. His owner, San Francisco real-estate magnate Harry Aleo, described as a "gruff octogenarian" by* Blood-Horse *magazine, endeared himself to US racefans by refusing to sell, despite huge offers for a colt who had cost him just $48,000 as a yearling, a relative pittance in the world of inflated bloodstock fees. "What the hell would I do that for?" Aleo asked. "I've been waiting all my life for a horse like this, and if I took all those millions I'd still be sitting here today doing what I'm doing, and I wouldn't have that horse that has given me all this excitement and enjoyment. I'm not in the selling business. I'm in the racing business."*

Although Lost In The Fog flopped when favourite for the Breeders' Cup Sprint, he still collected the Eclipse Award as America's outstanding sprinter for 2005. The Golden Gate giant with the crooked white blaze on his face stayed in training as a four-year-old in 2006 with trainer Greg Gilchrist, but his story did not have a happy ending. To the dismay of his connections, Lost In The Fog was found to be suffering from cancer and, despite efforts to save him, had to be put down in September. The bravest of horses, he had been running with three malignant tumours in his spleen, even winning a Grade 3 event at Churchill Downs in June just before his cancer was diagnosed. Vets considered the tumours had been growing for a year, which meant they were probably troubling him when he disappointed at the Breeders' Cup in 2005.

"I believe he was already feeling the effects of the cancer," said Baze, who was distraught at the loss of his favourite horse. "He had never run a bad race for me. We were on the lead at the eighth pole and he just faded badly from there. A horse like that just doesn't come along very often – it was sad that he had to go like that. He was just a fantastically talented racehorse."

To huge acclaim, Baze finally surpassed Pincay's world-record mark on December 1, 2006, when a four-year-old filly named Butterfly Belle became the 9,531st winner of his career at Bay Meadows. "Who would've thought 32 years ago a skinny little kid with no experience would be standing here today?" said the rider. "I could hardly believe this would happen. I'm not going to do a lot of celebrating – I'm going to do a lot of relaxing."

The refusal of the Maryland general assembly to sanction slot-machine gambling continued to hit Pimlico racetrack. The Preakness may have survived, but the Pimlico Special, the state's second-most-prestigious event, was not carded in 2007, its $500,000 prize being spread among other races in a bid to keep purses competitive. Ironically, the 2006 renewal was the best for a while, being won by Invasor, who went on to become the world's top-rated racehorse after an unbeaten streak in the US culminating in the Breeders' Cup Classic.

PUERTO RICO

VITAL STATISTICS

RACING		FINANCE	
Racetracks	1	Total prize-money	$20.4m
Fixtures	260	Betting turnover	$247m
Races	1,948		
Racehorses	850	All figures for 2005	

BREEDING	
Stallions	10
Mares	600
Foals	550

BY the time I moved on from the States, back home it was the week of Royal Ascot, albeit a Royal Ascot with a difference. Owing to a multi-million-pound redevelopment programme at its traditional base in the Queen's Berkshire back garden, the meeting was transferred, silly hats and all, to York. Contrary to popular opinion, this temporary venue was not chosen for its proximity to the Leeds branch of Harvey Nichols.

As the latest chapter in the story of a historic meeting was being written in Yorkshire, I was busy substituting the Bollinger for pina colada and examining the state of horse racing in the Caribbean holiday island of Puerto Rico, where the racecourse dress code is more easygoing, although the wearing of swimming trunks is discouraged unless they are covered by a respectable pair of shorts.

Opened in 1976, the nation's sole racetrack was El Comandante, which lay in the town of Canovovas 12 miles east of the capital San Juan, a lower-rent Miami. They race anti-clockwise around a one-mile sand-track oval, very much in the American style, like everything else in Puerto Rico, a nation that enjoys a slightly confused status. Although its inhabitants claim US citizenship, they have three times voted against becoming a fully fledged state of the union, preferring to remain part of the American commonwealth. Rather like Britain, as Ben Elton might have once suggested, except we don't carry the passports.

Puerto Rican horsemen have long made a home from home on the backstretch training centres of American racetracks, and the island has a rich racing heritage, dating back more than a century to the days when wealthy plantation owners bet against each other over whose horse could run faster. These matches turned racing into a spectator sport when third parties got involved in the gambling, resulting in a variety of makeshift venues across the island, including tracks in the San Juan area that remain part of the nation's racing folklore, like Las Monjas and Quintana.

The former was home to Puerto Rico's greatest bequest to the world of horse racing. Angel Cordero jnr, 'El Angel de Las Monjas' to his first followers in his native country, was brought up on the backstretch by his father, Angel Cordero Vila, himself a respected jockey and trainer. When the former moved to the US, he was to become one of the most celebrated names in the racing world, a daring stylist with a string of triumphs in the top races and plenty more besides.

"If the horse has got four legs and I'm riding it, I think I can win," Cordero once said. More than 7,000 of them did, making him one of the most prolific riders in US racing history. He won four Breeders' Cup races and all three legs of the Triple Crown, including three victories in America's most famous race, the Kentucky Derby (Cannonade in 1974, the ex-Puerto Rican-trained Bold Forbes in 1976 and Spend A Buck in 1985). Three times leading prize-money earner, he also topped the charts in numerical terms once, and won the Eclipse Award for outstanding jockey twice in the 1980s. For good measure, Cordero was the undoubted king at Saratoga, America's oldest and best-loved racecourse, where he was leading rider on 13 occasions.

Renowned as the most competitive of riders, Cordero was seldom far from controversy in a career defined by a fierce will to win. He pushed the rules to their outer limit, driving his mounts into holes others couldn't see and leaning on his rivals to a sometimes unacceptable degree as far as the stewards were concerned, resulting in frequent suspensions. But as well as being the toughest of competitors, he was also the showman who originated the flying dismount, jumping high off the back of his mount in acrobatic fashion after big-race victories. A generation later, the exuberant Frankie Dettori continued the tradition with his own version of the 'Cordero Leap', emulating his US-based predecessor by flying into the air after Group 1 victories. Dettori learnt how to perform the trick watching Cordero during a stint as an exercise rider in southern California in the early 1990s; he tried it out for the first time when partnering Barathea to victory for his mentor Luca Cumani at the 1994 Breeders' Cup at Churchill Downs in Kentucky.

Loved and loathed in almost equal measure, the volatile, immensely dedicated Cordero is a legend anywhere in racing terms, but in Puerto Rico he is regarded as one of its all-time sporting heroes, perhaps eclipsed only by the beloved Roberto Clemente, the baseball player killed in a plane crash in 1972 while en route to delivering aid to earthquake victims in Nicaragua. A long-serving right-fielder for the Pittsburgh Pirates, for whom he performed heroically in the 1971 World Series, Clemente provided the inspiration for the name of 1972 Epsom Derby winner Roberto, who ran in the colours of Pirates owner John Galbreath.

Even in retirement, Cordero was still making his mark in his 60s, helping to shape the career of his fellow countryman, the leading New York-based rider John Velazquez. The latter, who was introduced to racing at the Puerto Rico jockeys' school and rode his first winner at El Comandante in 1990, moved to New York when he was 18 under Cordero's guidance. The older man later became his agent, a partnership that blossomed to the extent that Velazquez emulated his mentor in becoming the US prize-money champion and winning Eclipse Awards and New York riding titles of his own.

The occasional Puerto Rican-trained horse has also left its mark in the US. The aforementioned Bold Forbes won his first five races at El Comandante before taking two legs of the US Triple Crown under much-admired front-running rides from Cordero, while Mister Frisky was 13-for-13 in Puerto Rico before coming unstuck behind Unbridled when favourite at Churchill Downs in 1990.

Such a rich legacy was ancient history by the time I visited El Comandante, amid suggestions that racing in Puerto Rico was on the skids. Reports of financial trouble emerged when the English-language *San Juan Star* claimed the track was bankrupt – and the evidence of a dreary Wednesday-afternoon card did little to argue a positive spin.

All but one race on a seven-race card was worth under $10,000, with unattractively small fields the order of the day, plus a pari-mutuel betting pool in which the odds were monstrously prohibitive to the punter. There wasn't much of a crowd, either. Although Sunday cards were expected to attract around 2,500 patrons, the attendance was so sparse that the top floor of the three-storey grandstand stayed closed. So did most of the bottom two floors.

Then again, racecourses all over the world struggle at the gate midweek and Marco Rivera, El Comandante's director of equine operations, claimed the paltry attendance was not a source of concern to him. "Ninety per cent of our handle comes from off-track betting these days so we don't depend on people coming to the track," he said.

The numbers supported his claims. El Comandante, which was run by a US company, habitually figured among the top 15 tracks annually in North America in terms of 'handle', or total betting turnover, largely as a result of 650 off-track betting parlours and the more recent innovation of internet wagering. These were augmented by a rudimentary five-hour TV broadcast of every meeting, fronted by a bald, bespectacled fellow who looked like a cross between former British Horseracing Board chairman Peter Savill and Jim Bowen from *Bullseye* with a permanently startled air, as if he was sitting on a porcupine. Perhaps the excessive heat was getting to me. As I quizzed him in his office, the moustachioed Rivera seemed to bear an uncanny resemblance to Big Bird's human friend in *Sesame Street*. It was unsettling.

Further investigation revealed that Rivera was a 51-year-old Chilean-born accountant whose father was a trainer. He had been around horses all his life, trained as a vet before turning to number-crunching, and joined the racecourse first in an auditing capacity. He had never appeared alongside a man dressed in a giant yellow ostrich costume on a Canadian-produced children's TV show. Or so he claimed, which was a shame, because otherwise perhaps he could have done a turn with the 'Hipikids', infants attached to the racecourse crèche. The children of racetrack employees, they were recognisable by their uniform of maroon T-shirt with 'Hipikid' logo and shorts, and they seemed to be having a fine old time running amok around the virtually empty stand. At least there was plenty of room for hide- and-seek.

The proposed installation of video-lottery terminals, recently passed by the senate, gave further succour to racecourse officials. Even without them, purses were generally less shabby than on the day I turned up, being said to average $14,000 at a track that operated five days a week, 52 weeks a year, hurricanes permitting. They don't always permit. Hurricane Jean, in 2004, forced a temporary shutdown, an occupational hazard in a tropical region where such storms are common, having got their name there, after the malevolent deity Jurakan, pronounced 'Hu-ra-kan'.

Although Puerto Rico has its own triple crown for local-bred horses, the most important race held at El Comandante is the Clasico del Caribe, the intriguing nine-furlong contest I had heard about in Mexico that successfully brings a national rivalry to bear on the issue by pitting against each other native-bred thoroughbreds from member nations of the Caribbean Racing Confederation. First held in 1966, when it was won by Venezuela's Victoreado, the race brings together Classic winners from across the entire region. The 2005 renewal, worth about $290,000 and held in December as part of a two-day festival, was won by a home-trained representative in the Sammy Garcia-trained Borrascoso under Alexis Feliciano, who prevailed in an international finish from Excelencia, representing the Dominican Republic and winner of all his 14 previous races. The latter was disqualified, which meant Shahid, another Puerto Rican, was promoted to second ahead of Mexico's Ruller Chief.

The Clasico was the most lucrative event hosted in 2005 by a venue that on its website proclaimed itself the "foremost racecourse in the Caribbean", a region providing homes for a surprisingly large number of racetracks. The best-known among the others are Garrison Savannah in Barbados, which provides a winter home to the better-heeled of the British racing set and hosts the Sandy Lane Gold Cup sponsored by the five-star hotel, and Jamaica's less elegant Caymanas Park. They also race in places like St Thomas, St Croix, Martinique and Guadeloupe.

Back at El Comandante, the track did its best to tempt potential customers away from the TV via free entry, although patrons were asked to spend a minimum of $10 per head (Puerto Rico's currency is the yankee dollar, of course) if they used the first-floor restaurant.

Facilities were fairly basic. 'Winners Sports Bar', the prime spot for a drink, could easily pass for a British Legion social club, with handwritten special offers inked on cardboard cut-out stars and small bulbs fitted into empty Johnny Walker miniature bottles blu-tacked above the counter to give a fairy-light effect.

You could ignore the dated interior, however, for a magnificent exterior was rewarding enough. Around half an hour away and visible in panorama from the stands was the mist-enshrouded El Yunque rainforest, while the racecourse itself sat in a densely forested area. Its own version of the Hollywood sign greeted visitors with a 'Bienvenidos' on the hillside. To enter the racecourse, you had to pass through a blanket of palms, more of which were cultivated on the infield and the backstretch, camouflaging a training centre of 38 barns and 1,500 stalls housing imports from South America, Ocala and Kentucky alongside the home-breds.

A couple of unique features were evident as soon as racing started. If green was the dominant hue elsewhere, the paddock was strikingly multi-coloured. As the five runners for the opener entered it in front of the stands, it emerged that their attendants were all dressed in shirts reflecting the owners' colours, more or less approximate home-made versions of the jockeys' silks. A horse carrying a jockey whose silks were yellow with green shamrocks was led around by a handler wearing a polo shirt of yellow, with green shamrocks. If a horse was wearing blinkers, these, too, were in the owner's colours, while a fondness for brightly coloured nosebands was also noticeable, with lime green, orange and shocking pink among the favourites.

Given that the parade ring itself was blooming with primrose and terracotta buds and housed a display of jockey figurines, even with only a handful of runners the paddock resembled an explosion at a fluorescent paint factory. Only the trainers, determinedly polo shirts and jeans, let the side down. Well, they and the handful of racegoers, almost exclusively male and sullenly middle-aged, bellies bulging out over the rails.

A look at the pari-mutuel board showed the punters had little to smile about, given the miserly nature of the returns on offer, a function of the percentage of turnover held back by the racecourse (including tax) and not redistributed among those who backed the winners. Take a look at the prices for the opener, the longest event on the card at a mile and a furlong: 1-2 the favourite, then 4-5, 5-1 and 70-1 (only four prices because a pair of horses were coupled in the betting). You don't need to be a mathematical genius to figure out that a betting market with two odds-on shots in the same race might not offer the greatest value in the world.

It wasn't the most alluring betting option in history – and that was without considering the unsubstantiated allegations of corruption among riders, with rumours of electric whips ('batteries') being found on the track. To be fair, my tiny sample hinted at nothing untoward, and Marco Rivera forcefully dismissed any suggestions of skulduggery. "I believe we are controlling it," he said. "We dope-test the first three home, and the government is responsible for all the regulatory functions." Mind you, some of the races were shocking, regardless of whether the riders were powered by Duracell.

On the plus side for punters, there was a big rollover in the poolpote, the track's jackpot bonus to its regular Pick 6, only 35 cents a throw. A lottery-style lucky-dip option was available, whereby the machine simply generated six random racecard numbers on your behalf. There was a major snag, though. Unless you were the only bettor to select all six, the poolpote fund rolled over – and it had been a long time since anyone won it on their own, as the pool was up to $8.5 million.

With no racecard available and virtually no form to go on – all-in-a-line past performances could be downloaded from the website, but I didn't work that out until afterwards – the wisdom of Gonzalo Ramirez, contained in two sentences in the *San Juan Star*, became imbued with near-scriptural significance.

Ramirez suggested the fifth race, a three-year-old claimer, looked the most interesting contest, pointing out that it featured a horse named Recomendado, an "invader from Panama". As the unlikely strains of Colonel Bogey were piped through the stands, the tote board seemed to speak against him: the Panamanian invader went on a march in the wrong direction, finally hitting 7-1, which meant he was a 10-1 chance in true market terms. Surely Recomendado would have been appreciably shorter if he had a live chance? Panama, after all, wasn't exactly next door. It didn't stop his winning by close to ten lengths, after which I commended myself on having had the restraint to resist the temptation to bet in such unattractive circumstances.

Come on now. With allegations of corruption, no form and a tote with an inbuilt takeout fashioned by Shylock, surely only a halfwit could have considered having any sort of bet. I was only $48 down on the day.

*

SUGGESTIONS of financial problems at El Comandante turned out to be well-founded. After the racecourse filed for bankruptcy protection, in the early days of January 2007, a US bankruptcy-court judge approved a $73 million reorganisation by the Camarero Group. After 30 years as El Comandante, the track was renamed the Hipodromo Camarero after the Puerto Rican horse who won a world record 56 consecutive races from April 1953 to August 1955 at Quintana and Las Casas.

"We know we have a tremendous task ahead of us but I have been a racehorse owner for 23 years and so have most of the members of our board," said Camarero president Ervin Rodriguez. "For the first time, the racetrack is owned by a Puerto Rican enterprise and we feel a great responsibility to excel and do our best to take the racing industry in Puerto Rico to its highest standard ever. That's why we chose Camarero as the new name – he is a symbol of success and consistency."

TRINIDAD

VITAL STATISTICS

RACING		FINANCE	
Racetracks	1	Total prize-money	$1.39m
Fixtures	38	Betting turnover	$8.02m
Races	345		
Racehorses	381	All figures for 2005	

BREEDING	
Stallions	29
Mares	350
Foals	165

INVIDIOUS as it is to resort to stereotypes, I cannot talk about Trinidad and Tobago without reference to the cultural phenomenon of 'liming', said to be virtually the official national pastime in the twin-island Caribbean nation whose inhabitants are renowned for their relaxed outlook on life, there to be enjoyed to the full.

Anyone can learn to lime. All it involves is hanging out with friends for a chat over a drink, possibly the local favourite Stag lager, marketed as 'a man's beer' in a region that wouldn't be batting high in the political correctness XI. My preference was for the less gender-specific Carib.

Although sunseekers descend in their droves for the mellow vibe and the vast golden strands of Tobago, this picture-postcard tropical paradise no longer has a racecourse, so I gave it a miss in favour of its tougher big brother Trinidad, which does. Even in high season, between January and March, Trinidad's unvarnished capital Port of Spain is not really geared up for tourists. The rainy season had just started when I arrived in June, and the city wasn't so much laid-back as comatose, denuded of life for the Labour Day bank holiday weekend. The explanation was simple. They had all buggered off to Tobago to chill out.

A deserted Port of Spain with only the dregs of society left behind wasn't the most immediately appealing place, especially around its ugly downtown central district around Independence Square and Brian Lara Promenade, and a large, heavily industrialised dock area. I didn't help matters by booking our least appealing accommodation so far. Generally speaking, we had spoiled ourselves on the first three months of the trip, splashing out occasionally on some high-quality hotels, such as a plush high-rise *Blade Runner*-type tower in Tokyo that offered a fantastic panoramic view out across the city from its top-floor bar, like in the movie *Lost In Translation*. It cost a small fortune just to sit in the bar, so we made do with a couple of cans of lager and a bag of crisps sitting in the alcove of our room next to a deeply recessed window. Same view for about $20 less.

There's a trendy buzzword for that type of journey, which has become known as 'flashpacking'. According to the Sunday supplements, it is popular among people in their 40s and 50s with heavy disposable incomes unencumbered by children. Budgetary constraints, however, soon meant that we could no longer indulge in upmarket treats. Flashpacker reverted to backpacker – yet while the Trinidad guest house was about $200 a night cheaper than the Japanese hotel, it sounded great value for a place described in the *Rough Guide* as an "old colonial mansion" with a "verandah overlooking picturesque Victoria Square".

You get what you pay for, and I hadn't paid for much, which possibly explains how Jane and I found ourselves the only customers in a dirty, overwhelmingly hot firetrap badly in need of renovation and redecoration. To say the facilities were spartan overstates the issue, though there was a bed plus a fan that worked occasionally.

This room was accessible only by a rickety staircase above the main homestead, where a voluminous landlady kept constant vigil over the television alongside her brother, possibly not the most energetic soul, given that in five days I never once saw him rise from his perch on the sofa. The only place less appealing on the entire trip was a Lima backpackers' hostel at which we arrived late at night to be met by a teenage crackhead who was supposed to check us in. To his credit, he just about managed it, and he got the double up by checking us out again the following morning.

Trinidad nights were scary enough at this candidate for the anti-hip hotels' guide. "Picturesque Victoria Square" proved such an attraction that a cross-section of the local homeless made it their base, while sleep was a precious commodity owing to a loud noise at irregular intervals outside the window. At first it sounded as if someone was trying to hammer down the door, and it continued all night, every night. All became clear in the morning when I was greeted by the remnants of a crab-apple shower at the bottom of the outside stairs, the fruit harvest having fallen on to the corrugated roof of the shed adjacent to our room.

Fortunately, with Port of Spain offering scant reason to stay out and the guest house even less incentive to stay in, the rest of the island had plenty to recommend it, notably the Caroni Swamp, a dense mangrove habitat home to the exquisite scarlet ibis, which can be seen in large numbers. Although the swamp also contains snakes and caiman, I saw neither; on the other side of the island, the Nariva Swamp is famed for manatee and anaconda.

Visitors stuck in Trinidad could also do a lot worse than heading inland to Santa Rosa Park, the nation's only racetrack about half an hour's drive on the East-West Highway from Port of Spain to the busy market town of Arima, where it is overlooked by the rainforest heights of the Northern Range.

It was here that I witnessed the greatest clash in horse racing history. Kind of. On paper. If you left out some salient points.

Anyway, how about this for a field? Among the seven runners for the nine-furlong Stud Farm Association National Stakes were a pair of Triple Crown winners plus two further Derby winners and the best sprinter in the land. OK, I have omitted to mention that we are talking about a very low standard of racing, and the three legs of the Trinidad Triple Crown – Guineas, Midsummer Classic and Derby – are all restricted to creole thoroughbreds (horses bred in the West Indies) and thus may not be the most competitive races in the world.

Still, there were enough domestic stars in this collection to get the crowd excited. There were cheers as the stalls opened; a rising hum throughout the race developed into fierce vocal encouragement as the favourite, 2003 Triple Crown winner Top Of The Class, asserted two furlongs out after being taken on for the lead for much of the race. He won convincingly from Glenn Mendez-trained stablemate Cardinal Messiah, the 2001 Triple Crown winner, who outstayed top sprinter Man Of Class for second.

So what if it was only Trinidad? The chunky Mendez seemed to know what he was doing – and it was also a good day for winning rider Ricky

Jadoo. With Trinidad number one Emile Ramsammy away riding in Canada, he bagged a treble.

To put the nature of racing at Trinidad into context, it is worth comparing it with Puerto Rico. As detailed in the previous chapter, on the moderate day I visited El Comandante, the biggest prize was worth the equivalent of about £6,000 and only a handful of people turned up, although the purse figure was unrepresentative for the Caribbean's number-one track where they race five days a week for average prizes of about £7,700 per race. In contrast, a couple of thousand joined me in attending the big Labour Day meeting at Santa Rosa – but the main event was worth only T&T$60,000, about £5,200 at prevailing exchange rates.

Racing in Trinidad has its origins in the early 19th century, when there are records of match races being held in 1828 on the Queen's Park Savannah, the largest open space in Port of Spain known colloquially as the 'Big Yard'. For well over 150 years until the racing scene was reorganised in 1994, the Big Yard was the focal point of racing on the island and home of the Trinidad Derby, restricted to Caribbean-bred three-year-olds. Mentone, voted Trinidad's horse of the century, broke a pair of track records at the Savannah during a 12-month spree in 1959-60, which saw the ex-British import pass the post first 15 times in 18 starts at varying trips, including six out of six in Barbados. Lester Piggott and Willie Carson both rode at the Savannah, while for a period in the 1970s the Derby was a closed shop for second-division British riders, with John Higgins, Geoff Baxter and Tony Kimberley among the winners.

Although the racecourse is now defunct, still standing is the grandstand, originally built in 1897 and rebuilt 50 years later. It is used today for various cultural events, including the annual carnival, for which the Big Yard provides the central location. For most of the year, however, the only sport you are likely to witness from the stand is the odd jogger.

Both Queen's Park Savannah and another track, Union Park, were closed before the 1994 season, when racing was centralised at Santa Rosa and the nature of the sport in Trinidad abruptly changed. Having been based on a European turf model, Santa Rosa's right-handed grass circuit was relaid as a left-handed dirt oval adjacent to a training centre designed to cater for 600 horses. In the year that Trinidad's favourite son broke records for the highest scores in both Test cricket and first-class cricket, the first winner of the new-style Derby was appropriately named. It was the Roger Hadeed-trained Lash Dem Lara. The same year, leading English rider George Duffield partnered five winners in a row on the Boxing Day card.

Although the Santa Rosa turf track was restored in 2000, US-style racing dominated the programme, which involved mainly anti-clockwise races around the sand oval, plenty of claimers, and free use of anti-bleeding drugs.

Race distances, expressed metrically, had the customary uninspiring range on the day I visited, from 1,100 metres up to just 1,800 metres. All eight races were on the dirt, because two scheduled for the inner turf track were shifted when the rainy season hit with a vengeance before racing. Mountains that were in plain sight behind the Larry Gomes Stadium towering majestically over the track minutes beforehand were suddenly hidden from view amid a torrential downpour that lasted nearly the whole afternoon.

Moving the first race on to the dirt required plenty of effort as the starting stalls were moved 50 yards up the muddy straight, a manoeuvre that sounds easier than it was given the marshy nature of the racing surface. Drenched commentators dived for cover as the warm tropical rain came down in sheets; the horses were excused parade-ring formalities and sent straight out on the track from saddling boxes, set behind a jockey figurine painted in the Derby winner's maroon-and-navy colours. The horses were partnered by jockeys who bombed out of the weighing room after their pre-race prayers to mount them in the stalls.

The racing surface took the rain amazingly well. The conditions might have been excessive, but such otherworldly storms are a hazard of the climate in Trinidad, and Santa Rosa still manages to race all year round, with a limited programme, comprising meetings on 50 per cent of Saturdays and bank holidays.

A day's racing there offered a miniature version of Trinidad society as a whole. A diverse, multicultural crowd of African, Indian and European descent mixed in a down-to-earth environment. It was basic and unfussy, a bit rough round the edges but totally uncontrived. Keeping it real, you might say.

The compact grandstand was divided into three floors. The bottom, which cost nothing to enter, was a raw place, featuring two rudimentary betting cages, beer outlets, a shark-and-bake stall, and a Kentucky Fried Chicken franchise. It was rammed with people avoiding the squall. As scruffy dogs roamed loose among discarded betting slips, a muscular security presence maintained a semblance of order among individuals whose charms were of the rough-hewn variety.

You had to purchase a ticket for the other floors – Level 2's Clubhouse even had a dress code, 'elegantly casual', allowing no shorts, denim jeans, sandals or sneakers. No-one seemed bothered enough to worry about enforcing it; the emphasis was more on the 'casual' than the 'elegantly'. It would be hard to imagine a less stuffy environment to watch a race meeting, although there was one formality to which everyone adhered: the national anthem, played before racing, was shown great respect by everybody.

While Trinidad's racing programme is intermittent, punters can also bet daily on North American racing – and there was extensive coverage of racing in Britain in the local daily newspapers, with previews, tips and reports. The worldwide web is one thing, but it felt strange picking up a paper on the other side of the Atlantic and considering a British-based journalist's selections for Beverley and Windsor, which could be seen live via SIS in a handful of off-course fixed-odds betting shops. On-course betting was exclusively pari-mutuel.

Among many welcoming officials, I found one with a distant expatriate link. Steward Roy Podmore was a Liverpudlian from Port Sunlight, who, in a former life, was a jockey in Britain riding for Peter Thrale and John Benstead in Epsom. "Where have you left your car?" was his opening gambit.

Just outside the front gate, I answered.

"That's as good a place as anywhere else. I just hope it's still there when you get out."

Aged 63, Podmore had been in the Caribbean for 40 years. His stepson,

Joshua Stephen, was an apprentice. "He should win the first, if he doesn't mess it up," Podmore told me.

Although he missed the break, Stephen didn't mess up thereafter in a display approaching competence to win on the 3-5 favourite Gray Admiral. It was the first winning tip I had been given for a couple of months, and the bug was catching.

David Loregnard, an affable stewards' secretary with a vast knowledge of British racing, introduced me to 'The Skipper' of the *Daily Express*. His real name was Shammi Kowlessar, but pseudonyms were much favoured among the tipping clique, where his colleagues include The Guru, Earl J and Mr Knowledge.

The Skipper exuded the self-confident air of someone who was about to give me the trifecta in the next. "I'm going to give you the trifecta in the next," he said, self-confidently. It paid just over 5-1. Grateful as I was to The Skipper, it's possible I might have found the winner Getdjobdone independently. Sent off 1-9 favourite, he was a US-bred three-year-old son of the Preakness Stakes winner Louis Quatorze who had comfortably won both his previous outings.

"As he was bred in America, he's not eligible for the Classic, but he could be the best horse in Trinidad," said The Skipper. He certainly won as if he was, Ricky Jadoo bolt upright like a stiff-backed Victorian gentleman as he crossed the line. The jockey wasn't showboating, having lost his irons two furlongs out, much to the merriment of one happy soul among the rougher necks on the ground floor who accosted me with a massive grin as he ran out into the rain to welcome the impressive winner.

"He ride backward and do the job," my new friend told me. Pleased with himself, he said it again, "He ride backward and do the job," and then went off to impart his wisdom to a group of his mates huddled nearby. They all had a good laugh about it over their tins of beer, soaked to the skin.

You can't let the weather get in the way of a good lime.

PERU

VITAL STATISTICS

RACING			FINANCE	
Racetracks	2		Total prize-money	$3.67m
Fixtures	260		Betting turnover	$20.43m
Races	2,216			
Racehorses	1,526		All figures for 2005	

BREEDING	
Stallions	52
Mares	710
Foals	386

UNLESS you are the sort of person who feels threatened by a change in the weather, there isn't much to match the thrilling sense of anticipation just before you touch down in a new continent for the first time. It is a feeling that cannot be encountered on more than five or six occasions in a lifetime, a mixture of excitement and anxiety rolled into one, a neurotic fear of the unknown interwoven with an almost overwhelming exhilaration.

All those emotions were coalescing when I crossed the equator and touched down in South America, specifically Peru, land of Andes and Amazon, Incas and Inca Kola. The last-named is a lime-green fizzy drink that tastes like Vimto. More Es than backstage at a Happy Mondays gig.

Before visiting Monterrico racecourse in the sprawling, squalid capital city Lima, there was time for a couple of weeks' break, during which the highlights included a visit to the ancient capital Cuzco and nearby Machu Picchu, the famed lost city of the Incas in the Urubamba Valley, known as the 'Valley of the Kings'. A four-day boat trip up the Amazon was also pretty special, featuring as it did piranha fishing, a trek across the treetop canopy, sleeping under a mosquito net in the heart of the jungle, and spotting pink river dolphins. Plus tarantulas, caiman, armadillo and capybara, all of them spotted by a bibulous basketball-shaped guide named Segundo, who insisted on stopping our motorised canoe to visit his cousin at a riverside hamlet for an early-morning libation. We emerged, many tins of beer later, after an audience with the mayor and half the town. All of them not slow to enjoy an ale. It was a long journey back down the river to camp; let's just say that when nature calls Amazon-style, it requires quite an effort to find a suitable tree.

*

ALTHOUGH horse racing is well established in many South American nations, the sport has not been immune to the continent's extreme economic problems, although horse racing doesn't seem much of an issue set alongside the twin evils of acute unemployment and devastating poverty.

Argentina's Gran Premio Carlos Pellegrini at San Isidro racecourse near Buenos Aires remains the region's most prestigious race, the South American answer to the Arc, but another important contest, the international Latin American Grand Prix (the Gran Premio Asociacion Latinoamericano de Jockey Clubes e Hipodromos, to give the race its full title), has suffered a troubled recent existence, enduring a four-year hiatus before being reinstated in 2004 with prize-money of $200,000 in the Chilean capital Santiago. When it is being contested, this peripatetic 2,000-metre event acts as a South American championship, featuring horses from Argentina, Brazil and Chile – the three leading racing nations – alongside Peru, Uruguay and, in the past, Venezuela. The last-named and Colombia, where they race at a tight dirt oval just outside Medellin, usually look to Puerto Rico and the Caribbean Classic for their rare international sorties. It seems no-one wants the hapless Ecuadorians, who, since Quito racecourse became the land on which an airport extension was built, have just a single racetrack at Buijo, outside the city of Guayaquil. Paraguay, too, has a racecourse in the capital Asuncion.

Peru has a decent record in the Gran Premio Latinoamericano with five winners in 22 runnings up to 2006, including a victory in Chile in the first contest of the new era in March 2004 with a horse named Comando Intimo, trained by Felix Banda at Monterrico. Argentinian horses won the next two.

The first recorded instance of organised racing in Peru dates back to a meeting held at Lima's port Callao in 1864 before the first permanent racecourse was inaugurated 13 years later between Callao and Lima. This was called Cancha Meiggs ('Meiggs Field') after Don Meiggs, the American engineer who constructed Peru's central railroad and built the stands. Although this venue lived long enough to witness the foundation of the Jockey Club del Peru in 1895, it was superseded in 1903 by Santa Beatriz, initial home of the Derby Nacional, the most important leg of the nation's Quadruple Crown. Clearly they like to go one louder in Peru.

Owing to the extraordinary growth of the capital, Lima's racetrack has been moved twice since, first to San Felipe in 1938 and then its current base, Monterrico, which opened in 1960. While this fine venue has hosted the Gran Premio Latinoamericano more than once, times were tough there in 2005, as evinced by a glance at the racecard in the sports paper *El Libero* ahead of my Thursday-afternoon visit. This midwinter card featured nine dirt races, from 1,000 metres to 1,600 metres, with truly pitiful purses. The most lucrative contest was worth a total of just 4,200 nuevo soles, the national currency, pegged closely to the dollar, also used everywhere in Lima. The dollar conversion for this prize was $1,300 at the time. This equated to just £730 – and connections of the winner received only £452 of it. Sundays, one of four racedays per week, generally offered better prizes, but even the most recent running of the Derby Nacional in 2004 had been worth only around £33,000.

Having said that, Monterrico was still more affluent than Peru's second arena in Arequipa, birthplace of leading US-based rider Rafael Bejarano, who spent a year and a half at the Peru apprentice school, winning the apprentice title in Lima before moving to the States and, in 2004, topping all riders numerically with 455 wins.

Monterrico lies in solidly middle-class territory in the wealthier eastern half of the enormous capital. Half an hour by taxi from the old town centre, it is, both socially and geographically, even further away from the slums, grim and vast, concentrated in the western half on the way to the airport and down to the docks. A pretty sight this was not, and Lima as a whole looked unlikely to win any beauty contests, which was unfortunate, given that its status as a hub in the air-travel network meant I ended up spending eight nights there altogether spread across three separate visits.

Far away from the slums (or far enough away), on entering the racecourse there were obvious clues to grander days gone by. After turning off the dual carriageway, following white-painted arrows on a red-brick wall letting, a regal avenue flanked by majestic tall palms ushered visitors past car parks into the chunky concrete grandstand, behind green iron gates at the end of the Avenida del Derby, the Wembley Way of horse racing in Peru.

Although entry to the main grandstand was free and there were nice-looking bars and restaurants – one of them was the *Bar Ingles*, improbably overseen by a man in a kilt – there couldn't have been more than 300 people in attendance, though I was told this was unusually small. An average Sunday was said to attract 3,000, a really big day ten times that, with racegoers also taking advantage of the infield behind the pari-mutuel board opposite the stand, on the other side of red-and-green striped running rails that turned blue and white 100 metres down the track.

The swish Jockey Club del Peru existed mainly as a social club, offering its 6,000 better-heeled members access to tennis courts, swimming pool and gym, as well as the best seats at the track, in the members' stand close to the winning line, where individual places could be purchased on a long-term basis by debenture-type arrangement, with owners' and stud colours etched into the seat upright. Behind the winning post, the numbers of the first five horses home were posted after every race beneath the Peruvian flag. Eleven more flags flying nearby represented the owners' association and the current top ten owners, whose colours were replicated; a change in position in the table meant a change in the order of the flags.

As this was midwinter, it was chilly by Lima standards, though not by ours, at 20C. Visibility, however, was terrible for much of the day as the sun tried vainly to pierce the armour of smog enveloping the track. It would probably have been easier to see the Cesarewitch start from the Rowley Mile stand than it was to discern the stalls for races started on the straight five-furlong chute, tacked on to a US-style oval. A turf track, badly in need of a trim, went unused.

They didn't mess about once racing began: nine races, only 25 minutes between each one. After the horses were led round from the training centre by attendants in green boiler suits, they appeared briefly for a perfunctory circuit of the parade ring before going straight out on to the track, down to the starting gate and back again. Then it was a quick photo of the winners, jockeys weighed in on a set of scales in front of the stand, horses rushed off to be hosed down.

All this was achieved with the minimum of fuss. Unfortunately, the same could not be said of my comedy-sketch attempts to find someone to break down the language barrier, a thin grasp of Spanish not being up to debating the finer points of the Peruvian thoroughbred in the local idiom. Midway through the day a lean-looking, suited-and-booted official named Elmer Cornejo started taking a keen interest. "You're from England?" he said. "But you have really good horses in England." (Translation: what the hell are you doing here then?)

Later, a ridiculous linguistic mix-up meant that, rather than being granted access to take a few photographs to accompany a piece on Peruvian racing for the *Racing Post*, Jane and I found ourselves shepherded into the winner's circle instead to have our pictures taken alongside fifth-race winner Duque de Anjou with his trainer Alberto Quimper and jockey Jose Enriquez. Understandably, they were as bemused as we were, but happy to oblige.

The farce ended with the appearance of a cigarette-and-shades woman of a certain age who introduced herself in near-perfect English as the racecourse public-relations manager Margarita Calderon. "Why didn't you let me know you were coming?" she asked. As if I hadn't sent a hundred emails warning the track about it, and telephoned ahead to alert them when I failed to receive any reply.

Speaking in the Jockey Club box – all oak panelling, fading portraits and trophies won abroad by Peru's top horses down the years – Margarita made no bones about Peru's problems. "The racing here is certainly below Argentina, Chile and Brazil. We've had a big recession and it has taken its toll but it's been like that for four or five years, and we are surviving. We are down to below 500 foals a year now, whereas a few years ago we were just below 1,000. We are definitely struggling, but it's getting a little better – the sales were quite good this year. People were spending $20,000 on a horse."

The betting boards didn't offer much financial relief. Though all the money bet in off-course outlets was pumped into the pool, the totals still looked as if someone had left a zero or two off the end. I pointed to the win (*ganador*) pool for a race less than five minutes away, scarcely able to believe a figure still short of 1,000 units. "That's everything," confirmed Margarita,

It takes more than a visor to keep traffic fumes away en route to the races in Bangkok (© Jane Godfrey)

A bike, a fag and a racehorse: a trainer arrives at the Saigon Race Club (© Jane Godfrey)

Is this the donkey derby? Schoolboy jockeys ready for action in Vietnam (© Jane Godfrey)

Above: *Destined for greatness: Deep Impact and Yutaka Take in full flight as they win the Satsuki Sho at Nakayama (© Japan Racing Association)*

Grand Hedge, yes, but no brick wall: Karasi (Brett Scott) en route to the first of three successive victories in the Nakayama Grand Jump (© Japan Racing Association)

Racing nirvana at Nakayama: nowhere are there bigger crowds or more betting than Japan (© Jane Godfrey)

Jockeys bow to the crowd before a race at Seoul racecourse (© Jane Godfrey)

Royal Ascot it ain't: the 'owners' and trainers' bar' at Beijing's now defunct racecourse. Standing in rear is our man in China, Nigel Smith (© Jane Godfrey)

The national flag flies high above the Hipodromo de las Americas in Mexico City (© Jane Godfrey)

Bottom left: All shades of life on the infield at Pimlico for the Preakness Stakes, second leg of the US Triple Crown (© Jane Godfrey)

Bottom right: The Pimilco weather vane is painted in Alfeet Alex's colours according to Preakness tradition (© Jane Godfrey)

The racecourse mascot prepares for action at Emerald Downs, just outside Seattle (© Jane Godfrey)

Me and Russell Baze: the author meets the world-record breaker at Golden Gate Fields (© Jane Godfrey)

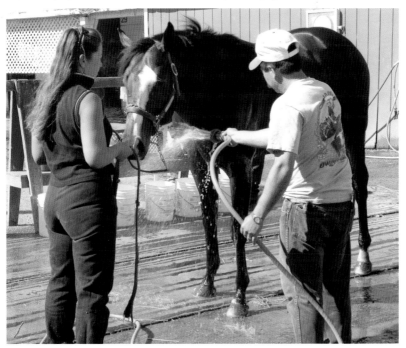

Star of the show: ill-fated Lost In The Fog, the best horse for years at Golden Gate Fields, is hosed down after a morning workout (© Jane Godfrey)

The Triple Crown winner that never was? Afleet Alex (Jeremy Rose) is imperious in the Belmont (© Uli Seit/Horsephotos.com)

Attendants are colour-coordinated at Puerto Rico's only racetrack (© Jane Godfrey)

Racing in the Caribbean at Santa Rosa in Trinidad; shame there wasn't any Caribbean-style weather (© Jane Godfrey)

Author and photographer in the spotlight for no apparent reason alongside a winner at Monterrico in Lima

Caracas averages between 35 and 45 murders every weekend – but the views are nice at La Rinconada racetrack (© Jane Godfrey)

Best view in the house: the famous statue of Christ the Redeemer overlooks racing at La Gavea in Rio (© Jane Godfrey)

Bottom left: *Brazilian riding legend Jorge Ricardo at his home track, La Gavea in Rio; in 2007, he broke the world record for career victories (© Jane Godfrey)*

Bottom right: *The veteran Jorge Valdivieso, the most celebrated jockey in Argentina (© Jane Godfrey)*

embarrassed yet inured to such paltry figures. "And 70 per cent of that comes from off-course. We are losing out to slot machines and casinos."

The pools for the *quiniela* (forecast) and *duplieta* (daily double) were slightly better, but not much. Outside the slums, there were slot-machine centres on every corner in Lima; in contrast, only a handful of tellers were working the on-course machines at Monterrico. There was never a queue in front of them.

Among the most famous Peruvian racing names are jockeys Edgar Prado, among the very best riders in New York, and Jorge Chavez, rejected as a child by his family and forced to roam Lima's mean streets before he took up riding, went to the States and won an Eclipse Award. He also won the Kentucky Derby on Monarchos in 2001.

Although he was nicknamed 'Chop Chop' Chavez owing to the aggressive-looking whip action he took with him to the USA, his compatriots at home seemed more docile. Benjamin Padilla, 40 clear in the jockeys' race, had little need for the whip on his only mount of the day, which won easily, but at other times I was forced to wonder if I hadn't unwittingly stumbled on the Lima round of the hands-and-heels series, a British concept for young riders who are banned from using their whip. This wasn't 'chop chop' exactly; it was more a case of 'stroke, stroke', and seldom even that.

The natives were restless on that score after the sixth race, where a photo was required to produce an outcome between the front two in the betting, separated by half the track. The favourite, up the middle, looked sure to win a furlong out. At least, his rider thought so – but, on the far side, the jockey on his market rival was slightly more vigorous. They crossed the line together; there was an audible groan when the photo was displayed on the screens around the stand, showing that the winner was on the far side, and catcalls for the rider on the second.

The laughable nature of the pools was made abundantly clear by a four-year-old named Baltimore Belle in a 1,000-metre handicap. She had done no better than seventh in her previous six starts, clocking a series of slow times in the process. Unmentioned in the paper, she attracted zero votos from the list of 25 tipsters (*pronosticos*, literally prognosticators) in the racecard. Even her rider seemed to have little going for him. He was called R Ponce, poor bloke. Then again, one of her rivals was ridden by A Arce.

Despite such unpromising antecedents, I was shocked to see, barely two minutes before the scheduled off-time, that there wasn't a single sol on Baltimore Belle, who was showing 999.9 in the ganador pool. With dividends declared to the two soles minimum stake, this was 500-1, the maximum price the board could show. This meant that, in the entire betting pool, on- and off-course, not a single cent had been risked on this horse. Not one.

I was sorely tempted to risk a couple of soles just to see what happened, but a couple of moments later someone beat me to it. Suddenly, there were three tickets in the win pool for Baltimore Belle, whose price was cut in half. The tickets crept up, reaching double figures before the off; that's ten tickets – 20 soles, the equivalent of £3.50 – looking at a return of 425.3, or just over 212-1.

After the stalls opened, Baltimore Belle valiantly fought to keep up with the leaders for the first two strides before falling away. Five lengths down after 200 metres, she lost more ground before staying on in the final furlong to finish eight lengths adrift of the seventh-placed horse. The race was won by Best Of Friends, the favourite with ten votos in the card, ridden by Senor Arce. He who laughs last, and all that. Then again, he could afford to smile, because he wasn't going to Caracas, reputedly one of the most dangerous cities in Latin America, in the next few days.

What exactly was I thinking when I put together that itinerary?

VENEZUELA

VITAL STATISTICS

RACING

Racetracks	1
Fixtures	312
Races	2,835
Racehorses	3,284

BREEDING

Stallions	182
Mares	1,936
Foals	1,132

FINANCE

Total prize-money	$23.75m
Betting turnover	$776.23m

All figures for 2005

THINK back to this book's introduction. You may recall my suggesting I would not be following the racing road anywhere near places likely to involve the slightest hint of danger. In that respect, the risky Venezuelan capital Caracas was possibly not the most obvious choice as a stopover between Peru and Brazil.

Sure, horse racing is extremely popular in a country with three racetracks, notably La Rinconada, on the outskirts of the capital, reputedly South America's largest racecourse. It was here that Canonero, winner of two legs of the American Triple Crown in 1971, was trained, while Javier Castellano rode winners in his native country before moving to the US and partnering 2004 world champion Ghostzapper and Sheikh Mohammed's 2006 superstar Bernardini.

What's more, Venezuela as a whole has much to recommend it, including a number of attractions that earn the country a few mentions in the *Guinness Book of Records*, such as the highest waterfall in the world, the 978-metre Angel Falls, and a cable-car system that takes the prize for both longest and highest at 12.5 kilometres and 4,750 metres. Lake Maracaibo is also the largest in South America.

I didn't see any of that on a three-day trip focusing on Caracas, home to around a fifth of Venezuela's 25 million population. The birthplace of South American liberator Simon Bolivar, the capital benefits from a beautiful location, shadowed by the exuberant forests of the El Avila mountains – but most travel advice did not centre on how best to consider such historical significance and supreme vistas.

"It's not just hype," offered *Frommer's*. "Caracas is one of the most violent and dangerous cities in Latin America. On Monday mornings, one of the prime statistics published in all the papers is the number of homicides registered over the weekend. The number averages around 35 to 45 in Caracas alone."

Latin American cities usually suffer from a bad reputation, and Caracas might well have been the worst. The Foreign Office website alerted potential visitors to "an incidence of street crime that is high and rising", detailing specific concerns such as kidnappings of foreign tourists for ransom by bogus taxi operators at the airport, carjackings and armed hold-ups.

"Foreign nationals have also been kidnapped for ransom or violently mugged in Caracas and visitors should be alert to this threat in hotels, taxis and, in particular, the airport," suggested the UK Embassy website. "The road to the airport is best avoided after dark due to the recent spate of armed robberies taking place on the highway at night. Maiquetia Airport, the international airport serving Caracas, is dangerous. Passengers arriving on late flights are particularly vulnerable."

US advice warned of "express kidnapping", the abduction of individuals for short periods of time in order to receive a ransom or other specific demand. "Kidnapping of US citizens and other foreign nationals from homes, hotels, unauthorized taxis and the airport terminal has occurred." While such information habitually errs on the side of caution, it seemed sensible to expect a more challenging holiday destination than the Hayling Island Butlin's. "Don't get too adventurous at night," added the American advice, somewhat unnecessarily.

Then there were the warnings of leftist leader Hugo Chavez, democratically elected president of the world's fifth-largest oil producer. The populist demagogue, demonised as a Hitler figure by US defence secretary Donald Rumsfeld, survived a Washington-backed army coup in 2002 thanks to the support of the masses, who have benefited from his social justice measures, paid for by oil revenues, such as a national education programme that has brought almost 100 per cent literacy for the first time in Venezuelan history. A couple of weeks before my visit, Chavez presided over a mass ceremony at La Rinconada for graduates of the Mision Robinson programme, designed for adults and teenagers previously denied an education because of poverty.

Although Chavez has made it on to the long list for the Nobel Peace Prize and Britain is the fifth-largest investor in Venezuela, he remained a hugely controversial figure in the west: witness the right-wing opposition to his visit to London in 2006 at the invitation of mayor Ken Livingstone.

Chavez himself was not averse to stirring the pot, having contended shortly before my visit that it was only a matter of time before the US launched an invasion or an assassination attempt. Although the US government ridiculed such allegations, it did not stop Chavez from taking the precaution of forming a civilian militia under the banner 'fatherhood or death' and stockpiling helicopters and rifles in readiness for conflict. "If I am assassinated, there is only one person responsible: the president of the United States," he said during his weekly radio broadcast, *Hello President*, in early 2005. Apparently Fidel Castro had warned him of a plot. "I will not hide," said Chavez. "I will walk in the streets with all of you – but I know I am condemned to death."

The meanest of streets and fears of an imminent military invasion? I couldn't help but wonder exactly what I was doing there. Suffice it to say that I wasn't entirely aware of the city's dismal reputation when I booked the ticket and, as the possibility of civil war in Bolivia had already forced one expensive change of flight plans, it remained a case of 'Caracas, here we come'. Oh joy.

*

JOHN PILGER visited Caracas in 2006, filming in the hillside barrios and breeze-block houses. "Caracas is said to be one of the world's toughest cities, yet I have known no fear," he wrote in the *Guardian*.

Then again, Pilger is more used to war zones than racecourses; after Mexico City, I had no plans to emulate him by checking out any of the edgier Caracas districts. No chances were taken, and, after being picked up by limousine at that scary airport, the weekend was spent cocooned in an upmarket hotel beside the pool, where sunburn was the most threatening thing to worry about. Unless Hugo had a point about George W Bush and the stealth bombers made an appearance, that is. The thought did cross my mind one particular night when an unexpected thunderclap disturbed the atmosphere.

As far as the disturbingly high incidence of street crime was concerned, a large security presence including military police armed with billyclubs told its own story at La Rinconada, half an hour from the city centre. Yet a visit there for ten races on the sand on a Sunday was to prove an unexpected delight.

There is racing nearly every day at one of Venezuela's three surviving racetracks, the others being Santa Rita, near the Colombian border in Zulia state, and Valencia, about 100 miles west of Caracas. La Rinconada, founded in 1959, was possibly the richest track on the continent for a spell when the oil started flowing, with leading European-based owners like Vernon's pools millionaire Robert Sangster and the Aga Khan reportedly among those to have had runners there.

Although those days have passed, purses were still far from shabby. Venezuela's most important race, the Clasico Simon Bolivar (he gets in everywhere, including the currency), is a mile-and-a-half event worth around 500 million bolivars (more than $200,000). A familiar name figures on the Simon Bolivar roll of honour in Laffit Pincay, although this is not the world-famous Panamanian, but his father. Also a rider, Laffit Pincay snr was based in Venezuela for a lengthy period between the late 1940s and the '60s.

Held in late October or early November, the Clasico Simon Bolivar was the ultimate domestic target for the nation's star of 2005, the Triple Crown winner Polo Grounds, ahead of a tilt at the Clasico del Caribe and, ultimately, a campaign in the US. Sadly, it wasn't to be. Although the colt was to receive a thunderous ovation when he scored next time out at La Rinconada in September in another Grade 1 event, Polo Grounds' glittering career came to a dramatic halt owing to a severe bout of colic. A subsequent testicular problem put all plans on hold. In his absence, the Simon Bolivar went to Rampe Carga, heading an unprecedented 1-2-3 for trainer Giuseppe Iadisermia.

Venezuelan-trained horses also have a decent record in the Clasico del

Caribe – as mentioned earlier, they won the first event in 1966 with Victoreado – while riders from the nation have left their imprint on the States. Not always in a creditable way, it has to be admitted. Seven Venezuelan jockeys were expelled from the Florida circuit in 1993 for falsifying documents. They included Jesus Bracho, who was forced to surrender the Eclipse Award he had won in 1992 as outstanding apprentice after stewards ruled that he was not qualified to ride as a 'bug boy', the US term for a claiming rider designated by the asterisk, or bug, that appears next to their name to identify their status in the *Daily Racing Form*. Eibar Coa, now a leading rider in New York, was also caught in the investigation, earning a 60-day ban after admitting he should not have been claiming a 5lb allowance. Coa claimed to have ridden only 11 winners in Venezuela rather than the 59 he really had to his name.

Although my visit to La Rinconada's dirt-track oval coincided with a run-of-the-mill card, there were still about 5,000 people in the track's three grandstands, where they were treated to a breathtaking view right over Caracas – it looked somewhat more enticing from a distance – and competitive, attractive racing. A rigid jacket-and-tie dress code was enforced in the Jockey Club *tribuna*, but baseball shirts were the order of the day elsewhere in samba-filled public stands, where punters waved racecards and screamed support for their fancies.

I was met by racecourse official Juan Martinez. "Weren't you afraid coming to Caracas?" he inquired, in excellent English. "I am sorry but the reputation is true and it isn't just tourists – a month ago, someone stabbed me in the arm for my mobile phone in the centre of Caracas, and I have lived here all my life."

According to Martinez, approximately 25,000 million bolivars (around £6.6m) was bet on average over a month's racing at the country's three tracks, including 3,000 off-course outlets where customers eat, drink and punt. A testament to racing's popularity was that it received a couple of pages in the daily sports paper *Meridiano*, which also had an extensive section on its website.

"After the oil, this is Venezuela's second-biggest industry," said Martinez. "This is the biggest thing for enjoyment that the people here do –

they love to go to the betting houses." It would be even more lucrative but for the illegal bookmakers, though no-one seemed overly concerned, Martinez suggesting the best the racecourse could do was to extract a levy from them. It seemed an odd way of doing things. "In our country, there is corruption everywhere," he said. "It is just the same with this president."

Martinez chaperoned me on an extensive guided tour around the track's nooks and crannies, past the statue of 1930s star Burlesco under the track to the one-man-operated pari-mutuel board and then the domed dope-testing centre, where a vet examined horses both pre- and post-race. Every runner was weighed on entering this facility before every race.

Next stop was the stewards' room high in the main stand, and a surprise: Gustavo Avila, a Puerto Rican native, and Juan Arias, jockey and trainer respectively of Canonero, the most famous horse in Venezuelan history, were on hand, full of smiles and warm handshakes. The story of Canonero is one of racing's true fairytales. Bred in Kentucky, the colt was no oil painting, beset with a crooked foreleg. He was sold for just $1,200 at a Keeneland auction and duly shipped to the owner's native Venezuela, where, though he won his share as a two-year-old, he was no superstar. As a three-year-old in 1971, he was shipped to Kentucky by his trainer, accompanied only by his owner's son and crates of ducks and chickens. After a troubled journey involving a missed flight, four extra days in quarantine in Miami owing to customs papers having been forgotten and a broken-down van en route to Louisville, Canonero lost a whopping 80lb in weight.

If he was a no-hoper for America's most famous race even before such a tortuous journey, this surely confirmed he might as well have stayed at home. Canonero was the least-fancied among 20 runners in the Kentucky Derby, in which he was bracketed with five other outsiders in the 'mutuel field', a device used at a time when tote boards couldn't accommodate fields greater than 14. Listen carefully and you could probably have heard the pins dropping as the Venezuelan-trained colt rounded the whole field from back in 18th place to swoop wide down the outside in the stretch and win going away by nearly four lengths. It wasn't a fluke, either, as his subsequent victory in the Preakness in track-record time testified. Large numbers of New York's Latino community contributed to the largest Belmont Stakes crowd in history as Canonero tried to complete the Triple Crown, but he could finish only fourth after a foot infection in the run-up. He had already done enough to warrant an Eclipse Award, and an everlasting place in Venezuelan racing history.

Given that neither jockey nor trainer spoke any English, the post-race interviews in 1971 weren't particularly illuminating, and I am afraid I did not fare any better 24 years later, although I can reveal that Avila remembered the Kentucky Derby as "fantastic". Arias doubtless agreed.

Recent Venezuelan visitors to the US haven't fared quite as well as Canonero. Three-time horse of the year My Own Business, winner of the Simon Bolivar in 2000 and disqualified after finishing first in that year's Clasico del Caribe, was virtually unbeatable at home, winning 37 of his 44 starts in either Venezuela or Puerto Rico. Sent to the States as a four-year-old amid much national fervour in 2001, he failed to make the first three in six starts at various tracks in New York and Florida, none of them Graded races.

From the stewards' room, it was a short walk across the roof and down a ladder into one of three bizarre concrete spheres stuck to the front of the roof on each of La Rinconada's three grandstands. Known as the 'Continental Ball', the only one of these in use was occupied by the racecourse commentator, afforded an amazing view through a giant slit in the front. It was from this three-dimensional Pacman that I watched the next race, a seven-furlong event that provided leading jockey Angel Castillo with the final leg of a treble aboard an easy winner called Fashion Parts, thereby underscoring his superiority on the day over fierce rival Emisael Jaramillo, the current champion and rider of Polo Grounds. The pair were inseparable in the current jockeys' title race; they declined to be photographed together.

My guided tour was interrupted just long enough to allow me a bet on the sixth and, having regaled you at regular intervals with the multiple ways in which I contrived to back losers, it is only fair to mention what must surely be the most ludicrous, flukey, undeserved winner I have ever found. In fact, it wasn't a winner at all, but they still paid out. Having abstained all day long, I had 20,000 bolivars (about $10) to win on a filly named Lady Elizabeth who had run just twice before, winning first time out before being outclassed in better grade, according to my understanding of an informative racecard. Although she was showing 8-5 second favourite when I hit the windows, she went to even-money as we ran off to the mile-high Pacman to watch the race from the best seat in the house. Mind you, there were only peanuts in the pool, and Lady Elizabeth started to drift, reaching 5-1 by the time we got to our eye in the sky.

Fashion Parts, carrying a weird number cloth with a zero on it, led from the off and won by about five lengths from Lady Elizabeth, a clear second, albeit well beaten. For some unfathomable reason, my guide was excited on my behalf, so, with regret, I informed him that I backed Lady Elizabeth win only. "No, no," he said. "You don't understand. Fashion Parts is invalid."

For betting purposes, it transpired, the winner never existed. It seemed that when such a horse is considered vastly superior to its rivals and likely to go off at long odds-on, the pool operated without it in a pari-mutuel version of betting without the favourite. That's why Fashion Parts was allotted no number in the racecard, and never appeared on the pari-mutuel board.

Having agreed that this was an ingenious concept, I went to collect my winnings. Lady Elizabeth returned more than 7-1; it was almost enough to make a man wish he could stay longer in Caracas rather than hurrying off for the overnight flight to Rio.

I said almost.

BRAZIL

VITAL STATISTICS

RACING

Racetracks	8
Fixtures	510
Races	5,105
Racehorses	7,017

FINANCE

Total prize-money	$13.94m
Betting turnover	$137.19m

All figures for 2005

BREEDING

Stallions	303
Mares	4,267
Foals	3,034

A SINGLE name is the Brazilian convention, a mark of intimacy and humility, especially among the working classes. That's why Luiz Inacio Lula da Silva, elected president in October 2002, is known to everyone simply as Lula.

Brazilian sportsmen often exist only via their nickname. Trivia buffs will recognise Edson Arantes do Nascimento as Pelé, whose predecessor Garrincha was christened Manuel Francisco dos Santos. It can get confusing. In the modern era there are the likes of Ronaldo and Ronaldinho ('Little Ronaldo'). The latter is widely known as Ronaldinho Gaucho at home to differentiate him from the previous Ronaldinho, who was actually the superstar Ronaldo, leading scorer in World Cup history, whose full name is Ronaldo Luiz Nazario de Lima. He was originally called Ronaldinho to avoid confusion with Ronaldo Guiara, a teammate at the 1996 Olympic Games known then as Ronaldo. When he fell out of favour, the younger Ronaldo (then Ronaldinho) became, well, Ronaldo. The full name of the best-known Ronaldinho, the toothy wizard whose free-kick put England out of the 2002 World Cup, is Ronaldo de Assis Moreira. Got all that? Good. There may be a quiz later.

Before the first race of a Saturday meeting at the elegant La Gavea racecourse in the very heart of Rio de Janeiro, I was introduced to 'Ricardinho', racing's answer to the nation's soccer giants. This was Brazil's leading rider, the prolific Jorge Ricardo, better known to the locals by his nickname after more than 20 years as champion jockey in Rio. Ricardinho means 'Little Ricardo', marking the rider out from his father Antonio Ricardo, who was also a successful jockey in his time. The latter's nickname was 'Banana'.

The poster boy of Brazilian racing for more than two decades, Jorge Ricardo is a phenomenon. A national icon, he won the Rio jockeys' championship for the first time in 1982 and did not relinquish it until he moved to Buenos Aires in 2006, often recording more than 400 winners per season. His best score was 477 in 1992-93, when he had 1,612 mounts – and this not at some minor leaky-roof circuit, but primarily at the foremost track in a major racing nation.

Ricardo's name was scarcely known outside South America, presumably because fewer than 200 of his winners prior to 2006 had come anywhere else but La Gavea, just a handful of them away from Brazil and none outside South America. He had appeared in Europe just once, when he partnered the Brazilian-trained star Much Better to finish 14th in the Arc won by Carnegie in 1994.

By the time I met him, Ricardo had his sights set firmly on recognition on an international scale. Although the US concentrated on Russell Baze's attempts to overhaul Laffit Pincay's world-record mark of 9,530 career winners, Ricardo was actually the closest to overhauling the Panamanian. I went racing at La Gavea in mid-July 2005, by which time Ricardo's score had reached 9,071, according to statistics provided by the diligent Bertrand Kauffmann at the Jockey Club Brasileiro. Then, Baze was around 60 behind Ricardo in a fierce battle conducted two continents apart that was set to run and run.

With the help of an interpreter, I was able to have a brief, stilted, chat to Ricardo. And one thing's for sure: if Baze wasn't fully aware of his South American rival, the latter knew all about him. "Russell Baze and I are closely matched together and I would like to reach Laffit Pincay jnr's mark before him," said Ricardo, born in 1961 at Leblon, a beach district near the centre of Rio. Apprenticed at the age of 15 in November 1976, Jorge quickly progressed to the fully fledged ranks only eight months later, when he was only 16.

"I never imagined when I started that I would ride anything like 9,000 winners," he added. "But when anyone enters any profession they want to reach the summit – and now my goal is to break the world record as soon as I can. It is my great dream to break the worldwide record."

To that end, Ricardo had turned down a lucrative riding contract in Saudi Arabia, but he was still being courted by Argentine interests. When I met him in July 2005, it looked certain to be a close-run thing between Ricardo and Baze in the race to surpass Pincay. They raced four times a week at La Gavea, Friday to Monday night, Ricardo averaging just over a double a day, while his rival could be relied upon to keep up his inexorable progress on the northern California circuit.

Bertrand Kauffman, possibly not the most impartial of observers, acted as unofficial cheerleader for his compatriot. "The great difference between Russell Baze and Jorge Ricardo is the fact that Baze is used to riding in just the San Francisco area," he said. "You know, they are low-class racecourses with a very few runners per race. Ricardo has ridden in Brazil and Argentina, both very competitive countries. He is an outstanding jockey, able to compete in all the world."

However, while Baze dutifully recorded a four-timer the day I met him at Golden Gate Fields, his friendly Brazilian opponent let the side down by managing just one winner from a full book of ten mounts when I visited La Gavea, which means 'Topsail', for an early-season midwinter card, South America's new term having commenced on July 1. In the first three races, Ricardo was beaten on a pair of odds-on favourites who sandwiched an outsider that needed scrubbing along for the entire trip before finishing last. Another fancied mount was withdrawn, leaving him to switch to a stablemate who came nowhere, and then he was out of luck on fancied horses in the day's premier events, a pair of Group races. He finally got on the scoresheet in the ninth.

Ricardo's performance was not the only disappointment at La Gavea, Brazil's showpiece track since its opening in 1926. The roots of Brazilian racing lay a century earlier, when a group of British merchants organised contests on Rio's Botafago beach that were attended by the young emperor, Dom Pedro II, whose surrogate father is said to have been an English stable groom named Richard Shelley. The first racing club, founded in 1847, acquired the land for the nation's first racecourse proper, Fluminense. At one time, there were nine racetracks operating in Rio alone, and La Gavea's top race, the 2,400-metre Grande Premio Brasil (Brazilian Grand Prix), dates back to the 19th century.

Under the 20-year presidency of the towering figure of Linnea de Paulo Machado, racing thrived in the early 20th century, reaching its pinnacle in the 1950s and early '60s, when a visit to La Gavea was the height of fashion and jockey Luiz Rigoni, three-time winner of the Grande Premio, was in his pomp. Such was Rigoni's popularity that he had at least two songs written in his honour, *O Homem do Violino* ('The Man with the Violin', after one of his nicknames) and the tango *Da-lhe Rigoni* ('Give us Rigoni'). Some of the greatest horses in Brazilian racing history also date back to this period, notably Escorial, authoritative winner of Rio's Triple Crown who went on to win one of the best renewals ever of South America's most prestigious race, the Gran Premio Carlos Pellegrini in Argentina, in 1959. There, he beat his top-class compatriot Farwell plus crack performers from Argentina and Peru.

Any brief history of racing in Brazil cannot go without mention of the jockey Juvenal Machado da Silva, Ricardo's predecessor as top dog in Rio. Juvenal was still in business when Ricardo started out, and his final career tally of 3,842 seemed unlikely ever to be bettered – until Ricardo doubled it. According to the latter's biographer Jessie Navajas de Camargo, "in footballing terms, Juvenal was Garrincha to Ricardo's Pelé".

For all La Gavea's historic past, when the brand, spanking new planned city of Brasilia became the nation's capital in 1960, the status of Rio dwindled in virtually every walk of life, racing included. In the modern era, it is merely one of two separate and equally important racing centres alongside Sao Paulo, the largest city on the continent, where the main track is Cidade Jardim ('Garden City'). While La Gavea's Grande Premio Brasil continues to dwarf every other race on the calendar in value terms with a purse of about $236,000, the other two races worth more than $100,000 were staged in Sao Paulo in 2006. There is only limited crossover between the cities, each community having its own discrete racing programme focusing on a Triple Crown at different times of the year. Other racecourses offering a decent level of racing include Taruma, in Curitiba, and Cristal, in Porte Alegre.

La Gavea's influence might have waned in the modern era, but it remains by far Brazil's best-loved racecourse and I was looking forward to going there. The track plays its joker even before you get through the door, creating the most positive of impressions with a stupendous location. Even allowing for the vagaries of Rio's one-way system, this was not far short of idyllic. Situated close to the Rodrigo de Freitas lagoon in the heart of the city, La Gavea is barely five minutes from Ipanema beach. While racecourses ringed by mountains had become a commonplace on the racing road, La Gavea trumped them all with its picture-postcard setting, directly beneath the Corcovado hill, overlooked by the arms-outstretched statue of Christ the Redeemer that is synonymous with Rio.

While any building would struggle to live up to this setting, there was also plenty to admire about the French architecture of the main clubhouse, resembling more a colonial hotel than a grandstand. A stately entrance, mosaic flooring and sturdy white pillars ushered racegoers into a lobby area with ornate chandeliers dangling from the ceiling. This was the main betting hall, where dignified wooden counters sat underneath bronze murals in front of a non-functioning tote board. A marbled staircase, bannistered and carpeted, led to a posh restaurant behind a wall of tall mahogany display cases housing around 300 foot-tall figurines of jockeys carrying silks of Brazil's top owners down the years. Elsewhere on its three floors, plush sofas and wicker chairs were the order of the day, while much of the ground floor is taken up with dignified wooden betting counters underneath candelabra. Throughout, a sense of antiquated glamour pervaded, redolent of a bygone era, more Raffles than Redcar.

Outside, horses paraded around a leafy paddock, jockeys chatting on benches surrounded by vine-encrusted tree trunks before taking part in a series of competitive contests around a left-handed circuit where the turf course sits outside the dirt, for once reversing the American model.

I expected much from Brazil, traditionally the foremost racing nation in South America supported by a breeding industry responsible for a drip-feed of top-level exports to the USA since the 1990s, when the bull-like pair Sandpit and Siphon, both as tough as teak, advertised the virtues of

Brazilian bloodstock with a string of fine performances at the top level. They were soon followed by plenty of others, among them Riboletta, five times a Grade 1 winner in California, top sprinter Pico Central and Hard Buck, who finished second in Ascot's King George VI and Queen Elizabeth Diamond Stakes on a visit to Britain in 2004. Another big name from Brazil was the top turf miler Leroidesanimaux, who was to finish runner-up in the 2005 Breeders' Cup Mile. He was owned by TNT Stud, the racing name of leading stud owner Goncalo Torrealba, who made a splash in the States when he purchased the historic red-and-blue colours of Calumet Farm the day the famous stud was auctioned in 1992.

Torrealba also owned the aforementioned Much Better, twice South American horse of the year. Much Better numbered a victory in the Gran Premio Carlos Pellegrini, plus a pair of Gran Premio Latinoamericanos, among numerous top-flight successes, although he and Sandpit were beaten into second and third by Villach King in a tight finish to the 1993 Grande Premio Brasil, one of the greatest races ever run on Brazilian soil. Among Torrealba's stallion band was Royal Academy, who earned a place in racing history with his spectacular victory in the 1990 Breeders' Cup Mile at Belmont under Lester Piggott only 12 days after the riding legend had returned to the saddle following five years in retirement, among them a year in prison.

This is all context, however. For all its elegant fittings and furniture, La Gavea promised hopelessly more than it could deliver. The nation's top race, the Grande Premio Brasil, is still worth around $100,000 to the winner and can attract a crowd of 30,000. This, though, is very much the exception to the rule, for otherwise the days of thousands converging on La Gavea appeared to have faded into distant memory. Though it cost absolutely nothing to get in, there cannot have been 300 people in attendance when I was there – and that for a Saturday card featuring a pair of decent Pattern races contested by good-size fields including a handful of multiple winners.

The clubhouse was virtually empty, and it was a similar story in the next stand along, another two-storey effort, albeit much more rundown, designed for the *hoi polloi*. The stand nearest the winning line was for owners, trainers and stewards; two more dilapidated stands farther down the track, towards a stage where concerts were regularly held, usually stayed shut for the racing.

It seemed a waste – and it hadn't always been that way, as English-speaking vet Mayra Frederico, my guide for the day, told me. "I am not old enough to remember it, but the older people here are always telling me what it used to be like," said Mayra. "There were thousands of people here every weekend to watch the racing. But now it's so sad – we don't see it."

Mayra moved to Europe soon afterwards as the first South American to be selected for the 'Flying Start' programme, a two-year course run by Sheikh Mohammed's Darley Stud operation for a few lucky hand-picked students from around the racing world.

She took me across the track to watch the start of a 1,100-metre event on the sand track, a journey that revealed how rundown the track had become. The infield was overgrown and unkempt and, after a week of near-incessant rain, there were pools of standing water all over the place, plus broken-down tractors and, bizarrely, what looked like an allotment.

The tote board was antediluvian, its figures operating slowly like reels on a padlock, while it was hard to work out whether a canal in the middle of the track was for decorative or drainage purposes. It succeeded in neither, being not particularly attractive to the eye, while six races had to be transferred to the sand track from the turf. With bare patches everywhere, this was itself hardly in pristine condition.

To be fair, it was little short of a miracle that any turf racing took place at all, as Rio had been submerged for much of the previous week amid downpours of biblical proportions. The lagoon burst it banks, while Christ the Redeemer was perpetually hidden by heavy grey clouds. Obviously, it isn't only Easter that the sky turns black. About the only place I could see this picture-postcard view during the week I was in Rio was on a picture postcard.

Back within the 'Tribune of Honour' in the clubhouse, I was joined by chief steward Paulo Pires do Rio (nickname unknown), who tried to convince me that his garden was rosy, pointing to betting turnover that averaged around $300,000 every weekend, bolstered by over 100 off-course betting parlours. "We are healthy here," he insisted. "Only ten per cent of our turnover comes from the racetrack; we have around 100 betting shops and most of the betting is done there or on the telephone."

And it was just about possible, I suppose, that appearances may have been a little deceptive, for crowdless La Gavea employed 1,500 in its training centre, where 1,000 racehorses were stabled. Around 1,500 more horses travelled in from satellite training centres, while the Jockey Club had 5,000 well-heeled members, though many of these were simply social members who used the attached country club, swimming pool, tennis courts and parking spaces. Pires was also anticipating a deal with a simulcasting company that he said would eventually see transmissions in the USA, something that would produce a major boost to purses.

Elsewhere in Brazil, however, the facts certainly spoke of an ailing industry, and a task force was set up in 2003 by the Ministry of Agriculture to address deep-rooted problems. A side-effect of the decline was an influx of horsemen to Europe in recent years, among them talented jockeys like Nelson de Souza and his friend Silvestre de Sousa (unrelated, and spelt differently), who have won plenty of admirers riding their share of winners in Britain. Back at home only half a dozen of 40 licensed tracks were operational on anything other than an irregular basis in 2005; many were not functioning at all. Even Cidade Jardim, which even superseded La Gavea for a time as Brazil's wealthiest, was in trouble, down to three days' racing a week from five amid administration problems and illegal betting. In that sort of context, La Gavea looked like a thriving concern.

There, the Group 2 highlight, the Grande Premio Onze de Julho, worth 40,000 Brazilian reals (around £10,000) and run on the doglegged 1,000-metre turf chute, was won by the 2-5 favourite Omaggio, an attractive four-year-old who had scored previously in Group 1 company. He was a powerful-looking colt of the type for which his nation is much respected, and it was a pity there was hardly anybody there to appreciate his efforts.

The meeting ended over half an hour late, the legacy of much fannying about at the stalls throughout previous races, a false start in one of the Group races and the need to regulate the simulcast broadcast with racing from Sao Paulo. This was by no means a rare occurrence – Monday-night cards, scheduled to finish at 11pm, often carried on until after midnight. Presumably the last person there at La Gavea would turn the lights out.

*

AFTER winning yet another Rio jockeys' title in 2005-06, Jorge Ricardo moved to the thriving racing arena of Buenos Aires in Argentina, enticed by both a lucrative retainer and increased opportunities as he continued his battle with Russell Baze to reach Laffit Pincay's world-record mark. Bertrand Kauffmann explained: "The prizes in Argentina have had a fantastic increase in recent years and they race all week. There are something like 40 races a week at La Gavea against 100 in Buenos Aires."

Initially, the move was to little avail when the American overtook Ricardo, and then reached Pincay's mark in December 2006. At the time, Ricardo, three years younger than Baze at 45, was only 27 winners adrift, and he duly passed the previous world-record mark four weeks later. The Brazilian made slight inroads into Baze's lead in January 2007, before his rival cracked ribs in a fall at Golden Gate Fields and endured nearly a fortnight on the sidelines. Ricardo did not waste his chance. Just two months after Baze became only the eighth jockey in 120 years to hold the world record for number of wins, Jorge Ricardo became the ninth when he rode the 9,591st winner of his career on February 5 at Palermo racecourse in Buenos Aires on a six-year-old called Minimal. "I dedicate this winner to my father and my family, who I must thank for everything I have achieved," he said.

When told he had lost his record, Baze offered his congratulations to his opponent. "I knew there was a guy down there who was close to me," he said. "More power to him – competition is the name of the game." It wasn't long before he once again overhauled Ricardo, and the number-one spot changed hands twice more before the end of February 2007, continuing to flip-flop in the months that followed. With both riders eager to be the first to hit 10,000, this titanic struggle seemed likely to continue for some years.

Brazilian horses also continued to demonstrate their worth on the wider stage, notably at the Dubai International Racing Carnival. Unquestionably the world's most cosmopolitan racing arena featuring horses trained on six continents, this compelling series is held annually at Nad Al Sheba racecourse in the run-up to the Dubai World Cup meeting at the end of March. Several leading South American performers left their mark in 2006 and 2007, both those who had been sold to race for owners and trainers based in the Gulf and others who were still handled by their original connections. Brazilians and ex-Brazilians figured among the winners, including some startling performances in richly endowed contests.

Trainer Pedro Nickel Filho was among the winners at the Dubai carnival from a team of nine horses at his temporary base at Nad Al Sheba. "South America has always produced very good racehorses but unfortunately the rest of the world has always been wearing blinkers," he said. "Some people don't even know where Brazil is on the map – it's mind-boggling."

Compatriot Cosme Morgado saddled Imperialista to win the first round of the Group 3 Maktoum Challenge. "The horse is part of South American heritage," said the multiple champion. "There are no short cuts, and the breeding side of it has taken years of painstaking planning. We have not suddenly got lucky – our success has been because we've earned it. Of course, football is the number-one sport in Brazil but you walk into many bars in Brazil and the racing will be on TV. It is a very popular sport, and South American success overseas means more and more people are taking an interest."

Having said that, many Brazilian horses in Dubai seemed to be racing with a price on their head, destined sooner rather than later to end up racing for others if they were any good. That's precisely what happened to Imperialista, a 25-1 chance with British bookmakers when scoring in Dubai. Three weeks later, Imperialista was 3-1 favourite when he reappeared for Round 2 of the Maktoum Challenge – trained by Dubai-based Ismail Mohammed and running in the colours of a member of the Maktoum family. He finished a dismal ninth.

URUGUAY

RACING		FINANCE	
Racetracks	18	Total prize-money	$4.38m
Fixtures	108	Betting turnover	$12.87m
Races	1,035		
Racehorses	1,635		

All figures for 2005; apart from number of racetracks, they refer to Maronas only

BREEDING	
Stallions	282
Mares	2,855
Foals	1,686

HOMESICKNESS was never a problem on the racing road. Thanks to the wonders of modern communications, it can be pretty difficult to cut yourself off unless a concerted effort is made to do so.

In any event, I had to keep in some sort of contact with the *Racing Post* office to file my weekly column plus the occasional report from major racing nations, while Jane seemed to be in almost daily contact with her family. Even some of the most remote places offered a degree of internet access, although it wasn't always straightforward in the depths of the Amazon rainforest or sailing down the Yangtze. Early in the trip, when I was still making a vague attempt to stay in touch with equine matters at home, trying to watch the Grand National on a Vietnamese computer screen proved an exercise in little more than futility, but I did obtain a commentary on Virginia Waters' victory in the 1,000 Guineas from a coach somewhere in China. I phoned the *Racing Post* newsdesk, where a helpful member of the team placed the receiver next to the TV screen so I could hear Simon Holt's call.

Being able to access my internet mailbox at regular intervals certainly had its drawbacks. The spam kept on coming, and I continued to receive every global email sent around the *Racing Post*. So much for avoiding office politics, then, but it was my own fault. You know that old joke about the bloke with alcoholic constipation who couldn't pass a bar? I had an electronic version. I couldn't pass a cyber café. On the plus side, I suspect such a round-the-world trip would have been vastly different, and considerably more difficult, as little as ten years earlier.

Though avoiding Royal Ascot at York hadn't bothered me unduly, there were a few things I missed from home, as I suggested in my column from Uruguay for the *Racing Post*, where I detailed a disparate and slightly tongue-in-cheek list. The King George VI and Queen Elizabeth Diamond Stakes, Glorious Goodwood, the Ashes, the Greyhound Derby, AFC Wimbledon's debut in the Isthmian Premier League, *Big Brother*, Belle and Sebastian doing their classic LP *If You're Feeling Sinister* in its entirety in London. All were forsaken in the cause of chasing racehorses on the other side of the world.

The truth was that I was somewhat more peeved by something I missed in Uruguay, an unexpectedly welcoming place for a brief visit, even in midwinter, with a thriving racing scene that appeared to be growing fast. Nearly every region in the country has its own track, like the *hipodromo* in the lovely, historic cobbled port of Colonia del Sacramento, a UNESCO site and Uruguay's oldest town 150 kilometres up the coast from the likeable capital Montevideo.

In Colonia, horses often gallop on the banks of the River Plate – but unfortunately, I learned all this only days before a visit to the port, where race meetings are held only on alternate Sundays. Last-ditch efforts to change travel plans came to nought, so, annoyingly, I had to be at the Iguazu Falls at the border between Argentina, Brazil and Paraguay. Looking back, it is clear my priorities had become a bit skewed. There I was, visiting one of the continent's most spectacular natural attractions, yet the missed opportunity to go racing at Colonia rankled enormously. Call it obsessive-compulsive disorder if you like.

Apart from a quick scout around the racecourse and its stables one Wednesday morning – ramshackle, not many horses, looked a rough place, probably would have been fun – I had to rely on a visit to Maronas racetrack in Montevideo to do the honours for Uruguay. As this is the only track in the nation with international pretensions, it was probably a fair enough place to start.

Having said that, most people don't bother with Uruguay at all, it seems. Travel guides suggested the vast majority of visitors to South America miss it out altogether and, set alongside the behemoths Brazil and

Argentina, the less-populous nation sandwiched between them remains somewhat anonymous, rarely registering on a global scale.

In horse-racing terms, too, Uruguay has long been regarded as a poor relation of its higher-profile neighbours, despite a tradition of horsemanship dating back centuries to the famed *gauchos* and their native *criollo* horses, an intrinsic part of an agricultural society. Gaucho is the term used to describe residents of the South American grasslands, the pampas, found principally in Argentina, Uruguay and the state of Rio Grande do Sul in southern Brazil. Originally cattle herders, they are the loose equivalent of North American cowboys, synonymous with horses, which are themselves ingrained in both Uruguayan and Argentinian culture more than anywhere else on the continent. It is no coincidence, despite both being Spanish-speaking, that these nations are closer in mindset to Britain and France. Even allowing for the odd war here and there.

Horse racing began in Uruguay as an entertainment among the rural population, the first jockeys being the ubiquitous gauchos who competed against each other without saddles in match races up and down hills, often over obstacles in a primitive local form of jump racing. The first recorded properly organised racing seems to have taken place in 1855 at a racecourse called Azotea de Lima in the Piedras Blancas district of Montevideo. As usual, the European influence was immediately to the fore: races involving saddles were usually advertised as 'English races', or sometimes 'foreign races'. Although the gauchos' 'national races' also continued as other tracks were constructed, 'English races' soon began to take precedence when the government recognised horse racing as an official sport in 1877.

In the next decade, a thoroughbred Stud Book was established, and the cross-breds and criollos were phased out. Popularity surged in the 20th century as racing became synonymous with high society: the Jockey Club built an ornate headquarters in central Montevideo, where an entire community grew around the main racecourse, which had been built in 1874 in the Ituzaingo district. Run by English descendants for the first few years, it became known as Maronas, after the owner of the farm on whose land it originally stood. At its height, the Uruguayan horse industry employed around 70,000 people, a huge amount in a small country, and racing was a hugely popular pastime. Irineo Leguisamo, known as 'El Pulpo' ('The Octopus'), was a national hero, winner of 21 jockeys' titles between 1923 and 1952.

However, the sport was by no means immune to the economic problems that hit Uruguay in the latter years of the 20th century, when the Jockey Club became a byword for decadence, running up millions of dollars of debt. Despite being designated as a national monument and chosen to host the inaugural running of the Gran Premio Latinoamericano in 1981, Maronas's marble colonnades and sculpted bronzes represented bombast rather than elegance when considered alongside the Jockey Club's management failures. The nadir arrived in 1997 when the unthinkable happened. The club closed its doors for the last time, and the bankrupt Maronas was closed down.

Neglected and barren, it was shuttered for five and a half years, though regional tracks ensured horse racing continued in Uruguay, with major races taking place at Las Piedras, north east of the capital. When I got to Montevideo, however, Maronas was back, owned by the republic of Uruguay and reborn with a new vitality after a $15.4 million revamp involving an injection of business acumen from a joint venture between Spanish and Argentinian concerns, with input from Lone Star Park in Texas. The latter possibly explained the bugle salute that accompanied horses on to the track.

The result was a revitalised racecourse offering something racing officials in certain other nations – not least neighbouring Brazil – could only dream about. Spectators. There were more than 5,000 of them on the Sunday I dropped in for a ten-race card, featuring contests at varying distances up to a mile and a half on a sand track. Maronas is situated in the north east of Montevideo, about 20 minutes in a dirt-cheap taxi from the capital's Old Town centre in a scruffy district that fell apart when the racecourse went bust, like a coal-mining community after a dose of Margaret Thatcher.

Now the track almost seemed out of place in generally unappetising surroundings, but while it did not benefit from a particularly attractive location – even what looked like a forest on the far side is a trick of the eye, as the trees are only two-deep – the facilities themselves were first-rate.

The main stand may have dated back to 1925, but while some original features had been retained, like the old-fashioned iron-cage lift that took you up to the fanciest restaurant and the bizarre statue of the wild boar that sat in front of the stand, it was by no means antiquated. Revarnished and refurbished, this building housed numerous TV screens, cashpoints and betting windows, including an international parlour featuring simulcasts from the top US tracks like Churchill Downs, Belmont and Hollywood Park – and Pleasanton, venue for the Alameda County Fair, where Russell Baze had recently returned from injury.

This stand, the *palco oficial*, functioned as a kind of club enclosure, and when I arrived ten minutes before the first, there was a queue of people lining up to pay 70 pesos (around £1.60) to get in. Later on a spring-like afternoon, the track's two operating stands were packed with customers: male, female, kids, many of them with flasks of the national beverage, maté, a kind of herbal tea drunk through straws from odd-looking bulbous containers.

They raced every Saturday and Sunday at Maronas, and this, it seemed, was considered no more than an average gate. Around 15,000 was a good one, and after some pretty lacklustre days at various venues in South America, it was a pleasure to be able to report on a nation where horse racing seemed to be flourishing, albeit after the stickiest of patches.

The racing had its idiosyncrasies, many of the riders appearing longer and taller than I was used to in Britain. There, everyone wanted to be Richard Hughes, the Irishman unusually tall for a successful rider in Europe. One gentleman in particular caught the eye with his extreme style. If Joao Severi wasn't known as the 'Human Right Angle', then he should have been. In the second race, the top half of his body, head to midriff, was almost completely flat, as if he was riding with a spirit level on his back. This horizontal jutted out from the perpendicular of his legs, rigid for much of the journey. It seemed impossibly straight and stiff, but appeared to work – Severi rode the winner with barely a twitch of a muscle.

The winning post at Maronas was a hoop hung out over the racecourse, rather like the Mayans used to favour in ancient Mexico for their ballgames on the pelota court, the best example of which is at the ruins of Chichen

Itza. Then, mind you, the winners were often beheaded as a reward, a practice long since discontinued at the racetrack, though Maronas punters might have considered it a fair outcome for one hapless jockey who was caught on the line in the third race, in which leading rider Wladimir Maciel, cutely judging the pace on an outsider, surprised a shorter-priced rival in the dying strides.

A semaphore system was employed to announce results, with a red flag denoting unofficial outcomes before the weigh-in, while green signified a photo and yellow a stewards' inquiry. When the numbers were in the frame, they were augmented by mystifying boards, depicting various shapes and letters rather like a look-and-learn educational module. Further inquiries revealed these to denote the winning margins: a full black circle represented one length (*cuerpo*, literally 'body' rather than length), two spots signified two lengths, while a 'C' meant a *cabeza*, a head, a lower-case 'p' the equivalent of a neck.

After the maiden, won by the favourite Aceptado, a huge horse who dwarfed his rivals, a spotted card went up: lots of circles, meaning many lengths, or *varios cuerpos*. Having backed the winner, I was pleased to see it, although as he was a 1-3 shot, I wouldn't be writing home to mother about it. Such odds-on favourites seemed the norm in Latin America, a result of unattractive takeouts across the region; no wonder the local punters seemed to favour exotics.

Midway through the afternoon, I was granted an interview with racecourse president Dr Martin Canepa. Straight away, he offered his condolences over the London bombings, which had taken place a week before. It was a strange moment. I felt the most unlikely ambassador for my country, perhaps not striking the most dignified of impressions in a black jacket that hadn't been dry-cleaned in months, and now featuring an attractive sweat line on the back that I hadn't previously noticed, while my cream slacks had ball-point pen marks on them. Neatly rounding off this ragamuffin effect was a pair of clumpy walking boots last used for the hike down the Amazon. They appeared at Maronas because my only other footwear in working order were two pairs of training shoes.

I wasn't expecting an official audience, but at least Canepa didn't turn his nose up at the smell as we shook hands, and neither did his silent sidekick, the vice-president Juan Garcia Docio. Silent because he spoke little English, and I spoke even less Spanish.

Fortunately, Canepa, an urbane Argentine, spoke English slightly better than me, and he ran through a swift history of racing in Uruguay – the gauchos, English stallions in the late 19th century, much history and tradition, ending with the problems of the 1990s when the track went bust, before he and his company brought a business plan to the table. "It was completely abandoned here," he said, showing photographs that confirmed the track's desecration. "It was all very rundown and took a lot of work."

Plus no little foresight, it seems. Canepa gave me a lavishly illustrated hardback book detailing the birth, death and rebirth of Maronas. In his introduction, he recalls his first sighting of the neglected track in March 2001. "Had we not been dreamers and business persons," he says, "we would probably have discarded the project that same day, since a great deal of imagination was needed to wake that dormant giant, unjustly abandoned."

Canepa suggested the reason so many South American racing operations were struggling in the modern era was because of their historical reliance on well-heeled Jockey Club members bailing them out. Maronas, the first South American racetrack to be broadcast in the US, employed 1,500 people at the track plus thousands more in off-course outlets and casinos, which were a crucial part of the business. Unusually for the region, there was no amateur members-only Jockey Club running the show. "Racecourses have relied on a few rich people to spend a few million dollars to keep them going," said Canepa. "Well, times have changed, and it doesn't work any more; it didn't work here."

He was adamant that relying on a social elite was commercial suicide. "The Jockey Club was high society but it wasn't a business," he said, although he conceded that Uruguay had certain advantages, given the status of horses as a significant part of the culture. "This is a country that loves horses. Around 20 per cent of the population is involved working with horses in some way – and we have more people here today than are watching the soccer. OK, soccer's struggling in Uruguay at the moment, but it is still quite something.

"This is a social thing, and all the family comes here, not just those who are here simply to bet. This is a racetrack for everyone. If you want to wear a tie, that's fine, but you don't have to. And the politicians come as well – the left as well as the right."

President Jorge Battle attended the first running of the reinaugurated Gran Premio Jose Pedro Ramirez in January 2004, the nation's most prestigious all-aged race. Both runnings of the race after its return following a seven-year hiatus were won by Argentine horses.

As I spoke to Canepa, racegoers crowded around the parade ring to examine the field for the afternoon's highlight, the Group 2 Gran Premio Presidente de la Republica, headed by a consistent four-year-old named The Best, who had a white pom-pom arrangement plaited into his forehead. Another contender had green ribbons embroidered into his mane like a dressage pony.

This race was worth 585,000 pesos (about $25,000) – not much in American or European terms, though it should be remembered that Uruguay's cost of living is probably around a third as high as Britain; it costs only $200 a month to keep a horse in training. Both the Uruguayan Derby (November's Gran Premio Nacional) and the Jose Pedro Ramirez were worth about $75,000. "Our prize-money now is similar to Brazil," suggested the secretary of the owners' association, before adding, mischievously: "The difference is that here you actually get the money – in Brazil they don't pay up!"

That's as maybe, but some of the horsemen over the border still know what they're doing. The main event was won easily by a mare named Necessaire, a former Group 1 winner who was bred in Brazil before being moved to Uruguay. She won by a lot of spots.

*

I WAS really impressed with Maronas, where the recovery continued apace in the months following my visit. Uruguay was formally admitted to the International Federation of Horseracing Authorities at the Paris conference in 2005, while the track hosted a successful renewal of the Gran Premio Latinoamericano in March

2006. Uruguay had never won the race, but Necessaire, by now a champion mare, came desperately close in being beaten only a length into second by Argentina's Latency. The race, attended by Uruguayan vice-president Rodolfo Nin, was simulcast across the continent and, for the first time, into North America, thanks to racetrack-owning giant Magna Entertainment Corp., the company behind Lone Star's involvement.

For all Necessaire's talent, she was nowhere near the best horse to race at Maronas in 2005. In a maiden race in February that year, an Argentine-bred two-year-old son of South American champion sire Candy Stripes had made his debut under jockey Gustavo Duarte. As a three-year-old, he went unbeaten in four more races that year at Maronas, stepping up from a comfortable Grade 3 victory to win all three legs of the Uruguayan Triple Crown by a combined total of nearly 16 lengths, including a six-and-a-half-length verdict in November in the Gran Premio Nacional, after which he was named horse of the year.

His name was Invasor, and he caught the avid eyes of the Maktoum empire, the most powerful and globally minded racing operation on the planet, who bought him and sent the colt to New York-based trainer Kiaran McLaughlin. Running in the colours of Sheikh Hamdan Al Maktoum, Invasor was beaten for the first time in his life when he finished fourth, in retrospect seriously undercooked, behind the wonderful Discreet Cat in the UAE Derby at Dubai's Nad Al Sheba racecourse in March. Shipped back to the States, Invasor was not beaten again in 2006, winning four Grade 1 races culminating in a fantastic victory in the Breeders' Cup Classic, the most valuable race on the continent, to take his lifetime record to nine wins from ten starts. In March 2007, he went back to Dubai to win the World Cup, the world's richest race, before injury forced his retirement in June. Even if he was a one-off, there couldn't have been a better advert for the newfound strength of the Uruguayan racing scene.

The month of March 2007 was a good one for Uruguyan racing. As well as Invasor's Dubai World Cup, the nation finally broke through in the Gran Premio Latinoamericano when Good Report was ridden to victory by Jorge Ricardo at La Plata in Argentina.

ARGENTINA

VITAL STATISTICS

RACING		FINANCE	
Racetracks	24	Total prize-money	$26.15m
Fixtures	*unknown*	Betting turnover	$132.29m
Races	7,268		
Racehorses	12,762	All figures for 2005	

BREEDING	
Stallions	884
Mares	11,500
Foals	6,783

GETTING to Buenos Aires from Uruguay wasn't difficult; just an hour on the ferry from Colonia del Sacramento across the River Plate. I liked Argentina's capital very much, considerably more than expected considering its relatively recent history of right-wing death squads, dictator-generals and thousands of 'disappeared' dissidents. They were prevalent during the years of military-junta rule in the 1970s and early 1980s, but gross economic instability remained the norm even after the restoration of democracy in 1983, reaching its nadir at the turn of the century, when chronic inflation and further currency crises sent the nation into another downward spiral. Fierce recession led to civil unrest and riots on the Buenos Aires streets.

Things were looking a lot brighter by the time I got to South America's third-largest metropolis, a city of many and varied neighbourhoods, from the bustling centre and its French-style architecture to the brightly painted wooden and corrugated-iron houses of La Boca, the southern working-class district where Diego Maradona was the local deity. The nocturnal lifestyle of the typical inhabitant of Buenos Aires had much to recommend it. No self-respecting *Porteno* would consider going out for their steak – and chances are they would be eating beef of some kind, this not being the most attractive place for vegetarians – before at least 10.30pm.

They could go there straight from the racetrack if they felt like it, despite the average meeting starting early in the afternoon. Go racing in Buenos Aires and you are in it for the long haul, as I found on a visit to a reasonable

Saturday card at Palermo racecourse in the heart of the capital. There, a 16-race card started at 2.30pm – and ended under floodlights seven and a half hours later at 11pm. I had already worked out that UK racegoers faced the highest entry fees in the world; given that most British cards feature six or seven races only, I was also beginning to wonder if we were still being short-changed. Then again, it is possible to have too much of a good thing, and 16 races on a chilly day in the middle of the Argentine winter was quite a test of endurance, not least because Palermo was my fifth racecourse in five separate countries in a dizzying fortnight. I had begun to realise how the blue-arsed fly might have felt.

*

IN the early years of the 21st century, after its own share of turmoil inextricably linked to problems on a national scale, Argentina was again vying with Chile as South America's most prosperous racing nation. In the context of the other countries I had visited in the previous few weeks, its prestige was similar to that of Brazil in the past, but with a history almost identical to its neighbour Uruguay, where Argentine influence is felt in almost every walk of life, including racing. Both countries have a celebrated gaucho tradition, but Argentina has always been by far the more significant horse-racing nation. It seemed to be retaining that status in the modern era.

Equine matters of all shapes and sizes have long since played a significant role in Argentine life. One obvious way in which the legacy of the gauchos tearing across the pampas manifests itself comes via the nation's tourist industry, seldom slow to promote the virtues of holidays on horseback in the interior with images of Argentina's answer to Roy Rogers lassoing stray cattle ahead of extraordinarily large steak dinners chargrilled over a campfire barbecue.

Argentina is renowned internationally in many other equine disciplines beyond racing, most obviously polo, in which it is a world leader. You would struggle to find a sport with more snooty connotations, and racing in Argentina also still carried traces of the same sort of class-based social cachet as a pastime for those who consider themselves somewhat superior to the general riff-raff.

Alan Patrick, author of an excellent user-friendly Buenos Aires travel guide on the internet, approached this subject in an article detailing a visit to Palermo in 2006. "I think the horses are given English names because the rich, horsey owners believe all things English are a cut above the rest in terms of class and breeding," he suggested, though it should be added that the blogger spoke of his afternoon in glowing terms. Like him, I found a mix of all types among the Palermo clientele, from hardened punters to family groups, to obvious representatives of the social elite that has traditionally provided the movers and shakers of the Buenos Aires racing scene.

Argentina's most internationally renowned racecourse, however, is not Palermo. That title belongs to suburban San Isidro, which opened in 1935 and is around 14 miles north of central Buenos Aires. Arguably the most celebrated racecourse on the continent, San Isidro features both dirt and turf racing, though the latter provides both its focus and its highlight in the weight-for-age championship event, the 2,400-metre Gran Premio Carlos Pellegrini, South America's answer to the Prix de l'Arc de Triomphe in mid-December. This race dates back much farther than San Isidro itself, having been inaugurated in 1887, five years after the foundation of the Jockey Club, and named after that body's initial president. The father of the Argentine turf, Pellegrini must have done a decent job: he was to become president of the republic between August 1890 and October 1892.

Palermo opened in 1876, making it nearly 60 years older than San Isidro. If anything, the latter's city-centre cousin appeared in the ruder health of the two showpiece venues thanks largely to its underground slot-machine emporium, open 365 days a year. Both Palermo and San Isidro hosted an annual total of about 120 meetings, but the former had just about surpassed its more famous sibling in terms of prize-money. Palermo's premier race, the Gran Premio Nacional, Argentina's dirt-track Derby held on a Saturday in early November was worth about 520,000 pesos ($175,000), virtually the same as the Carlos Pellegrini, but the city track habitually drew bigger crowds and attracted larger fields.

Situated on parkland opposite the polo ground across a busy main road, the Avenida del Libertador, Palermo is officially known as the Hipodromo Argentino. No-one ever uses that title, however, the racecourse preferring to share its name with the neighbouring district, a Buenos Aires version of

Islington: gentrified, artistic, bohemian, full of cafes and boutiques. Close by is the Jorge Newbery domestic airport and the banks of the River Plate, while the back straight runs parallel to a railway line. The nearest metro station was, unsurprisingly, Palermo itself, about half a mile away on Line D, but the vast majority of patrons drove to the track. Anyone caught in a traffic jam and missing a couple of races could console themselves that there were plenty more where they came from.

Designated drivers weren't needed either, as alcohol was banned under a law that bracketed racing venues with football grounds. There was a suggestion that the mayor, who must have been a barrel of laughs, was miffed at the track's being allowed to introduce the slots a couple of years previously and decided to hit back with a booze crusade.

An English expatriate journalist based in Buenos Aires for a few years explained the niceties. "It all comes down to tax payments and illicit kickbacks, of course," he said. "The mayor has been throwing his weight around among the football clubs as well, giving them all sorts of problems as he thinks they are not paying enough taxes to the city. He is locked into a long-term fight with the president of Boca Juniors – he's closed the ground more than once on security grounds that many consider to be trumped up."

Betting levels had actually increased during prohibition, but racecourse president Antonio Bullrich, a fifth-generation racing man and owner of Argentina's foremost sales company, hoped the liquor ban would soon be rescinded. "This is a recent thing and I hope it will change in a couple of months," he said, claiming not to know exactly what was behind the ban. "They've been drinking here since 1878 – I don't know if they think racegoers are turning into hooligans."

Bullrich, a young 48, looked like he had a few quid; perhaps it was the roadsign near the track saying 'Avenida Intendente Bullrich' that gave it away. Meeting him on the racecourse, you would immediately peg him as a bloodstock agent: he had that gift of the gab, fluent in English with a strange Irish twang, knew everybody, mobile phone ringing constantly. A major figure in Argentinian bloodstock, he was closely involved in building up the Haras Clausan, the Italian-owned stud that bred 2006 Breeders' Cup Classic winner Invasor.

Bullrich also had the smell of the playboy, having just returned from a trip to Europe where, among other things, he attended the St Tropez wedding of Anthony Stroud, Sheikh Mohammed's racing manager for a long period before returning to his roots as an independent bloodstock agent. It was difficult to imagine another world in which the pair of us would be found sitting together having a laugh over not having a drink, but racing makes for strange bedfellows, and Bullrich was fine company, self-deprecating and informative.

Warming to his subject, he went on: "When I was in Ireland recently, I asked someone what they would do if drinking was not allowed. They said there would be no racing. Argentina is not really a drinking country but at 7pm here everyone starts shaking. I could do with a drink myself." It was 6pm.

We chatted in the *tribuna oficial*, a sort of club enclosure building behind the imposing entrance, which was nothing short of a mini Arc de Triomphe. Wrought-iron front gates, patrolled by a ridiculously heavy armed security presence, opened on to an ornate marble walkway and a truly *grand* stand – think phrases like Art Nouveau and *belle époque* – built in 1908 in the French style best illustrated by the city's wonderful Recoleta cemetery. After such a grand start, Palermo's other virtues were more prosaic: a muddy mile-and-a-half dirt circuit skirted by a train line.

Three and a half hours into the programme there was an unexpected reminder of home in the shape of former leading apprentice Gustavo Clemente, a doppelganger for Jamie Spencer, Britain's champion jockey in 2005 well known for an in-the-saddle sangfroid evinced in his habitual reliance on audacious come-from-behind tactics.

The seventh race at Palermo was the Clasico Old Man, a Group 3 race over 1,400 metres named in honour of one of Argentina's greatest horses, a Triple Crown winner who also took the Carlos Pellegrini in 1904 and 1905. Regarded as a major trial for the first Classic of the season, this 15-runner contest featured a hot favourite in the shape of Gold For Sale, a Clemente-partnered chestnut who had won both his starts as a two-year-old in decisive fashion. Carrying 50 pesos of my money, Gold For Sale was settled wide and deep in the field by his red-cheeked, baby-faced rider. Gold For

Sale stayed wide, and was five lengths adrift of his two main market rivals as they fought it out at the furlong pole. The man on his back exuded no sense of urgency whatsoever; he simply let his horse stride on down the middle of the track. Gold For Sale cut down his rivals close home, Clemente motionless on his back, as cool as duck in an icebox, the personification of arrogance in the saddle.

"He is going to be really good," suggested Bullrich. "We think he could be our new superstar – he is only 19 and he is very cool, and the good thing is that he doesn't realise yet how good he is."

Ask anyone in Argentina to name a racing celebrity and chances are they'd answer Jorge Valdivieso, the nation's answer to Lester Piggott and something of a heart-throb in his time. This riding legend's flowing blond locks were a thing of the past, but the 48-year-old multiple champion was still appearing regularly at the Buenos Aires tracks, though he selected his rides carefully after a bad fall. In March 2005, the veteran partnered Don Incauto to a popular home victory, giving Argentina its third success in the history of the Gran Premio Latinoamericano as it stopped off at San Isidro. Indeed, it was an Argentine 1-2-3, as Classic winner Latency and top racemare Halo Ola chased home the winner.

Valdivieso spent much of his time at Palermo posing for photographs with children, as did Pablo Falero, himself many times champion in a competitive jockey colony. This Uruguayan-born rider made the most of umpteen chances with five winners, among them Ronronero, who took the 11th race of the day, a Group 2 event over 2,500 metres. This race started at 7.30pm, when people were still arriving at the track. I examined Falero closely after another of his victories, in a 1,200-metre event named the Premio Dorian Gray. It's funny; he looked older in his pictures.

Evidently, reports of Argentina's revival were far from exaggerated. They spoke of a racing industry once again making the most of natural advantages offered by the wonderful pasture of the southern pampas. In 2003, an article printed in *International Gaming and Wagering Magazine* quoted Antonio Quintella, a breeder with horses in Brazil, Argentina and Chile. "The Mar del Plata region is the best place in the world for horse breeding," he claimed. "The quality is unmatched."

A home-town verdict, perhaps, but Argentina's bloodstock industry, which produces nearly 7,000 foals a year, certainly possesses a fine reputation. As with the rest of the continent, it is a fair bet that anything that looks any good on the racetrack at home may well end up abroad, usually in the United States. Such exports were relatively common back as far as the 1930s and 1940s, but probably the best horse ever to join the exodus was Forli, still unbeaten in 1966 when he won the Carlos Pellegrini on his final outing in Argentina before being shipped north. Unfortunately, injury meant that he was to make more of an impact at stud than on the track in the US, but he still retired with a record of nine wins and one second from ten starts. Forli and Telescopico, the hero of 1978, remain the only two horses to win all four legs of the Argentine Quadruple Crown, featuring a Guineas and Derby equivalent on the turf at San Isidro plus the Gran Premio Nacional on the dirt at Palermo, rounded off with the weight-for-age Carlos Pellegrini.

A distinguished list of top-flight performers to have thrived after leaving Argentina in the last couple of decades is headed by the fantastic Bayakoa, the unstoppably courageous parrot-mouthed supermare, a top-level winner at home as a three-year-old who went on to win 12 Grade 1 races in the States in a two-year spree in 1989-90, including a pair of Breeders' Cup Distaffs. Her top-class fellow exiles include Paseana, who also scored at the Breeders' Cup, and star older horse Gentlemen, an Argentine Guineas (Gran Premio Polla de Potrillos) winner in 1995 with half a dozen American Grade 1s to his name, plus Candy Ride, who looked a world-beater in two top-level Californian victories in 2003 before injury ended his career.

For all this, though, Argentine racing as a whole, and Palermo in particular, faced an extreme crisis as the nation went into (another) financial meltdown in the late 1990s. The Carlos Pellegrini lost much of its value in real terms, while the game was nearly up entirely for Palermo. "We had five years of struggling and in 2001 we were just months away from closing the track," recalled Bullrich.

International Gaming and Wagering Magazine examined the turnaround in Argentina's fortunes. "The general improvement in the country's economy is the driving force, but flexible horse racing regulations have also played a major role," said the magazine. While the broader economic recovery cannot have hurt, you needed only to go downstairs upon entering the track to see the main source of the turnaround. "This is Las Vegas," said the PR girl who showed me around a huge underground parlour of slot machines at basement level, running the full length of two stands.

Since all racecourse staff not directly involved in operating the slots were not permitted to visit this part of the facility, it was also the first time my guide had been there. From the way her eyes lit up when she entered a neon-lit cavern of around 7,000 noisy, gaudy machines with names like 'Mystical Mermaids' and 'Fairy Fortunes', it was probably just as well she was normally barred.

Though there were about 5,000 paying customers at the track, a high proportion of them behind glass in the restaurants, the free-to-enter slots parlour was absolutely swarming all day long with a crowd that could have been attending a completely separate event. It could almost have *been* Vegas – except drinking alcohol was banned here as well, so there was a distinct lack of scantily clad females offering to bring drinks every ten minutes.

Such scenes have been responsible for the survival of many tracks in the USA, and they certainly saved Palermo after the dark days. The evidence was in the racecard, where the list of runners and riders for each race carried a breakdown of where the prize-money was derived: at least 50 per cent of every race came from slots. While purses still weren't up to much by European standards, with the richest race worth only 39,000 pesos (about £7,500), they more than held their own in a South American context.

The financial boost provided by slots was also responsible for the ludicrous magnitude of the card as Palermo catered for a vast supply of horses well beyond the 900 actually trained at the track itself, tempting runners from San Isidro and La Plata, the region's third, slightly lower-grade venue, and even the country's interior. "The introduction of slots in 2002 really saved the industry here," said Bullrich. "I took over just before they changed the law, and now everyone thinks I'm a genius! We put up our prizes, and now we are ten per cent higher than San Isidro on average. As a result, we are absorbing everything. I would love to be able to have just eight or nine races like the good old days but if we have less racing, we would make a lot of people in the industry very unhappy."

On that particular Saturday at Palermo, fewer races wouldn't have pleased me either, as I managed to back four winners from six bets, all of them favourites, but not at all bad given the indecipherable nature of the form supplied in the racecard and *La Nacion* newspaper. I came out about 100 pesos up: it was around £20, the equivalent of five good-sized *filet mignon* at a fair Buenos Aires *parilla*.

I had just been playing about in South America when it came to gambling, not just because of my total ignorance of the form, but also owing to the horrendous takeouts that habitually resulted in a plethora of odds-on favourites, the curse of Latin American punters. Soon, though, it was back to the United States, where I intended to go full tilt.

At Palermo, though, I left after the 13th race of an excellent day's racing, when the old gent hawking the evening paper containing latest news of Boca Juniors' transfer speculation shouted about the card for the following day's meeting at San Isidro, also a mixture of turf and dirt.

It sounded like a tempting variety. Mind you, I wouldn't have paid to go there – there were only 15 races and it ended before 9pm. Bloody rip-off merchants.

*

IN *December 2005, Pablo Falero went on to win the Carlos Pellegrini on the Juan Bianchi-trained Storm Mayor, who scored by a head over the favourite Forty Licks in front of a crowd of 50,000.*

Three months later in the Gran Premio Latinoamericano, held that year at Maronas in Uruguay, Storm Mayor could finish only a disappointing tenth, veering inward just after the break and hitting the rail. However, the continental championship demonstrated Argentina's relative strength as Latency, a half-length behind Don Incauto the previous year, used his late kick to score from my old friend, the Uruguayan-trained Necessaire. The race was worth $150,000.

In December 2006, after returning to form with a pair of Group 1 wins, Storm Mayor won his second successive Carlos Pellegrini, beating Peru's Shuaily to cement his status as the No.1 racehorse on the continent. He was the first horse to win back-to-back editions of Argentina's signature event since Filon in 1944 and 1945.

Gold For Sale, so impressive at Palermo, returned to the track later in the season to win Argentina's version of the 2,000 Guineas, after which he was sold to Prince Sultan Al Kabeer, a first cousin to the king of Saudi Arabia. He re-emerged in 2006, when he was trained by Englishman Ian Jory in Riyadh to win a race at the Dubai Carnival in impressive fashion under multiple Irish champion Mick Kinane. Jory also saddled Simpatico Bribon, a Group 1 winner in Chile, to a spectacular victory in Dubai, but the pair flopped in mysterious circumstances when both were strongly fancied in the richly endowed UAE Derby on the Dubai World Cup card. In a race won by Godolphin's nascent superstar Discreet Cat, neither South American star showed a glimmer of their previous form. Jory later conducted private urine tests on both horses, which revealed traces in their systems of a drug closely related to valium. "I'm pretty sure it wasn't accidental and we have to suspect foul play," said the trainer. No further explanation was ever made public. In due course Forty Licks, the 2005 Carlos Pellegrini runner-up, also joined Jory's team.

USA (2)

FEARS of civil war in Bolivia had receded by the time the itinerary was due to hit La Paz, the highest capital city in the world, but it was too late to revert to the original schedule without incurring hefty financial penalties attached to the round-the-world ticket, even if seats had still been available. Such tickets are excellent value: the less flexible you are, the cheaper they are. Let's just say I went for cheap over flexible, so no Bolivia. Lake Titicaca would have to wait.

Instead, after just over five weeks in South America and another stopover in Lima – just try to avoid it if you're zigzagging across the continent – it was time to return to the land of stoopers, chalk-eaters and hangin' pigs. The United States, in other words, a nation in which racing has its own distinct argot.

A 'stooper' is someone who searches the floor of a racetrack looking for winning tickets thrown out by mistake, haunted-looking sallow-cheeked individuals easily recognisable by their undernourished appearance and crooked backs. 'Chalk-eaters' are those who habitually play the favourites, while 'hangin' pigs' are horses who challenge the leader without bothering to go past and win. In Britain, we would just call them dogs.

Not that I expected to encounter many such porcines (nor, for that matter, canines) on this particular leg of the journey, which involved two of America's best-loved racecourses, Del Mar and Saratoga, storied summer venues where the standard of racing is invariably vertiginous.

Both are classy joints, each of them extremely popular, the mention of their very names being enough to elicit a beatific smile from American racing enthusiasts. Yet they could hardly be more dissimilar in certain significant respects. Separated by the breadth of the entire country, these celebrated tracks represent the opposite power bases of American racing. This is California versus New York, West Coast versus East Coast; *nouveau riche arriviste* against old-money breeding and wealth. Those who favour Del Mar might also suggest the trade-off is laid-back versus stuck-up; the Saratogan faithful would possibly aver that it's timeless elegance against vulgar upstart.

Fortunately, no-one is forced to identify any preference. I thought they were both fantastic.

*

AMERICAN punters habitually refer to individual racecourses as 'the track' – and in the Californian summer, everyone's a beach boy for seven weeks as the track moves south to Del Mar, an upmarket coastal village about 20 miles north of San Diego, where horseracing provides the most noteworthy attraction of the annual county fair.

As the home turn is virtually on the beach, the racecourse has always played heavily on its proximity to the Pacific in promotional terms. Del Mar is billed as the place 'where the surf meets the turf', while the highlight of its brief season is the $1 million Pacific Classic in August. It was in this race that Cigar's winning streak was snapped in 1996 after he had equalled Citation's 20th century American record of 16 successive wins, when the Bill Mott-trained superstar and his rider Jerry Bailey were beaten by rival trainer Richard Mandella's three-card trick. Mandella's apparent first string, Siphon, hooked up Cigar in a speed duel, while Dare And Go bided his time well off insanely fast fractions. Cigar duly bettered Siphon, but had nothing left to fight off the late closer Dare And Go, who won the race at odds of 40-1. "I felt I had let everyone down, starting with Cigar," said a disconsolate Bailey.

When I visited Del Mar on a blazing Sunday afternoon, the highlight of a ten-race card was another of its Grade 1 contests, the six-furlong Bing Crosby Handicap, named in honour of the long-departed crooner who was among the track's founders in the mid-1930s, when Del Mar became the Hollywood set's summer playground, synonymous with a relaxed, easygoing atmosphere. Eddie Read, the track's publicity executive for years, accurately summed up Del Mar as a place "where nobody's in a hurry but the horses".

That particular quotation, as well as some of the anecdotes that follow, is shamelessly pilfered from a brief potted history by novelist William Murray entitled *Del Mar: Its Life and Good Times*, a volume written by a Del Mar regular that comes replete with an array of photographs of the famous horses, jockeys and film stars that feature in the racecourse's past. The Del

Mar raceclub was founded after a meeting between Bing Crosby and his Hollywood cronies at the Warner Brothers studio in Burbank. One of the best photos in Murray's book shows the opening day in July 1937, with Crosby, sucking on a briar pipe, welcoming the first customer through the entrance gate.

The track wasn't an immediate success. In those days, San Diego was hardly a major conurbation, while the 100-mile journey south from Los Angeles via the Sante Fe Railroad could be tortuous indeed. Crosby and his pals had a straightforward scheme for attracting the crowds and it worked. Bring in their celebrity friends. For its first couple of years, Del Mar was almost an extension of a Hollywood movie society, with some of the biggest names in pre-war movies and showbusiness among racecourse patrons. Just look at some of the names: WC Fields, Al Jolson, Jimmy 'Schnozzle' Durante, Mickey Rooney, Dorothy Lamour, George Raft, Edward G Robinson, Ava Gardner, Barbara Stanwyck and Robert Taylor. The seed of Crosby's professional relationship with comic Bob Hope that resulted in their series of 'Road' movies is also said to have been planted at Del Mar.

Crosby, of course, was a singer, and he left an indelible mark in 1938 when he sang for the first time the famous Del Mar racetrack ditty:

"Where the surf meets the turf
Down at old Del Mar,
Take a plane, take a train, take a car
There's a smile on every face
And a winner in each race
Where the surf meets the turf at Del Mar"

Originally performed live by Crosby, a recording is now aired during every day's racing.

Movie stars were one thing, but they were nothing without the horses to match. Del Mar really put itself on the map in 1938 with a match race between the fabled Seabiscuit and the six-year-old Argentinian import Ligaroti, owned by a partnership involving Crosby. Around 20,000 fans witnessed a fierce duel up the straight reputed to have been one of the dirtiest races anyone could recall with the two jockeys climbing all over each other. Seabiscuit, who was giving his rival 15lb over a nine-furlong trip, won by a nose and broke the track record by four seconds. He went on to beat the Triple Crown winner War Admiral in the most famous match in US racing history; his rival Ligaroti won top-level races before failing as a stallion. According to Murray, he collapsed while covering a mare named Last Bang, which seemed an appropriate name.

Although Crosby sold up soon after the war, the celebrities kept on coming, with patrons including Maurice Chevalier, Jack Dempsey and FBI chief J Edgar Hoover. Del Mar also developed a reputation as a place for racing legends. In 1956, John Longden partnered the 4,871st winner of his career at the track, thereby surpassing Sir Gordon Richards' mark as the leading jockey of all-time in terms of races won. Fourteen years later, Del Mar was the venue when Bill Shoemaker broke Longden's record with the 6,033rd winner of his career. For Shoemaker, it was a return to old haunts. In 1949, at the age of 18, he had established a track record when riding 52 winners at the summer meeting.

Nowadays, they race at Del Mar for just 43 days a year, six days a week in summer with cards featuring good-class horses competing for the state's highest average purses. And if my brief visit to its packed stands was anything to go by, then its laid-back reputation is fully justified. A jeans-and-polo-shirted crowd enjoyed the racing amid palm trees and attractive hacienda-style buildings, all ochres, creams and pinks, as a jaunty Mexican trio played mariachi. It was a welcoming environment in which to play the horses – and, after more than a month messing around for peanuts in South America, I *really* fancied playing the horses.

While there are those who can watch horse racing without ever feeling the urge to bet, I am not one of those weirdos. A coarser individual might describe racing without betting as a dry hump: not to be entirely dismissed, but you can't shake the sense that something fundamental is missing.

Although the odd half-baked wager in places like Venezuela and Peru provided entertainment value in the preceding weeks, serious action could never be part of the equation in such alien environments. Not so the slightly more familiar arenas in the United States, where I could kid myself that I had a vague notion of what I was doing.

In the vernacular, however, I didn't possess a 'bubble-gum ass'; I just hoped a return to the betting windows wouldn't leave me 'on the schneid'. (Translation: I couldn't sit stuck to my seat during races without getting up off my seat until an attractive betting opportunity arises; such a compulsive attitude could easily result in a losing streak. But if you are going to lose, there are surely few better places to do it than Del Mar.)

Chances are you might lose, though. Del Mar, with one of the shortest finishing stretches in the country outside the county-fair bullring circuit, is renowned as an idiosyncratic venue, a track for which the 'horses for courses' dictum might have been devised. "When they can run there, they run like hell or they can't run at all," said US training legend Charlie Whittingham, a regular over the decades.

There are those who take issue with the suggestion that Del Mar can often be a law unto itself, among them Brad Free, the *Daily Racing Form* expert responsible for most of the advice contained in the paper's invaluable 'players' guide' to the meeting. "The California racing calendar is a 12-month deal," he said. "Past performances from LA-area tracks definitely apply at Del Mar."

Nevertheless, outside posts could mean ruin on this tightest of tracks, while even Free didn't argue against the idea that Del Mar's racing schedule was slightly odd compared to other top American tracks, with distinct trends and an unusual programme generally geared towards turf and two-year-olds at the top end. Bob Baffert's dominance as leading trainer had recently been broken by Doug O'Neill, but the Andy Warhol lookalike's juveniles remained hard to catch – and priced to match. Patrick Valenzuela, a brilliant rider whose career had been littered with drug problems, had overcome his personal demons long enough to claim top spot among the jockeys.

Having spent much of the previous night taking apart the card over a few beers in San Diego's Gaslamp District, I got into position early at the track, allowing ample time for an early pint in the Charlie Whittingham Sports Bar before moving on to the top floor of its Mexican-style grandstand near Bing's Celebrity Grill, where pictures of Hollywood icons to have visited the track adorn the walls, Bette Davis and Walt Disney among the most prominent.

The card kicked off with a couple of low-grade claimers on the dirt, just the type of mysterious races to be ignored by anyone with a semblance of self-control. Statistics gleaned from the *Daily Racing Form*'s players' guide steered me towards a pair of horses at decent prices, thanks to compelling trainer-trends involving a pair of handlers unknown to me beforehand.

Art Sherman and Carla Gaines, a plague on both your houses. The former was hitting at a 36 per cent strike-rate with horses straight off a claim, while Gaines was 28 per cent with her second-timers. There was a Sherman qualifier showing 9-1 in the opener, and a potential Gaines 'special' in the second, later sent off around 12-1.

Complimenting myself on my undoubted shrewdness, I dived in on both and played a few exotics. The Sherman mare got caught in a speed duel and was spent after four furlongs of five and a half, while Gaines's gelding undermined his trainer's average by producing a carbon copy of his previous moderate effort.

So much for the smart-alec stuff. But if I was guilty of trying to be too clever in front of the windows, there was definitely a wise guy taking bets behind them. "I recognise your accent –which part of LA are you from?" he inquired before the next.

"Straight outta Compton, blood, and are you calling my bitch a ho?" That's what I wish I had said. Instead, resisting the urge to ask this accomplished humorist what he was doing wasting his time at Del Mar when the stage at the Comedy Store was so obviously beckoning, I upped the ante in a better-quality mile event that looked straightforward enough.

Four of the seven runners, all first-timers from South America, looked either hopelessly outclassed or running over the wrong trip. Then there was a Baffert trainee stepping up in grade – too far – and leading trainer Bobby Frankel's only runner of the day, a four-year-old who kept on finishing second. A hangin' pig, perhaps? As the Frankel horse was even-money favourite, it all pointed to Richard Mandella's Megabyte, showing

3-1 and worth a decent bet. The Frankel colt led all the way and won untroubled.

Time to take the tram to the infield, a margarita – $10 in special commemorative shaker – and a look-see. Though there was a bouncy castle, this was the only minor aggravation among the ice-cream and cotton-candy sellers, and that probably only because of its unfortunate associations with embarrassing family fundays at British racecourses. Believe me, there's nothing 'fun' about most of them. 'Desperate' might be nearer the mark.

While over there, I might have backed the fourth-race winner, but horses drawn one hadn't been winning very often at Del Mar prior to this card so I avoided it. On the positive side, I spotted jockey David Flores enjoying an ice lolly with his daughter, and senator John McCain turned up for the last few races.

The fifth offered hope of redemption thanks to a significant Del Mar trend involving ex-European-trained animals. "A fresh import, typically adding Lasix and receiving improved veterinary care, can be dangerous", suggested Brad Free in the *Form*. Could "improved veterinary care" be a euphemism for juiced up, I wondered?

This race, a turf event over a mile and a bit, featured a filly formerly trained in France by the esteemed Criquette Head-Maarek. As the horse was well drawn – ignore outside posts in all turf 'routes', races of a mile and over, warned Mr Free – she looked well worth another good lump in a race where the locals had done little to distinguish themselves. I saw the window marked 'large transactions only' and advanced towards it with purpose. If only Wakired, the filly in question, had done the same on the track two minutes later. No show.

Next up was a two-year-old contest with an unraced Baffert trainee named Air Ace sure to start hot favourite. I couldn't justify backing him at odds-on, even though published workout times showed him to be sharpish. Anyway, Baffert had a second string who had already had an outing, a very promising run at that. He was called Gold Maker, and he was on offer at 5-1, so I backed him to win, plus an exacta for him to finish second behind his stablemate Air Ace. Gold Maker finished third behind his stablemate Air Ace, who was none too impressive in just lasting home under a punishing drive.

Another loser followed, beaten by a horse I considered closely who got free on the lead under a 10lb-claiming bug boy. It seemed appropriate for a quick drink in the 'Coulda Woulda Shoulda' bar ahead of the main event, a good place to avoid Del Mar's daily ritual 'Sing with Bing' slot, where some C-list celeb or perplexingly enthusiastic member of the public takes the microphone to belt out the track's theme tune alongside a recording of the ubiquitous Crosby, long gone but clearly not forgotten. So, Bing, there's a smile on every face and a winner in each race, is there? You would have found neither if you'd come near me.

At last we came to dear old Bing's race, the Grade 1 sprint bearing the old crooner's name. Now, if nothing else that day went right, I was absolutely certain about one thing: Pico Central, among the best sprinters in the world in 2004, would not win. Not only had he not appeared since running in Dubai in March, his trainer was on record as saying that he needed the run and later targets were much more important. If that wasn't enough, there was also the not-insignificant detail that he was giving away 7lb and more to a field of decent sprinters. At level weights, an unfit Pico Central might have been good enough to beat these less-exalted rivals, but giving away half a stone? I put a line through him and made it a big black one.

For some reason, such weight issues, meat and drink to UK punters, seldom seem to affect the US betting market. Pico Central duly started favourite at 5-2. All I needed to do was identify which one of his rivals looked best to dig me out of the hole, and there weren't that many plausible candidates, to judge from the Beyer (rhymes with 'flyer') speed figures. I settled on Top Commander, who had recorded a couple of big Beyers in recent outings and was trained by Cole Norman, who shipped in Beau's Town to win off a similar profile in 2003. For good measure, my old mucker Brad Free tipped him as well, and he was 6-1.

Pico Central bombed – he was later found to have burst a blood vessel – and Pat Valenzuela showed his mastery of the track on Battle Won by forcing rivals wide on the home turn, among them Top Commander. He left the door open, though, for progressive Greg's Gold, who made the most of the weight concession under lolly-sucking Flores, Battle Won keeping on for second. While Top Commander wasn't disgraced, he wasn't placed either, so with one race to go I decided that discretion was probably the better part of valour and, none too early, shut up shop.

Though it might be considered a trifle vulgar to reveal the figures involved, such coyness could only be an aggravation in a section of the book designed as a punting diary. I left Del Mar $800 down, without a single winning wager. It was easier in South America.

*

CROSS the George Washington Bridge out of Manhattan and head north into upstate New York in the direction of Albany. Shortly before you get to the state capital, a slight detour off the main highway, lies the village of Woodstock, full of new-age nonsense, tie-dyed tea towels, Jimi Hendrix posters and postcards of pillocks prancing about on chestnut mares. Which is strange, because the 1960s music festival that inspired such necessities took place 60 miles away near the town of Bethel. Never trust a hippie.

Saratoga racecourse, on the other hand, was exactly where I expected it to be, in the spa town of Saratoga Springs, 40 miles past Albany and about 200 miles north of New York City. Established in 1864, America's oldest racecourse is nothing short of an institution, renowned as the keeper of US racing's spiritual flame. Come late July, the cream of the nation's top trainers and jockeys move to Saratoga en masse for its 36-day season, highlight of which is the Travers Stakes, the 'midsummer derby', the closest thing to a Classic outside the Triple Crown and imbued with similar prestige.

After the carefree delights of Del Mar, it is fair to say I was apprehensive of my visit to Saratoga, loins fully girded for somewhere with a reputation as a bastion of privilege and tradition, long-term home of the US racing aristocracy epitomised by their version of royalty, the 79-year-old heiress Marylou Whitney, who spent much of her time at the course indulging in regal waves and walkabouts. On the eve of the nine-furlong Whitney Handicap, the Grade 1 feature that bears her family name and was to provide the highlight of my weekend at Saratoga, Queen Marylou hosted a gala ball. Fortunately I wasn't invited to this affair, as it cost $5,000 a head. Always one for the big entrance, in previous years she had arrived in a hot-air balloon and coronation coaches. This time she turned up in a flapper-era Model T Ford with a new accessory on her arm, a 32-year-old husband. Wonder just what it was that attracted him to the millionaire socialite?

Add to this guide-book warnings about the town being a sleepy, fading resort peopled mainly by visitors keen to bathe in its magical spa waters, and I was prepared for an unappetising cross between the unfortunate side of Royal Ascot and the genteel torpor of a city like Bath. I really should have known better. The US, for all its faults, is never going to be able to give Britain a lesson in stuffiness. Saratoga might creak with history, but this was no loopy antiquated celebration of wealth and status, though both were, undeniably, hardly in short supply amid the parties and balls.

In short, I loved it. The town might have been mordant during the rest of the year, but during the race meeting it felt like a much more attractive, vastly less scuzzy version of Newmarket, with horse-racing ephemera everywhere, from the equine statues that dotted the high street to the hotels and motels with screens showing racing on cable television. All the restaurants and bars did the same. When Ms Whitney was hosting her big 'do' the Friday before 'her' race, I was among a crowd of racefans enjoying the evening on Broadway, the town's central artery, specifically in the Stadium Café, a fine sports bar featuring framed jockeys' silks on the walls (among them Khalid Abdullah's green and pink, Michael Tabor's blue and orange and Ghostzapper black and red) and a bank of screens offering a veritable cornucopia of delights: thoroughbreds from the western states, including Del Mar, quarter horses at Los Alamitos in Long Beach, and harness racing from just down the road at Saratoga Raceway, where the trotters continued all-year round. There was baseball as well, and the burgers and beer were more than acceptable.

Walking past clapboard houses and decorative gardens to the racecourse known as 'The Spa' was a joy in itself. In any event, there seemed little reason to drive. Everyone other than officials and dignitaries parked somewhere in the vicinity of the training centre, which left you about half a mile distant unless you were obscenely early. Saratoga's huge barn area was divided into two sections, with barns attached to the racecourse itself and many more across the road opposite the racecourse entrance, where they backed on to a second circuit, the Oklahoma training track. "No autos on the path at anytime," read a stark notice. "Violators will be fined." That was a surprise: given the primacy of the horse in Saratoga, you'd have thought they would be shot.

The names of Triple Crown winners were painted on wooden boards nailed on to trees lining the roads en route to the racecourse; approaching from the town centre, barely half a mile away, you passed the sizeable houses on Union Avenue to be greeted by roadsigns naming more recent stars, Travers winners such as Funny Cide, War Emblem and Birdstone.

I visited the track four afternoons in a row, from Friday to Monday, with the aforementioned Whitney Handicap proving an enthralling contest won by a new star in the Nick Zito-trained Commentator, a gelding who stepped up from impressive victories in lesser company over seven furlongs – regarded as sprints in the US – to steal a valuable Grade 1 over nine.

The Whitney, which started bang in front of the stands on the Saturday, was just the type of enthralling tactical contest that provides the most intriguing facet of American racing. Gary Stevens produced a brilliant example of pacemaking on the winner, kicking in a blazing fraction early in the race before giving his mount the breather that just kept enough gas in the tank to stretch him out to the wire. As a result, Commentator just held the fierce late charge of the favourite Saint Liam, the best older horse in the States, resplendent in shocking pink blinkers that resembled the masks worn by Lucha Libre wrestlers in Mexico City. They matched his colours, while his owners, William and Suzanne Warren, did their bit with pink tie and frock respectively.

Afterwards, as a sweaty Stevens drenched himself in water from the trackside cooler, the Brooklynite Zito offered high-fives to the crowd. Though Saint Liam was a valiant loser, giving weight away to the victor, Commentator's victory was a popular one two days before his trainer was inducted into the Hall of Fame across the road at the National Museum of Racing, which housed a wonderful exhibition of the work of racing cartoonist Pierre Bellocq ('Peb'). One particularly incisive satirical effort from 1993 entitled *Magic Trainer* showed a jockey riding in on a syringe, led in by a wide-boy trainer beaming a grotesque ear-to-ear grin.

Saratoga racecourse is something of a museum piece itself, notorious as the 'Graveyard of Champions' over the years. It was the scene of the legendary Man o' War's sole defeat, beaten by the famously well-named Upset in 1919, while Secretariat, perhaps the greatest of them all, went down to a horse named Onion in the 1973 Whitney. In 1930, another Triple Crown winner, Gallant Fox, suffered his only defeat in ten three-year-old starts in the Travers Stakes when he was beaten by Jim Dandy, himself now remembered in a Grade 2 event at modern Saratoga. When considering Saratoga as the 'Graveyard of Champions', the literal-minded might also point to champion filly Go For Wand's having been buried on the infield after breaking down at the Breeders' Cup at Belmont in 1990.

This was a wonderful place to go racing, albeit with a hint of the surreal about it. If a racecourse were constructed in Portmeirion, it wouldn't be entirely dissimilar from this, where form cards were studied beneath red-and-white-striped parasols overlooking TV screens and restaurants. The prize for kitsch went to the 'Carousel' restaurant, where fairground horses circled the central bar on the back of the ancient wooden-framed stand.

Virtually any winner is considered special at Saratoga, where the racing pitch is impressively high, like a six-week Glorious Goodwood. While national leader Todd Pletcher was clear among trainers, those vying for supremacy among the jockeys included John Velazquez, Edgar Prado, Javier Castellano and Eibar Coa. The last-named earned a lasting place in my affections for his display on the Sunday on an unraced two-year-old named Shelterfromastorm, who took a one-mile turf race. Unlike the two market leaders, neither of whom seemed to have an obvious turf pedigree, this filly was sired by Chester House, a horse I knew from his racing days in England when he was trained by Henry Cecil. While I had never heard of Shelterfromastorm's trainer Tom Bush, this was more than compensated for by the generous price. He won at 18-1, carrying $40 of my money, virtually eradicating Del Mar losses at a stroke. No wonder I liked Saratoga.

*

WHEN it came to Saratoga, one jockey stood head and shoulders above the rest. Jerry Bailey, who topped the all-time list for career victories at the track, was riding his final meeting at the historic venue six months ahead of his eventual retirement in January 2006 at the age of 48.

No-one was aware of this at the time, however, other than perhaps Bailey himself, and he was showing few visible signs that he was losing his edge. During my visit, he rode a treble on the Whitney undercard on the Saturday and stayed on long enough the next day to win another race on potentially top-class two-year-old First Samurai before rushing off to New Jersey to win a prestigious race there four hours later.

It was a privilege to see Bailey in action that weekend at Saratoga, an all-time great excelling yet again on a famous stage he had made his own: like Olivier at the Old Vic, Pavarotti at La Scala or Joey Ramone at CBGBs. Any discussion about the identity of the best jockey in the world, if not entirely pointless, is always likely to be hopelessly one-eyed. We all like what we know and whom we know. For a decade, though, few would have had better claims to that exalted status than Bailey, unquestionably the No.1 rider of his generation in the world's most powerful racing nation. The Texan was revered as the most tactically astute jock in North America: the most reliable, the least likely to mess things up, a ferociously competitive embodiment of the ideal of the consummate professional. The winner of six Triple Crown races, including a pair of Kentucky Derbys, and more races at the Breeders' Cup than anyone else, he had also won the Dubai World Cup four times.

It was quite a record, which made it all the more startling that such details are treated as only of secondary importance in Bailey's autobiography, *Against The Odds*, published earlier in 2005. The primary subject of an unflinching account is the one struggle that Bailey can never be certain he has finally won: a lengthy fight against alcoholism.

When I caught up with the rider for an hour-long chat, he made no attempt to avoid discussing what became an ugly dependence in the 1980s, when his drinking jeopardised rather more than just a promising career before he took steps to control the problem in January 1989. After gruesome fights with his wife Suzee – whom he abused verbally and psychologically but never physically – he visited Alcoholics Anonymous for the first time and undertook an outpatient programme that enabled him to achieve sobriety.

"I'll always be an alcoholic," said Bailey, relaxed and friendly demeanour a world away from the troubling subject matter. "I'm just an arm's length away from a drink and all I have is a daily reprieve, that's all I consider it. There is no cure; there's just an arrest for it."

The stories of Bailey's wild drinking days were hard to square with the business-like figure he cut on the racecourse after he stopped. How he was formerly known as the 'Two O'Clock Jock' by his colleagues for never taking an early ride to avoid having to arrive early at the track after the night before, a lack of focus he blamed for losing a lucrative contract in New York riding for Mack Miller, trainer for leading owner Paul Mellon's Rokeby Stable.

"I grew up in an era when it was almost encouraged for jockeys to go out and drink and have a wild time," he explained. "I just got hooked up in it, and it went over the edge for me, I went over the line. I started riding in 1974, and by 1976 I was in that lifestyle, partying and getting drunk, for 13 years. I was pretty good at hiding it, but even though I wasn't falling down drunk every day, there was some alcohol in my system. My thinking wasn't clear so it handicapped my riding by taking away my biggest asset, which was my mind. It was a damning thing for my career, even though I was so secretive that for the last two or three years I wouldn't go out in public, I would drink at home."

Worse still were the related relationship problems. "It affected not only my riding but my personality," said Bailey. "I knew I was going to lose my wife, and any little piece of respect that people ever had for me, so I had to do something about it. There was a tremendous amount of pain and I did a tremendous amount of damage to my marriage."

Most US racing professionals consider dealing with the media as an important part of their job. They are generally a journalist's dream, much easier to deal with than, say, some of their British counterparts, a proportion of whom still seem determined to treat the press as bottom-feeders. Even so, I was amazed at Bailey's candour, which was extended to other aspects of his life and career, not least when he discussed the fertility problems he and his wife had to overcome before the birth of their beloved son Justin. One treatment required fresh sperm samples, for which Bailey was prepared to go to any lengths, including, he said, withdrawing to the privacy of his car in a remote parking lot at Belmont Park to 'do the necessary' after morning workouts.

"It was probably the most embarrassing thing I could bring up to the public," he laughed, "but the things you will go through to have a child are limitless, really. You'll do whatever it takes and that's what it took, so I had to do it."

Bailey's career started to look up in his mid-30s, almost from the very moment he kicked the bottle in January 1989 to become both the rider and the man who went on to grace the racing scene for the next 16 years. It wasn't long before Bailey started to enjoy a regular supply of high-profile mounts, among them Sea Hero and Grindstone, aboard whom he won the Kentucky Derby in 1993 and 1996.

"Winning the Kentucky Derby really left me speechless," he said. "When you become a jockey, when anybody comes up to you on the street, it's the first question they ask, 'Have you ridden a Kentucky Derby?' When they find out you've won it twice – the look on people's faces, all of a sudden, says 'this guy's important'. It stamps you in your profession."

I wasn't surprised with his answer when I asked him for his most memorable moment in the saddle, however. He recalled a race that took place thousands of miles from Kentucky, Cigar's unforgettable victory in the inaugural Dubai World Cup in 1996. "He was injured before he went over, and his training schedule was a little off," said Bailey. "He showed that day that he was a champion – well, I knew he was a champion, but I could feel the engine start when Soul Of The Matter came to challenge him. I believe it was his greatest moment because he wasn't at his best."

Cigar, understandably, held a very special place in the affections of a man who still visited him every year at the Kentucky Horse Park. "He's the horse who made me love horses," said Bailey. "When I started riding I didn't do it because I loved horses. I mean, I liked them well enough, but I loved the competition, getting in there with other guys and winning. Cigar made me want to be around horses, to truly fall in love with them. He was truly charismatic, plus he was tremendously talented.

It was such a feeling of power with him. In every race I would come to the competition with so much horse under me. It was like pulling up to a stoplight in a Ferrari next to a Volkswagen."

Remarkably, Bailey considered that Cigar never showed absolutely everything of which he was capable. "I really mean that," he said. "I think he was at his best leading up to the Breeders' Cup in 1995, but I never asked him to run full out then, as I always wanted to save something for next time. I had to ask him to run full out in Dubai but he wasn't at his best, and by the end of his career he wasn't himself, so I could never really do it. I was never able to feel what I wanted to feel."

Another superstar ridden by Bailey was Dubai Millennium, the best horse produced to date by Sheikh Mohammed's Dubai-based Godolphin operation, the most powerful racing stable in the world. Bailey rode the colt to win the Prince of Wales's Stakes at Royal Ascot in 2000, when retained rider Frankie Dettori was injured.

"It was a learning experience for me," he said. "I was completely honoured that Sheikh Mohammed reached out to me, as there are certainly many capable riders over there who could have done the same thing. Believe me, I didn't do anything special to win, just didn't make any mistakes, that's all."

Bailey was renowned as the thinking person's rider, celebrated for a tactical nous that often put him a jump ahead of his rivals. He suggested the key to his success was meticulous preparation – plus the motivation provided by another riding legend in his early years. "I never thought I was as physically gifted as other riders," he said. "I tried to compensate in other areas: working harder, preparing better, and always looking for any edge I could get."

This determination was accentuated when he came up against the great Angel Cordero on a daily basis when riding in New York. "Angel was a very intimidating rider," Bailey explained. "He would push people out, trap people in. He would concentrate as much on other people as his own horse, so I tried to plot what he would think and do, and avoid it. If Angel was on the lead and I knew I was going to have to approach him, I was always trying to figure out who else I might use to distract his attention. If there was another horse he might interfere with, then I could take advantage that way, maybe slip through on the rail. That was the way I thought."

As Bailey matured, he became as familiar with his rivals' tendencies as with his own. To illustrate, he pointed to weighing-room rival Jorge Chavez. "He'll come off the rail 99 times out of 100 turning for home. So, if he's on the lead, I feel very confident sitting right behind him. Instead of going around him, I think I'll get through. Angel forced me to start thinking like that. I learned a tremendous amount from him – he was the best rider I've ridden against day in, day out."

Bailey also spoke very highly of Pat Day, who retired in 2005. "He was probably the epitome of Mr Cool. He would wait, and wait, and wait some more. He would come last of all. He would ride a smart race, but you couldn't follow him. If you did, you were going to finish second at best because he would be the last to challenge."

Not that Bailey believed there was really any great secret to his trademark tactical mastery. "More often than not I had a better horse, so I just kept them out of trouble," he said. "Because I had a choice of great mounts, my philosophy was that if I put them in the right spot, they would win."

*

EVERYWHERE you turned at Saratoga, it seemed, there was a racing legend. Jerry Bailey's old rival Pat Day was also in town, saying an official farewell to the Saratoga crowd after his retirement. Day was expanding his role with the racetrack chaplaincy. "He'll be a good ambassador for the Lord," said his agent Doc Danner.

Secretariat's rider Ron Turcotte spent the best part of two days signing books and shooting the breeze with fans, plenty of whom were in attendance. Even though the Sunday card boasted only a relatively minor Grade 2 event, the crowd was an incredible 61,709, most of them laying their blankets on the ground for the backyard picnic behind the stands.

Cigar-puffing Turcotte, wheelchair-bound since being paralysed from the waist down in a fall at Belmont in 1978, was well used to spending his days fielding inquiries about 'Big Red'. "People ask me about him every day, usually several times a day," he told me. "I get four to five dozen letters a month. I've got a huge backlog – they're on the table, under the table, everywhere – and people get me on the email, on the phone." He didn't seem overjoyed at the prospect.

On day one of Turcotte's mammoth signing session, he was joined by another Triple Crown-winning jockey in Jean Cruguet, who rode Seattle Slew in 1977. On the second afternoon, a tiny, dapper-looking old gent showed up. Turcotte's face lit up, and the two of them were straight into animated discussion. This was the camaraderie of the weighing room, a friendly rivalry still at work a third of a century after the fact, for the new face, it transpired, was another former jockey named Johnny Rotz. He rode the two-year-old Stop The Music, awarded the Champagne Stakes at Belmont back in 1972 when Secretariat barged into him.

This lovely interlude somehow encapsulated Saratoga, a living crucible of racing history still as compelling in the 21st century as it must have been in the 19th. I would go there every year if I could. And not just because I managed to back a few winners.

*

JERRY BAILEY, one of the most intelligent riders in the history of the sport, rode his last race at Gulfstream Park in Florida on January 28, 2006, at the Sunshine Millions raceday. After 31 years in the saddle and 5,893 winners, Bailey's timing for once let him down on the big occasion as his final mount, the Bill Mott-trained Silver Tree, finished second, three-quarters of a length behind the winner Miesque's Approval, who went on to take the Breeders' Cup Mile in November. "I hope more people bet on me to place than to win," said Bailey. "You're either a hero or a goat – I guess I'll go eat hay tonight."

The best rider of his generation in the States, Bailey went on to a new career as a race analyst for NBC Sports and ESPN.

NEW ZEALAND

VITAL STATISTICS

RACING		FINANCE	
Racetracks	52	Total prize-money	$22.24m
Fixtures	283	Betting turnover	$290.63m
Races	2,807		
Racehorses	5,975	All figures for 2005	

BREEDING	
Stallions	212
Mares	8,871
Foals	4,600

TO suggest New Zealanders are fond of sport is like saying OJ Simpson had a few issues with his missus. It is a national obsession. Unfortunately, my visit coincided with the national rugby and cricket teams both being away from home, so I had to make do with the basketball team. Less celebrated they may have been, but they managed to raise a smile before even entering the court on account of their nickname. They were known as the Tall Blacks. They would be, wouldn't they?

Horse racing is considered a major sport with its own devoted satellite TV channel *Trackside*, which also covers greyhounds and harness racing, plus plenty of pages in the daily papers. New Zealand has long been home to a respected breeding industry, but its status in racing terms relative to neighbouring Australia – a neighbour over 1,300 miles away, that is – is broadly comparable to the relationship between Ireland and Britain before the rampant Celtic Tiger economy meant the former could afford to keep its better prospects at home instead of habitually putting up the 'For Sale' sign.

Records suggest the first horses to be introduced to New Zealand arrived in 1814, a gift to the Maoris from New South Wales governor Macquarie brought from Australia to the Bay of Islands by one Reverend Samuel Marsden. Although early details are sketchy, many more subsequently arrived with military garrisons in the early part of the century, but the first acknowledged thoroughbred was Figaro, who landed in Wellington in 1840, the year the Maoris ceded sovereignty to Queen Victoria. He was beaten by a horse called Calmac Tartar in what is thought to have been the first formal race meeting on Petone beach in 1842, a ten-guinea sweepstake run in heats over a mile and a half.

It didn't take long for racing to establish itself in New Zealand as early settlers from Britain and Ireland brought their passion for the sport with them, and racing clubs sprang up across an infant nation. A feature of celebrations in new settlements like Wellington, Auckland and Canterbury, the sport soon found permanent homes, such as Hastings racecourse, home of the Hawkes Bay Racing Club on the North Island's beautiful east coast, which dates back to 1845. Hastings is now home to the Grade 1 Capital Stakes, the nation's most valuable race, worth NZ$1 million in 2005 (about £350,000). Christchurch's Riccarton Park was founded in 1854 and Ellerslie, home of the Auckland Racing Club, in 1874. The latter remains New Zealand's premier track, home to both the NZ Derby and the Auckland Cup, run in March after being moved from their traditional Christmas date in recent years.

From this patchwork start of various racing clubs spread across a rural nation developed a proud racing and bloodstock industry with a rich heritage. Even if it has always been overshadowed by Australia, New Zealand still houses more than 50 tracks – many of them of the small 'country' variety and racing only rarely – and can point to more than enough racing heroes to call its own, although they tend to have to prove themselves on the other side of the Tasman Sea to truly leave an indelible mark.

A quick look at international statistics illustrates the significance of New Zealand's bloodstock industry in relative terms. Despite a downturn, in 2005 the nation stood 15th in the world in terms of numbers of races held (below such racing hotbeds as Turkey and Venezuela), while it stood a lowly 20th in purses. However, New Zealand ranked eighth in terms of foal production, with an annual figure of just under 5,000 not far off Britain, which stages four times as many races every year.

Australian racing would certainly be the poorer without New Zealand imports. Before Makybe Diva added her name to the pantheon with an historic third win in the 2005 Melbourne Cup, three equine legends would have dominated any discussion of Australia's greatest racehorses in the shape of Carbine, Phar Lap and Tulloch. All of them were bred in New

Zealand, and Carbine, foaled in 1885, also raced there as a two-year-old, going unbeaten through five races before being switched to Australia and making racing history with a barely feasible weight-carrying effort in the 1890 Melbourne Cup. The horse known as 'Old Jack' carried 10st 5lb, a huge burden, giving weight to a field of 38 rivals – and won Australia's most famous race in track-record time. That day, Carbine carried 53lb more than the runner-up in what may well have been the greatest handicap performance of all time.

Not that New Zealand is short of big names trained at home. Look through the annals and you will find horses like Gloaming, who won both the AJC Derby and the NZ Derby in 1918, and retired at the age of nine with a race record of 57 wins – 19 of them in a row – and nine second places from 67 starts. His efforts mirrored those a couple of years earlier of the brilliant mare Desert Gold, part of whose career was contemporaneous. She too won 19 races in succession.

In latter years, no New Zealand-trained racehorse has achieved more than the redoubtable Sunline, one of the best racemares in history. Known as the 'Queen of the Turf', this spirited front-runner captured the hearts of the public with her bloody-minded determination, racing in four countries during a long career at the beginning of the millennium. Few could withstand her relentless galloping style. Among Sunline's most famous successes were a pair of victories (1999-2000) in the Cox Plate, Australasia's weight-for-age championship at Moonee Valley in Melbourne, and the Hong Kong Mile, where sheer doggedness enabled her to hold local star Fairy King Prawn.

In human terms, the biggest names in New Zealand racing history include trainer Richard John Mason, who sent out 30 Derby winners between 1880 and 1932, and modern giant Lance O'Sullivan, winner of a record 12 jockeys' titles. However, breeder Sir Patrick Hogan and his Cambridge Stud operation has probably had more influence than anybody. At the top end, Hogan's Cambridge Stud is New Zealand's flagship operation, based largely on the now-deceased stallion Sir Tristram. A son of 1968 Epsom Derby winner Sir Ivor, he sired nearly 50 individual Group 1 winners, including the winners of three Melbourne Cups, and was the continent's champion stallion on several occasions. Although Sir Tristram died in 1997, his son Zabeel has kept up the good work, winning sires' championships of his own thanks to champions like Octagonal and Might And Power. They are quite a family.

*

ENOUGH of the history lesson. New York and New Zealand might be almost next to each other in the index to your atlas but they are about 8,800 miles apart as the crow flies, assuming that bizarrely direct avian is blessed with stamina to match its legendary bullet-like trajectory. Far enough in a single hit, and I had to fly back to Heathrow to start a second round-the-world ticket before doubling back across the Atlantic to Los Angeles, a few hours waiting around in the airport lounge, and then another flight to Auckland.

Spectacular country, boring cities. That is what people will tell you about New Zealand, but there was no time to test the latter half of the maxim in Auckland after I arrived there in the early hours of a bitter midwinter Saturday morning. There was still one more little tiddler of a 760-mile internal flight to the country's more remote South Island. If this schedule was lunacy, it seemed necessary at the time. I had to get to Christchurch for that specific Saturday because the New Zealand Grand National was taking place at Riccarton Park racecourse. Mind you, after 17,000 miles in two days of flying broken only by the odd few hours at airports changing flights, the prospect did not enthuse me quite as much as it might have done in other circumstances.

A new Flat-racing season had started only a few weeks previously on August 1, but with heavy-ground conditions prevailing in the winter weather, the major contests were still some time away. As a result, while there were only a couple of jump races on a ten-race card at Riccarton, this was day three of the Grand National festival. It featured the big race itself, the Grand National Steeple, to use its proper title, thereby distinguishing it from the Grand National Hurdles (and that plural is not a mistake), which had taken place at the same venue two days earlier.

Jumping is considered very much a poor relation in New Zealand, a second-class novelty item generally involving clapped-out former Flat-racers. The 131st National, worth only about £23,000, was one of the highlights of a season that ran from March to August, with just one or two races added to Flat-dominated cards like the one at Riccarton. There weren't many races in total – so few, in fact, that Jonathan Riddell had just been crowned champion jockey with only 14 winners.

If the meagre status of New Zealand jumping is by no means unusual in racing jurisdictions outside Europe, the Kiwi branch of the sport is not without its heritage. In the 1970s a number of imports thrived in Britain, where they became renowned for their athleticism. Many of them were handled by trainer Derek Kent, whose best horse was that fantastic jumper Grand Canyon. He broke course records in five consecutive races in his mid-'70s prime, and won the Colonial Cup in the States in 1976 and 1978 back in the days when US jumping still meant something, while more than a decade later, David Barons trained the NZ-bred Seagram to win the Grand National at Aintree.

Riccarton is situated in the suburbs of Christchurch, largest city on New Zealand's South Island with 330,000 inhabitants and considered the most 'English' place in the nation – albeit a fairly genteel version of England, where punts are punted gently down the meandering River Avon. The mile-and-a-half left-handed turf circuit is one of New Zealand's foremost venues, home to a pair of Classics (both Guineas), yet still a notch below Ellerslie, the country's number-one track, and Trentham in the capital, Wellington.

According to Riccarton chief executive Tim Mills, the racecourse also has a rival on its own doorstep in Christchurch, which also houses the nation's top trotting track, Addington. "There are not many places in the world where harness racing is more popular, but the South Island of New Zealand is one of them," said the 42-year-old, a dead ringer for the taller of the *Fast Show*'s two camp tailors.

With a large proportion of a 5,000-strong crowd chowing down on car-boot picnics and the booze flowing freely in fresh, spring-like conditions, the initial impression was of a point-to-point, something the appearance of the Christchurch Hunt parading down the track did little to disperse. Neither did a tinny, barely functioning public address system.

In the posher enclosure, in rooms named after former Kiwi stars like Arc runner-up Balmerino and Phar Lap (inevitably, still claimed by them on the grounds of his breeding), women in silly fur hats and tweedy suits mingled with gents middle-aged and upwards. Later, Riccarton could have been Kempton Park's scruffy baby brother as a younger crowd enjoyed a pint and a punt, indistinguishable from their UK counterparts apart from the predilection for All Blacks sweatshirts, or sometimes the red-and-black stripes of Canterbury province.

Although there are no licensed bookmakers in New Zealand, the local TAB tote operation offered pari-mutuel and fixed-odds betting, both on the track and via a network of off-course outlets, many of them in pubs and clubs. The on-course facilities were not immediately attractive. One betting outlet looked like an ill-conceived conservatory tacked on to the backend of the stand, while a defunct odds board overlooked the paddock, still displaying ancient odds in bar-chart form for a race that must have taken place decades ago. Perhaps it was a museum piece.

Riccarton's ten-race meeting started at 11.40am with a hurdle, the only other jumps race on the mixed card; the temporary flights, synthetic nylon brushes, were easily knocked out of the way. Three hours later, the three-and-a-half-mile Grand National Steeple began from a starting gate, also used for the Flat, and more of a barrier than a stall. Far from being a 40-strong mishap-strewn contest like its vastly more famous Aintree predecessor, the race featured only five runners who barely put a foot wrong between them over the 21 fences, some of which barely deserved the name, particularly the Stand Double, a pair of small, narrow temporary obstacles 100 yards apart either side of the winning post.

Before the race, Tim Mills took me out on to the track to have a look at some of the more impressive obstacles. "We have to be careful with them," he said. "People like to set fire to them. Three of them went up in one night a few years ago on Guy Fawkes night – first he had a go at parliament and then he came back hundreds of years later to have a go at Riccarton."

Although these fences were regarded as the toughest in the country, they certainly wouldn't have frightened anything that had jumped safely around a British park track. The biggest of them all, named Cutts Brush, looked a sturdy enough obstacle, however. It was made of packed manuka, a native bush, and painted green. Mills illustrated its height. He was just over six feet tall, and could easily see over it. It wasn't quite so easy for his guests from the Japan Racing Association, on hand to scrutinise potential invitees to the following year's Nakayama Grand Jump.

Although there weren't many runners in the Grand National Steeple, the race had attracted a degree of publicity. It wasn't a tall black making the news, but a regular-sized grey with the most inappropriate of names. No Hero, a nine-year-old gelding trained by Paul Nelson, was bidding to establish a modern-day steeplechase record with his seventh consecutive victory over fences. The Desert Orchid of New Zealand was reminiscent of his esteemed counterpart in the northern hemisphere in more ways than one. An outstanding jumper, this admirable horse was also renowned for his courage, not least in that his winning run had been interrupted by a tendon injury that sidelined him for a two-year period. To the heartiest of receptions, No Hero beat his rivals pointless, making no semblance of a mistake before taking command on turning for home and winning as he liked.

His rider Jonathan Riddell was delighted. "I can't say enough about him, just enjoy him," he said. "I think you have witnessed a champion steeplechaser today, he's just a pleasure to ride."

The result was hardly a surprise as No Hero, sent off a generous 1-2 favourite, had done the same only a week previously in another race featuring virtually the same field. Well, there weren't that many opportunities, I suppose. You were bound to bump into the same horses.

And not just over jumps. Racehorses in the southern hemisphere habitually race more often than those in Britain, trainers often using shorter events as lead-up races. For example, before her retirement in 2002, superstar mare Sunline raced 48 times in six seasons at an average of eight times a year, despite one injury-curtailed season – and she was regarded as quite lightly raced. Best at around a mile, Sunline usually returned to action after a winter break with a preparatory outing over six or seven furlongs in mid-August in New Zealand.

Her exploits were still recalled with immense fondness – not least because New Zealand racing was going through a relatively lean period. If success in Australia is regarded as the pinnacle of achievement, it had been thin on the ground since the glory days of Sunline, and such greats as Bonecrusher and Horlicks before her. Add in a downturn in the bloodstock-export business, largely due to New Zealand having missed the boat when it came to 'shuttle stallions' annually flown down from Europe during their own off-season, and the natives were getting restless.

Racing's administrators were busy lobbying politicians for a break. Many horses at Riccarton were forced to run with an unsightly stencil reading 'Fair Tax Now' painted over shaggy winter coats on their flank, a gesture aimed at publicising the racing industry's point of view in the run-up to a general election in which Labour prime minister Helen Clark was seeking a third term. I asked Mills which party he considered would be the best news for racing. "Not the socialists!" he said, firmly. I didn't argue.

Others were less impressed with the protest, however, among them David McCarthy, racing editor of the *Christchurch Press*. "It's a bit childish, isn't it?" he said. I didn't argue.

New Zealand racing folk probably didn't need any further causes for consternation, which was unfortunate as the new champion jockey Lisa Cropp had recently become embroiled in a drug-related scandal. The first woman to win a jockeys' title in a major racing nation, she was notable only for her absence at a glitzy awards ceremony the night before I arrived in New Zealand, her jockey-of-the-year gong having been withheld.

Cropp's toughness, resilience and relentless will to win had already become the stuff of legend. Her championship had been achieved only after overcoming life-threatening injuries sustained in a fall in Macau in July 2001, by which time the rider already had more than 1,000 winners to her name. Thrown to the ground like a rag doll in the fall, Cropp rode trackwork the next morning before being told she had broken her neck in four places. She did not ride again for three years – but when she came back, she did not just ride more winners than anybody else in New Zealand, she rewrote the record books, smashing a mark set by multiple champion Lance O'Sullivan, the top rider in New Zealand history, with her total of 197 winners in the season that had just ended.

Then the racing world caved in as Cropp returned a positive test for the methamphetamine 'P', an illegal recreational drug described in some quarters as the scourge of New Zealand society. A highly addictive stimulant that affects the central nervous system, it is more commonly referred to as crystal meth or 'ice' in Britain, where it is common on the gay club scene. Seen as more of a safety issue than a performance-enhancer in racing terms, the drug's effects can include both the boosting of stamina and aggression and the suppression of appetite.

Cropp vehemently claimed her innocence, blaming diet pills. Her impressive record, though, was under intense scrutiny as sceptics questioned exactly how she managed to pursue a hellishly frenetic schedule, casting a huge shadow over her achievement. Inquiries were ongoing.

There was more. Former leading apprentice Michael Walker, a champion at the age of 16, had recently spoken on Australian TV about having cocaine for breakfast, while harness-racing circles had been rocked by the 'Blue Magic' scandal, involving performance-enhancing drugs. The latter resulted in shattered reputations and suicides.

It was a pity that so few people seemed to care about jump racing in New Zealand, or perhaps the gallant No Hero might have given them a compelling reason to be cheerful amid all the doom and gloom. It looked like they could do with a few.

*

IN the subsequent general election, Helen Clark's Labour Party again won more seats than anyone else and formed a coalition government. Michael Walker started to get his career back on track after his drug and alcohol excesses and again figured among New Zealand's leading riders in 2005-06, but the saga of Lisa Cropp's positive dope test seemed never-ending as her lawyers issued legal challenges at every turn. By the end of 2006, the case had been to the High Court – or, rather, a challenge against the right of the racing authorities to rule on the matter had been thrown out there – but there was still no resolution. Early in 2007, Cropp's lawyers lodged an application in the High Court for a judicial review of the racing authorities' drug-testing procedures. On the track, Cropp retained her jockeys' title in 2005-06 with 146 winners. The jockey-of-the-year award was again withheld.

No Hero added an eighth consecutive steeplechase victory to his tally with a 26-length victory at Riccarton in April 2006, after which his trainer Paul Nelson was said to be considering a bid for the Cheltenham Gold Cup in England in 2007. However, the grey's winning run ended at Te Rapa in May 2006 when he fell at the first fence, and then he flopped at Hastings. "He's just knackered," said his trainer.

AUSTRALIA

VITAL STATISTICS

RACING		FINANCE	
Racetracks	471	Total prize-money	$280.08m
Fixtures	2,752	Betting turnover	$8,564.58m
Races	19,968		
Racehorses	31,037	All figures for 2005	

BREEDING	
Stallions	916
Mares	27,882
Foals	17,178

ALTHOUGH I liked New Zealand, it would be idle to suggest the country's midwinter racing scene was the liveliest in living memory. This was unlikely to be an issue at my subsequent destination, however.

Racing has been part of Australian culture since settlement and it remains a hotbed, where around 250,000 people are reckoned to participate in the industry.

I spent nearly a month there, visiting three among its panoply of racetracks, including Birdsville, totally isolated about 200 miles from the closest 'neighbouring' settlement in the middle of the Outback and by far the most notorious example of the once-a-year 'country' meetings that pepper the racing calendar. The other two racecourses were Caulfield in Melbourne, one of the nation's best, plus Townsville's Cluden Park, a popular northern Queensland track with no pretensions to the highest level. While the latter wasn't exactly without its idiosyncrasies, compared to Birdsville it seemed almost normal.

*

HORSES aren't indigenous to Australia, which meant there were none there until the first draft of four mares, three yearlings and a stallion arrived in 1788.

They've made up for it since. If Australia is sparsely populated for its huge size, with just under 20 million inhabitants compared to Britain's 60 million, the nation is no longer wanting for racehorses. With over 31,000 in total, there are more racehorses in training *per capita* than anywhere else, servicing hundreds more courses than any other country in the world. After the initial introduction of horses into the new colony at the end of the 18th century, it didn't take long for match races to develop along its roads before the nation's first official race meeting, said to have taken place in Sydney's Hyde Park in October 1810. Now there are more than 350 racing clubs holding meetings at over 450 tracks – and that's not including harness racing, which takes the figures up to nearly 44,000 horses and 470 racetracks.

Racing competes with rugby league as Australia's second-most-attended spectator sport behind Aussie-rules football. There cannot be many other places where horse racing is seemingly so interwoven with everyday life, intrinsic to the fabric of society. Ireland is the obvious comparison. There, too, rather than being treated as some odd, outré diversion doodling in the margins, the sport is treated as part of the mainstream.

In this respect, the Melbourne Cup provides all the evidence anyone could require. To borrow a phrase that long ago entered the realm of cliché, this 3,200-metre handicap remains the 'race that stops a nation'. First run in 1861, the world's richest handicap is Australia's most valuable race, worth A$5.1 million (£2.05m) in 2006. Nothing short of a phenomenon, the Melbourne Cup is a totally unique event that evokes improbable levels of interest when it is run at Flemington on the first Tuesday in November as the highlight of the city's spring carnival.

Melbourne's Racing Hall of Fame, inaugurated just before my visit in 2005, is not shunted away to some discreet racing centre. Featuring the skeleton of Carbine, the heart of Tulloch and many and varied bits of Phar Lap memorabilia – national icons each of them – it is located right in the centre of town, on the banks of the Yarra river, opposite the distinctive orange-and-brown façade of the central railway station, Flinders Street.

Virtually every one of the humans featured in the museum is a household name, among them another triumvirate of all-time greats in trainers Tommy 'TJ' Smith, Sydney's champion trainer for 33 consecutive seasons, Colin Hayes and Bart Cummings, known as the 'Cups King' owing to his remarkable haul of victories in the Melbourne and Caulfield Cups and still producing winners from his Sydney base about 250 Group 1 wins into a fantastic career. Scobie Breasley, the 'Ice Man of Wagga Wagga', and George Moore head the list of Australian riding legends in the Hall of Fame, alongside poet Banjo Paterson – he of *Waltzing Matilda* fame whose racing-based ballads are part of the national folklore – and race-caller Bill Collins, known as 'The Accurate One' for his unerring ability to call photo-finishes correctly.

Australian racing is structured as a pyramid, with the Australian Racing Board (ARB) overseeing individual state jurisdictions that preside over the racecourses falling within their borders. The metropolitan powerhouses of Melbourne and Sydney figure at the summit, each with their own distinct racing community and programmes, both focusing on a prestigious carnival (spring and autumn respectively) featuring big races spread around their top tracks. In Melbourne, these are Flemington, Moonee Valley and Caulfield; in Sydney, Randwick and Rosehill Gardens top the list.

Besides Victoria and New South Wales, other states have their own top-level tracks, headed by Queensland's Eagle Farm and Doomben in Brisbane, while beneath them are a plethora of tracks whose meetings are regularly broadcast in TABs (Totalisator Agency Boards), the off-course betting outlets across the country often attached to pubs and clubs. Another grade down come the vast ranks of country racecourses, many of them in far-flung remote regions hosting ramshackle meetings just once a year, like Birdsville.

Though there is plenty of cross-pollination for showpiece events, each metropolitan centre has its own set of regional 'premierships' imbued with the status of *de facto* championships for trainers and jockeys. Naturally, the city titles at Melbourne and Sydney carry by far the greatest prestige. In the 2004-05 season that ended before I got to Australia, trainer Lee Freedman – who was to saddle the great Makybe Diva for her historic third Melbourne Cup in November 2005 – and jockey Nicholas Ryan topped the lists in the former. In Sydney, the jockeys' title went to Darren Beadman, who had retired for two years in the 1990s to concentrate on religious studies, while Tommy Smith's charismatic daughter Gai Waterhouse – a former model and actress who played the rebel timelord Presta alongside Tom Baker in *Dr Who* in the 1970s – kept up the family tradition among trainers. She and rival John Hawkes, who was to regain the title the following season, had between them won the previous 13 Sydney premierships up to the end of the 2005-06 season.

Although the Melbourne Cup never struggles to retain its grip on the national consciousness – unlike, say, the Epsom Derby in England – its status as a handicap means it is not really Australia's most prestigious race. While in the US, the majority of top races for older horses make up the 'handicap division', on account of most of them being handicaps, in Australia and New Zealand the same type of horses compete in the weight-for-age division, at trips ranging between 1,400 metres and 2,400 metres. Top of the tree here is the 2,040-metre W S Cox Plate, a weight-for-age contest at Moonee Valley worth A$3.14m (£1.25m). Inaugurated in 1922 and named after Moonee Valley founder Sam Cox, it has been won by a host of Australasian greats like Phar Lap, Tulloch, Sunline and the outstanding Tommy Smith-trained gelding Kingston Town, who took this championship event an unprecedented three times on the trot between 1980 and 1982.

Australia also hosts the world's most valuable two-year-old race, the Golden Slipper, run at Sydney's Rosehill just before Easter and worth A$3.5m (£1.4m) in 2006. Sydney's other major showpiece is the AJC Derby (or Australian Derby), a three-year-old race following the Epsom blueprint, over 2,400 metres on turf at Randwick.

Caulfield, roughly triangular and anti-clockwise, also has more than its share of top-flight races. Although it was September when I visited and still another few weeks until the Caulfield Guineas and Caulfield Cup, the course's most significant race, a richly endowed Dubai-sponsored nine-race card featuring a pair of competitive Group 1s and three Group 3s was hardly to be sniffed at. The racecourse is just five miles south east of the city centre, only A$3.10 (£1.25) on the metro. Sandown racecourse is a little further down the same line, whereas Flemington and Moonee Valley are close to each other to the west, both easily accessible as well.

Any obvious differences between Caulfield and a good-class track at home, which it closely resembled, stemmed mainly from where Australian racing as a whole differs from the British model. The metric system dominates in Australia. As well as all distances being expressed in metres, weights came in kilograms, and bookmakers – legal on course here, their pitches under cover inside the stand – displayed their prices electronically as tote dividends, so 33-1 was shown as $34.

There were other distinguishing features. On a bitterly cold, windy afternoon, a youth band serenaded racegoers to both *Waltzing Matilda* and *Tie Me Kangaroo Down, Sport*. They seldom do that at Newbury. Then there were the palm trees, oddly out of place in the Melbourne winter, and the air-raid siren that sounded an unnerving screech after one contest. The Martians hadn't landed; rather, the rider of the fifth had lodged a 'protest' (objection) against third and fourth.

A 224-page racebook fashioned like a pulp paperback offered runners and riders from distant-sounding places like Kembla Grange and Morphettville, while an unusual number of people were wearing trilby-style hats, pink and beige as well as black, females as well as males. Further investigation revealed these to be the 'Gleeson', a racecourse promotion involving headwear that has become the trademark of chief steward Des Gleeson, something of a fashion icon in these parts. Seemingly all minor racecourse employees were compelled to wear them on racedays; another edict seemed to involve their never being allowed to say Caulfield without adding the adjective "classic" beforehand.

The gift shop also offered sweatshirts in the colours of recent stars like the awesome Might And Power, twice Aussie champion, and dual Cox Plate winner Northerly. The latter in particular was an excellent purchase if you fancied parading down the street in a sweatshirt of bright yellow with a black Maltese cross. And that was just the front. The back carried details of the colt's career record with particular reference to Caulfield, where he won seven out of 13 starts.

All the major players on the Melbourne scene were in evidence, including Makybe Diva's esteemed trainer Lee Freedman, who was plainly well used to the Melbourne weather pattern, the 'four seasons in one day' often cited in travel guides. Standing in the 'mounting yard', or parade ring, he wore both a huge raincoat and sunglasses. Freedman trained two of the winners of the first three races, all of them being won by front-runners, an early indication of a distinct track bias on the heavy ground.

It didn't take long for the jockeys to overcompensate. Leading rider Danny Nikolic produced a brilliantly judged front-running effort on all-the-way winner Perlin in the Group 1 Underwood Stakes over 1,800 metres. In attempting to complete a Group 1 double in the next, the 1,400-metre Dubai Racing Club Cup, he kicked his mount Regal Roller into the lead from wide in stall 15. Regal Roller used up far too much of his juice to get to the front, folding tamely after turning for home. The race was set up for the fast finishers, headed by Barely A Moment, a four-year-old trained by David Hayes, scoring his first Group 1 triumph since returning from a decade-long sojourn in Hong Kong, and ridden by an even more familiar face in Craig Williams. "I've been very fortunate to win Group 1s all over the world but now at last I've had one at home," he said.

Williams won the Dewhurst Stakes on Tobougg for Mick Channon in 2000 during a spell in Britain, following a trend established decades earlier when the likes of Breasley and Moore enjoyed huge success on the other side of the world, winning Derbys and Arcs. Kerrin McEvoy, employed as understudy to Frankie Dettori by the Godolphin operation, is the most recent Aussie recruit to thrive in Britain.

Though superficially it might look fairly similar, the nature of Australian racing is hugely at variance with its British counterpart. Of supreme importance are rest periods, known as 'spells' and indicated in newspaper form guides with either a small 's' or 'x' to denote more than three months away from the track, while a typical campaign involves a horse racing on a regular basis, usually at varying trips before a major target, and sometimes once a week once they get there. The latter strategy is known as 'backing up'.

Nowhere was this approach more evident than in the Underwood Stakes, worth A$350,000 (£140,000). Won in recent years by future Caulfield Cup winners Elvstroem, Mummify and Northerly, this was regarded as a major trial for the Cups and the Cox Plate. Among the runners was Victoria Derby winner Plastered, early ante-post favourite for the Melbourne Cup, on his 'first-up' run after a spell.

It was the wrong trip and the wrong ground. No-one tipped Plastered, whose trainer virtually told the press the horse wouldn't be winning.

Unsurprisingly, Plastered's price drifted on course from 5-1 out to double figures. Settled at the rear, the four-year-old gelding made a derisory move turning for home six horses wide before finishing unplaced behind the New Zealand-bred Perlin. In Britain, this half-cocked display would probably have attracted the attention of the stewards, who might have asked questions about whether any attempt had been made to win the race. Not here, though, where everyone seemed delighted and, to be fair, no-one in their right mind could have backed him over an inadequate trip after such negative pre-race publicity.

Plastered remained ante-post favourite for the Melbourne Cup a few weeks hence. I'm sure there was no truth in the rumour that Sir Mark Prescott was considering ending his training career with a stint down under.

*

YOUNG people don't go racing – it is a well-established fact. Unless, that is, you go to Townsville, the biggest city in northern Queensland.

I visited Townsville's racecourse Cluden Park, about six miles inland on the Bruce Highway, for the second day of a two-day meeting called the Townsville Amateurs that dated back to the days when country folk in the city's hinterland descended on the track for their own designated series of races. While the Townsville Amateurs still existed only as members of a social club, their fixture had long since assimilated into the mainstream in racing terms and was more popular than ever with the public.

At midday, the wind-battered car park was packed with hedonistic locals clambering across its dusty scrubland in droves and their finery. It cost the same as Caulfield, only A$20 (£8) to get in, and more than 5,000 people took advantage; at a rough guess, at least 50 per cent of the crowd must have been under the age of 30, most of them dressed for an evening at a nightclub or wine bar. There probably wasn't much else to do in Townsville, a place for which the appellation 'shithole' might well have been coined. Nevertheless, such a startling demographic was the result of concerted marketing by the racetrack, featuring TV adverts between programmes like *Big Brother* and *Australian Idol*, alongside tie-ins with the radio stations.

"It is a generational change and we have been focusing on a younger crowd," said James Heddo, the track's chief executive. "Racing is booming here in northern Queensland. We had 15,000 here for the Townsville Cup – we charged $30 for a party, and we did a lot of promotional work with the nightclubs and the university. It holds 1,500 and it sold out in a week.

"When we put five races on here on Melbourne Cup day, thousands get dressed up and pretend they're in Melbourne. We also have a ladies' day in July that's very popular – we get a good-looking male sort of celebrity off the TV to show up."

The Townsville Race Club hosted its first meeting in 1884. Cluden is one of about 140 racecourses in Queensland, the vast north-eastern state that sprawls from the sea into the heart of the Outback, and stretches thousands of miles up from the Gold Coast tourist haven south of Brisbane, its biggest city, next to the Great Barrier Reef through tropical rainforest to the country's northern tip.

Queensland's premier tracks are Eagle Farm and Doomben, both in Brisbane, but Cluden's diehards-only midweek meetings featured regularly in the daily racing broadcasts to the nation's official off-course tote outlets, the TAB. On the other hand, Saturday meetings – even a popular one like this – were usually designated as 'country meetings' and denied to off-course punters. Instead, much more prestigious stuff elsewhere dominated the screens, like Makybe Diva scoring at Caulfield in a Group 1 event over 1,400 metres on her first outing of the season. It was a bit like a prospective Ascot Gold Cup horse winning the Lockinge.

Many of the horses at Cluden had more in common with their amateur predecessors than high-faluting Group-racers in Melbourne and Sydney, a hefty proportion being stabled in the owner's backyard and driven to the track every morning to work on its sand training circuit, situated inside the racing surface itself, which was a nine-furlong grass oval, racing clockwise.

The card consisted of four sprints, a mile, and then the Townsville Amateurs' Cup, a 1,960-metre event worth A$25,000 (£10,200). Featuring mainly ageing geldings, the standard of racing could be nobody's idea of quality. From a total of 63 horses, 54 were geldings; the rest, except one, were mares. The one, who had survived undercarriage intact until the age of five, finished a reluctant-looking third. Probably needed gelding.

Australia differed from nearly everywhere else I had visited in that on-course fixed-odds bookmakers are legal. Townsville boasted 12 of them, in two semi-circles around the central pari-mutuel booth under a shelter behind the stands. Five of them took bets on the 'away' meetings being broadcast on the screens in sight of an antiquated electronic board hanging from the roof that became illuminated for either the weighed-in signal, or an objection in Melbourne, Sydney or Brisbane. More layers, on the other side of the tote, like Dylan Tamblyn and TJ Byrnes, labelled themselves as 'local' and concentrated on matters closer to hand, with prices on their boards for both the next race and the main event later in the afternoon.

For betting purposes, anything approaching a hint of class seemed worthy of interest, which was how I ended up backing a horse called Ruhlmann, a five-year-old son of Green Desert out of a Lyphard mare down for the day from Cairns. He had finished a close second in his last two and looked a fair bet at 2-1 against a field of his fellow maiden geldings who had achieved even less. Ruhlmann was ridden by David Crossland, the leading rider at Cluden, who endured a round trip of ten hours three times a week to ride at TAB meetings but usually stayed away on Saturdays for country meetings closer to his home town of Atherton.

His presence on Ruhlmann seemed a tip in itself, but they could finish only second, sprinting home off the final turn in hopeless pursuit of a rival who gained first run after being allowed an easy lead, a pattern that continued throughout the afternoon.

Not that everyone was paying close attention, however, for this was a major social occasion in Townsville, an ugly, rundown coastal town where the most attractive option for the hip, swinging young locals was hanging around the unremittingly drab and grey shopping precinct failing to look hard but succeeding in looking bored. Only rarely did Townsville register at a national level in sporting terms, thanks mainly to the Cowboys, its strangely successful rugby league team. The place looked depressed, and it was certainly depressing.

Still, at the track the locals certainly didn't believe in half-measures in the sartorial department. This was perhaps the only racecourse in the world where the dress code appeared stricter the further away you get from the finish. By choice rather than compulsion.

Adjacent to the winning post was the members' stand, peopled by the soberly dressed regulars, many of them in open-necked shirts and slacks, and the usual racing crowd: mainly male, middle-aged and up. Here is where you'd find a plaque commemorating one of the track's most memorable days, when a horse named Picnic In The Park set an Australasian record with his 20th consecutive victory in 1985. He won 21 in a row in the end, and was injured when attempting to extend the sequence.

Moving down the straight at Cluden took you to the 'Party King' grandstand, where the average age dropped appreciably and people had dressed for the occasion: girls in their best frocks, strappy dresses and hats, plus the ubiquitous shades, guys in suits of all shapes and colours, sleeves rolled up Miami Vice-style, white, fawn, bright red, bright yellow, bright orange, often with trainers on their feet, a hen party dressed in *Blues Brothers*, a stag party in long black coats like understudies for Keanu Reeves in *The Matrix*. Dyed hair seemed a popular accessory, along with Mohawk haircuts. And shades.

They had clearly made an effort – and so had the denizens of the tented village further down the straight, where a white-boy rapper, who plainly knew no shame, 'entertained' a suited-and-booted crew from the Embassy nightclub alongside a rotund pony-tailed accomplice manning the decks.

Finally, down at the furlong marker, came the Hot FM enclosure, where a local radio station hosted an afternoon bash for a crowd of revellers, all of them dolled up to the nines. It could have been a wedding party as a rock covers band belted out recent hits to a juiced-up crowd.

Quite what the racecourse regulars made of all this was hard to imagine, though the band had the good grace to stop for the start of the main event, which started right in front of the marquee. Having examined the form, I backed a 5-2 chance called Snippety Snip. According to the local paper, this gelding had finished well last time out from a wide draw to finish second to likely favourite Magritte, ridden by David Crossland. Snippety Snip had been bought for just $1,500 by Gold Coast trainer Nathan Schofield a few weeks previously before making hay on the northern carnival circuit. "He's been a great buy and it's been a great holiday," said Schofield. Snippety Snip had a pull at the weights and was drawn inside this time around. It sounded good.

The race started well enough when Magritte fell out of the stalls and lost five lengths. The evidence of earlier races suggested he had no earthly chance from that position, even though a pedestrian pace allowed him to rejoin at the rear. Yet again, the race developed into a 300-metre sprint off the home turn; this time, though, the two outsiders who made the pace gave way, like *domestique*s in a cycling team setting things perfectly for their sprint finisher just behind. Snippety Snip, however, was not there to take advantage – like Ruhlmann, he finished well to take second behind outsider Russell O, who rushed clear under a female jockey named Kharma Penrose, silks bright orange with a white 'H'. (I preferred Lindys Groom, completely red but for a white lightning bolt, like Captain Marvel in Shazam! comics.)

It didn't take long after the race for things to hot up again on the temporary dancefloor, where a version of *I Believe In A Thing Called Love* by spandex-clad progressive-rock novelty band The Darkness inspired a particularly animated bout of frugging.

Without wishing to perpetuate a national stereotype, there was plenty of alcohol flowing in every enclosure, from beer containers that could accurately be described as tinnies; Toohey's, XXXX Gold or Bundaberg rum were the favoured accompaniment to Mrs Mac's 'famous' beef pies. None of which displeased the racecourse. The Townsville Amateurs kept the gate money, the track got the beer profits.

Late in the day one particular gentleman, not among the most elegant in vest and shorts, attracted a degree of attention thanks to a wide-brimmed sunhat advertising the Preston Youth Group, and bearing the slogan: "Christ is the answer." With a six-pack in one hand, he swigged from a bottle held in the other, staggering around amid a sea of crumpled beer cans.

And who knows? He might have been right. Perhaps Christ was the answer. At the Townsville Amateurs, though, it must have been doubtful if anyone could remember the question.

*

LEGENDARY gonzo journalist Hunter S Thompson described the Kentucky Derby as "decadent and depraved". It is probably just as well he never made it to Birdsville.

The tiny Outback township lies towards the dead centre of Australia, at the far western reaches of Queensland where that vast state almost becomes South Australia. For 363 days of the year, the population of this hot, dusty, unwelcoming place numbers no more than 100. There are significantly fewer during the summer months, which are hotter, dustier – and even less welcoming.

For just one Friday and Saturday in September, however, more than 5,000 people descend on this remote outpost of humanity for the duration of two days of horse racing at a rudimentary track that is little more than a set of running rails planted around a big patch of desert next to a couple of tin shacks.

None of the 12 events is longer than a metric mile, and only two of them reach that 1,600-metre mark, including the highlight, the Birdsville Cup, a handicap on the second day first contested in 1882, worth A$25,000 (£10,200).

Yet this ostensibly nondescript meeting has assumed mythical status in the nation's culture, where a visit to Birdsville, at least 1,000 miles from any coastal city, is regarded as a near-sacred pilgrimage, an Australian trip to Mecca. Such notoriety has virtually nothing to do with the horse racing. Birdsville is famous – or infamous – for monstrous doses of mayhem. Imagine the Oktoberfest held in the Wild West and you might be getting the idea.

Birdsville felt like the centrepiece of my trip down the racing road. If it lived up to its billing, it seemed perfect for a spot of fear and loathing, as trademarked by the late Hunter S. What follows is a derivative non-fiction based on true events as they actually happened. Only names have been changed to protect the guilty.

*

FOR reasons best known to my financial adviser, who doubled as my photographer, I was booked on a coach rather than flying in on one of the light aircraft chartered for the occasion.

Disturbing intimations of the horror in store during a scheduled 24-hour journey arrived as I ordered a drink in the pub attached to the off-course betting outlet at the Brisbane Transit Centre. The barman asked where I was going. When I said Birdsville, he gripped my arm, looked me straight in the eye, and said: "I feel I ought to warn you: it is pretty full-on out there. I'm not sure you're the type to survive."

The sense of foreboding wasn't eased by the ragged queue lining up beside the McCafferty's Greyhound Special. Seldom have I come across such a wanton-looking bunch as that which pushed and shoved its way up the steps on to the coach.

"Do you seriously expect me to get into a bus with this group of filthy degenerates?" I asked a man in a schoolboy's uniform, shirt, tie and shorts, who ticked my name off a list.

"No, sir, I don't," he replied. "This is the dry bus. I expect you to get into a bus with that group of filthy degenerates over there. That's the wet bus and you're supposed to be on it."

The wet bus permitted alcohol, a liberty grasped double-handed by my fellow travellers, who planted gigantic cooling boxes, known as 'eskies', up the aisle. The bus held about 40 people; most of them were already there, swigging away. It soon emerged that the touring party had been composed by a sadist: about half of them, mainly curdled, bibulous geriatrics, were travelling together from a hamlet somewhere off the Gold Coast, Goatshag Island or some such.

Another ne'er-do-well climbed in, huge-gutted in a tight-fitting vest, downing a beer as he went. "Christ, I'm on a bus with a bunch of piss-pots," he said, as he dumped his esky next to the driver, who quickly alerted us to the limitations of his 'luxury' vehicle.

"We'll be stopping frequently," he said. "You probably won't want to use the toilet at the back there as it gets a bit bumpy when the road gets dusty. If you do, I'd be grateful, gentlemen, if you'd treat it like a night at the opera and stay seated for the entire performance."

I asked Warren, a man in his early-40s with a Birdsville 2004 T-shirt, what to expect. "The first rule about Birdsville is you don't talk about Birdsville," he said. "What goes on tour stays on tour."

Either he had seen *Fight Club* or was suffering from a severe mental disorder, or quite possibly both. Further queries were plainly out of the question, though this was by no means the last I was to hear from this Warren, who had two party pieces. The first was a country-tinged yeehaw song entitled *The Boys From The Bush Are Back In Town*. Its first line went "The boys from the bush are back in town," and it was the only line Warren knew. Soon, we all knew it as well as him – as well as every word of his mock racecall involving Beau Zam, Rough Habit and Makybe Diva. Not too bad at first hearing, it palled a little by the 25th.

I was seated a few rows away from the Goatshag crew, which offered momentary succour until a middle-aged woman in purple shell suit took the seat in front. Named Brenda and clearly borderline psychotic, she dived straight into a cardboard wine box. "Anyone who doesn't want to enjoy themselves shouldn't be on the wet bus," she explained menacingly, glaring at me through vulcanised eyes.

Barely a couple of hundred miles towards the bush, this vindictive individual started demanding a sing-song, proceeding to regale us with her renditions of *Take Me Home, Country Roads, Coward Of The County* and various ditties by Anthrax and Napalm Death. "My advice to you is to start drinking, heavily," suggested my photographer.

The evening progressed, via coffee at a service station at a godforsaken fleapit called Miles to a similar facility in the middle of the night at Morven, where it was hard to see outside owing to the thick blanket of moths and flies that congregated on the window.

By now, the road was virtually single track, and the landscape bleak, scrubby bits of bush on a red rocky surface that soon became featureless. Breakfast came at Quilpie, lunch at Windorah, after which the local constabulary helpfully set up a roadblock to breath-test the bus driver before he moved off the bitumen on to the dirt track.

An uncomfortable 140 miles away from our destination, we stopped for a call of nature at woebegone Betoota, a ghost town where a dilapidated hotel stood forlorn in front of car wrecks, the legacy of failed attempts to traverse such a vast, unforgiving plain. The hotel had been closed since the previous year when Ziggy, Betoota's sole resident, popped his clogs; we stopped to use a rattletrap toilet, where it wasn't advisable to look under the floorboards. Natural facilities were available, if you were prepared to risk the bogum fleas, nature's version of the nailbomb. Small balls of needles, they attach themselves to your clothes and make their presence felt days afterwards.

After only a slight delay when a suicidal kangaroo bounced off the door shattering a pane of glass, we arrived at Birdsville on Thursday night at dusk, ready to hole up at our campsite, opposite the caravan park. Nearly everyone had to do this because the handful of rooms at the Birdsville Hotel, one of the most famous pubs in the country, were commandeered by race officials.

A troubled, sleepless night ensued, broken by various noisome interludes from my malodorous companions. One particularly memorable episode involved a pair of Irishmen repeatedly asking two girls to reveal their chests. "Show us your boobs!" they demanded for an age, until someone, presumably one of the Goatshaggers, intervened. "For Christ's sake show them your tits, will you, then perhaps we could get some sleep."

The horror resumed in the communal shower block the next morning. Each cubicle had two walls and a door, none of which reached the floor, so water flowed along from one to another. Birdsville generates its electricity from mineral springs under the desert, where the water is so hot naturally that it needs cooling. Whether that was responsible for the ghastly yellow tinge of the slightly pungent stream that seeped into my cubicle from next door was unclear. Like the water.

As well as the so-called hotel, a quick sortie around town in the morning revealed a few ramshackle houses, a bakery, two petrol stations, a police station, airstrip, flying doctor station, café, cricket pitch, small museum and community centre, the raceclub's base of operations over the weekend.

These permanent attractions were joined by a fish-and-chip van, pancake vendors, T-shirt stalls and the like, among them a tiny charity stand operated by a pony-tailed character who looked like a Hell's Angel and had a name to match. This was the comedian Dirty Pierre, a disgusting reprobate raising money for a nearby children's hospital in Mount Isa (that's nearby as in 350 miles away) by penning felt-tipped insults on souvenir T-shirts.

"Heat, dust and flies but the beer's worth it," read this year's official slogan. Any female visitor was told to "Party till your nipples tingle!" Dirty Pierre did not spare me his sagacity. "Get a dog up ya!" he advised. I had absolutely no idea what he meant. Doubtless it was unspeakably vile.

Not before time, racing beckoned, so I walked the three miles out of town, via billabong and coolibah tree, to the place where someone had stuck rails and a winning post in an expanse of desert and called it a racecourse. It would be a mile and a half if they ever bothered to race all the way round, which they don't. Look out over the track and there's nothing. Dubai's camel racetrack had more features. And that has none.

This was not the first Birdsville circuit, the now defunct original having been situated three miles to the west of town. Remarkably, they used to programme steeplechases there, but the course was abandoned as it was prone to being inundated with floodwaters. Looking out now across a painfully arid landscape, such a prospect was hard to credit.

Facilities at the modern Birdsville were scarce to non-existent. The main enclosure was little more than a frame with a roof, an open-sided barn that housed the bookmakers and a few television screens showing races from elsewhere, never Birdsville itself. Racegoers brought their own deckchairs to secure a slightly sheltered spot, though it provided scant respite from the heat and dust. A corrugated iron shed housed both weighing room and stewards' room behind three small rows of temporary seating.

This was back-to-basics racing, with runners and riders scrawled on a blackboard before each race, ditto results afterwards. There was no tote betting, and no need for starting prices since there was no off-course betting either.

The small betting ring on course was heaving all day; in the first, an appalling maiden sprint over just 800 metres, I took 5-2 about the second favourite. He had an odds-on shot to contend with, though quite why this gelding, Sirgates, was such a short price was hard to fathom after even a cursory glance at the form in the racecard, which showed that he had been running over at least three furlongs further recently.

My selection, Little Lynx, beat the favourite comfortably – but finished second to an outsider. I cannot offer a race description on this or anything else, as the only way to tell the contest had begun after the red light started flashing on the gate was by the duststorm that moved around the track, and the commentary stepping up a notch. The last furlong or so was visible enough if you could get a pitch on the rails.

The winner was trained by George Dawson, a Birdsville regular from Port Lincoln in South Australia, who had won the Cup itself on several occasions. Of his three runners on the first day, two won and the other went down in a photo.

After racing, a wander back into town was punctuated by a little detour down to the banks of the Diamantina river, where most of the horses were stationed. A mile from the racetrack, a number of trainers made this area their temporary home for the weekend, each setting up a temporary base, sleeping in a tent or caravan like the rest of us.

Most of these racehorses tied to fences along a muddy brown riverbank were regulars on the country-racing circuit trained in some back-of-beyond township, a tiny spot somewhere in the empty middle of the map, although some travelled from much farther afield, like Victoria.

I walked down to the base of trainer Craig Smith, third in the state premiership in 2004-05. Based in the town of Roma, about 700 miles towards Brisbane, the stocky Queenslander told me that it cost around A$1,600 (£665) to bring a team of six horses to Birdsville, with feed, staff and their own generator for electricity.

"I came a couple of years ago and we had a few winners, and the owners were on at me to come again so here we are," he said. "It's a bit different, isn't it? The horses don't like it much but at least it's a level playing field for everybody."

Smith, who trained 31 horses altogether, had saddled a Group 3 winner in the past. "Like everyone else, I'd love to win a Group 1, but we won't be doing that with any of these guys," he said, gesturing towards his hand-picked Birdsville team. "They've all had their chances at the big tracks and failed." Smith had no winners on the Friday but suggested that his chestnut gelding Murdsa, third in a 1,000-metre event, might win the last race the following day over 1,200m.

All too soon, it was with a feeling of deep trepidation that I returned to the Birdsville Hotel, where the raucous main bar had come to resemble the OK Corral after the gunfight. Neither this nor the external beer 'garden' were places for the faint-hearted, peopled as they were by everybody within a thousand miles capable of holding a glass, as well as the odd addled specimen from even further off.

I found myself chatting with a 24-year-old Brisbane builder named Brad. "What did you think of the racing?" I asked him, innocently enough.

"Racing?" he replied. "You must be the only bloke who's come here for that."

Despite having noted his slurred enunciation and whisky breath, I unwisely decided to take the conversation forward, though the subject, travel, seemed harmless enough.

"It's overrated," said Brad. "I went to India last year – didn't like it. Too many fucking Indians."

Time to move on to the evening's special entertainment in the community centre, titled 'Acoustic Heaven' and wrong on both counts. The electric band playing country music to square-dancing septuagenarians was no-one's idea of paradise. Named Haybaler or Shitshovel or something, they reappeared the following night at the same venue for the Birdsville Ball, which appeared less of a misnomer, as it did indeed take place in Birdsville. You might not have had a ball there, though.

On the way back to camp, my photographer reflected on events so far. "I don't know what all the fuss is about the flies and the dust," she offered, unkindly.

We awoke to a dustbowl accompanied by swarms of flies. On the way to the racecourse, having ignorantly resisted the charms of the racetrack shuttle once more, the twin plagues battled for supremacy. If you copped a mouthful, it was a relief when your teeth ground down on something gritty; unpleasant enough, but better than the meaty alternative.

Back at the track, the more extreme conditions upset some of the horses in the saddling boxes: flynets and eyeshades were not enough for some, who, visibly disturbed, clawed at the sand incessantly to the extent that some managed to dig out quite a pit in front of them. The wide-open track on unprotected desert offered no reprieve as they raced into the teeth of the wind, jockeys with the bottom half of their faces covered in handkerchiefs. Even in the stands, the sand stung the backs of your legs.

This must have been even more unwelcome to those few members of the crowd who had glammed up today for the 'Fashions in the field' competition, a ridiculous concept at the best of times that some diabolical genius figured would go down a storm in the middle of nowhere.

Scrutinising the racecard, I was aware of a strange sense of having been there before. Of course, I had been there the previous day – and so had around 50 per cent of Saturday's scheduled runners, who were 'backing up' after running on the Friday card. It made sense, as the programme was virtually identical: Sirgates, tried over 1,200 metres this time, got a bit closer but still finished only second.

I located the chief stipendiary steward, Reid Sanders, and quizzed him as to whether this predilection for running the same horses two days in a row is a charter for cheating, a quiet run one day lining horses up for a more active effort the next.

"No, that doesn't happen much," he said. "These races mean a lot to people and they've travelled hundreds of kilometres to be here, so they're trying."

Then again, Sanders himself, who was actually the chief steward of the entire state, exuded a laid-back, off-duty vibe, this being his weekend away from his day job in the Brisbane office. Perhaps it was the baseball cap and shades that created that impression, even though he wore a tie. "I flew in today and I'm here for two nights," he said. "I've been coming here for a few years," he added, unmistakeable glint in his eye.

The tin shack that passed for a bar was doing a roaring trade on its 'buy 11 for ten' promotion, and midway through the afternoon an unholy alliance developed in the betting ring between 15 men clad in orange boiler suits and hard hats for 'Mitchy's Bucks Bash' and another smaller gathering in orange suits emblazoned with the question "Where's Wally?"

As I struggled to manoeuvre around them a quarter of an hour before the Birdsville Cup, the staggering, horrific enormity of the situation finally hit me. Two stag parties had found each other, and they were forming a circle to serenade the blameless public from the middle of the ring. I was thoroughly drunk, surrounded by dangerous, threatening types who might be even more drunk, and hadn't even studied the form for the big race that was the focal point of the entire enterprise. I looked to my photographer for support but some godless yahoo was busy tattooing a Castlemaine XXXX cartoon figure to her left breast, a process enhanced in some mysterious way by pouring lager down her front.

I resolved to abandon her to her fate and fought my way to a pitch to back George Dawson's representative Mapua. I am pretty sure he finished the race, but as I could barely see my own feet in the dust and the horse was out of the frame, I cannot tell you precisely where he came.

The 2005 Birdsville Cup was won by the favourite, a six-year-old gelding named Monee Lane, from 2004 victor Vain Joe. According to a local expert, the winner would have been a good handicapper at better-quality Brisbane tracks. "These open handicaps out here do take a bit of winning," he alleged.

Winning trainer Jeff Dixon, from Oakey, was not the sort of fellow you would want to meet in an arm-wrestling contest. He looked like golfing whale John Daly, a huge figure alongside winning rider Chris Maund at the post-race presentations.

After five losers, the predicted victory of Murdsa in the last spread a little happiness ahead of the journey back into town for a visit to Birdsville's final attraction. This was Fred Brophy's boxing troupe, the last of its kind in Australia, banned in Victoria and New South Wales but still a regular visitor to places like Birdsville. Its very existence seemed an anachronism, an echo from freakshows gone by. Though I instigated a wide-ranging search just to be on the safe side, there was no bearded lady or cockfighting to accompany it.

The 60-year-old front man Brophy, silver-grey hair greased back 1950s style, was a carney huckster extraordinaire. On a raised platform at his Victorian-era booth, he stirred up a 500-strong crowd, exhorting the local toughs to take on members of his team who flanked him in gold dressing gowns and rejoiced in stage names like The Cowboy ("All the ladies love him") and White Lightning.

Brophy enjoyed particular sport with a tall Dutchman who climbed the ladder to fight White Lightning. Leaning forward towards him, Brophy feigned a close, conspiratorial exchange with his latest customer. "What did you say?" he said. "I'm not sure that's a good idea, you know, calling him a poof. He might not like it."

Following this Saturday night cabaret – not dangerous really, only one nose broken – and a final night under canvas, the journey back to Brisbane proved relatively uneventful. One fellow passenger asked me if I knew Norwich, before revealing that his daughter-in-law had absconded there. "I hope they bomb the place with her in it," he added, charitably.

Tedious Warren kept fairly quiet, Brenda the psycho threatened to send me an email and members of the Goatshag party invited me to stay on their island, wherever it was. I might even go. They all enjoyed themselves. Some even watched the racing.

Although the kangaroos appeared to have learned their lesson and kept their distance, various problems with fan belts and air conditioning managed to extend the trip to 26 hours. Then, five days after it started, my unforgettable fatigue-inducing odyssey to Birdsville was over. "It wasn't as good as usual," said Warren. "It was a bit quiet, too many police – I might not come next year."

I wasn't sure if I would ever return, but if I do, one thing is for certain. I won't be taking the bloody bus.

*

ALTHOUGH Plastered finished a disappointing seventh on his next outing in the Caulfield Cup, worse was to follow for those who had supported him for the Melbourne Cup. He suffered a foot infection and did not run, but his absence wasn't much lamented as Makybe Diva ensured her place in racing history with an unprecedented third consecutive victory in Australia's most acclaimed race. "We'll never live to see that again," said Lee Freedman after watching her defy top weight in front of a 140,000 crowd at Flemington. "I don't want to run Phar Lap down but I never saw Phar Lap win three Melbourne Cups."

Makybe Diva was retired after the race by her owner Tony Santic, a South Australian tuna fisherman who named her from the first two initials in five of his employees' names (Maureen, Kylie, Belinda, Diane and Vanessa).

"I think to ask any more of this mare would not be fair," said Santic. She certainly could not have done a lot more in 2005 – before taking the Cup for the

third time, Makybe Diva had won the Cox Plate as well. She was quite a racehorse. I still can't believe I managed to miss her.

INDIA

VITAL STATISTICS

RACING		FINANCE	
Racetracks	9	Total prize-money	$13.72m
Fixtures	435	Betting turnover	$250.43m
Races	2,981		
Racehorses	4,141	All figures for 2005	

BREEDING	
Stallions	107
Mares	2,518
Foals	1,429

JUST a month spent in India was enough to suggest most of the clichés about this vast, over-inhabited chunk of Asia are well founded indeed. There are people everywhere, they all love cricket and you do need to be careful with the food. Yet whatever I thought I knew about this utterly vivid society and its unsettling contradictions, nothing could have properly prepared me for such a full-frontal assault on the senses.

Enchanting and exasperating in equal measure, this was like nowhere I had ever seen, a place of violent contrasts where the modern is mixed with the medieval, extreme spirituality sits uneasily alongside blatant materialism, and gaudy displays of wealth are set against unrelenting mass poverty. India figures among the world's fastest-growing economies, but you don't need to be a financial expert to work out that it is starting from a low base. Only the most insensitive of western visitors could have gone there without being made to feel acutely aware of their relative privilege.

For much of the time, this was the most challenging of destinations. Well, perhaps not during a fortnight's holiday within a holiday when I was being driven around the walled cities and ancient forts of wondrous Rajasthan with my in-laws. Then again, even that luxurious portion of the trip to the new Chianti-shire for the slightly more adventurous had its less straightforward moments, with corrupt policemen demanding bribes from our driver, barely functional roads overwhelmed with traffic bursting at the seams, pushy touts hassling you from every corner and rip-off merchants trying to palm off shoddy gimcrack trinkets while twice swiping the credit card.

Away from Rajasthan, I spent the remainder of the time in various cities – Delhi, Kolkata, Hyderabad and Varanasi – in different corners of the country. All of them were overrun with people, and it certainly took a while to become anything like accustomed to such a ceaseless stream of humanity.

Take Varanasi, for example, the sacred city on the banks of the Ganges reputed to be the oldest on the planet and revered in Hindu mythology as a 'crossing point' between earth and heaven, where devotees have access to the divine and gods come down to the people. Huge numbers of pilgrims bathe daily in the river's holy, polluted waters while bodies are cremated daily on its *ghats*, the steps down to the waterway. The regulars develop a resistance to the bacteria, but it's best for tourists to avoid emulating them.

I stayed in a budget hotel overlooking the Ganges (caged balcony to keep out the monkeys), from where a boatman took us down the busy river at dawn to witness a scene that cannot have changed for hundreds of years. A warren of narrow alleyways and ancient bazaars, Varanasi's Old Town was an unforgettable place, straight out of the Middle Ages. It was also a pestilent, disease-ridden hole, with flies and other insects everywhere fighting over the cowshit, dogs copulating in fetid passages. You had to avoid your nose to avoid the overpowering stench. Varanasi was breathtaking in every respect.

India could hardly have been more vibrant, but seldom have I felt farther from home. It felt like anything really could happen, and it frequently does. A day after I landed in Delhi, there was an earthquake. I stayed in Connaught Square in the heart of New Delhi; soon after I left the country, it was bombed. Maybe the feeling of being well outside my comfort zone had some basis in reality.

People rave about India. After I flew back to Heathrow to start the final leg of my round-the-world trip, it was at least six months before I could contemplate ever going back. Now, as I write this, I can hardly wait to return.

*

ORGANISED horse racing in India, well over two centuries old, is a legacy of the British Raj maintained after independence by local social elites, headed by the historically pre-eminent Royal Calcutta Turf Club.

Yet racing's roots in India were laid long before British political dominion was formally establishéd in the mid-19th century. Around 100 years earlier, British cavalry officers had taken their love of equine sport with them to the subcontinent alongside the military might that accompanied the commercial acumen of the East India Company. Early records are more than a little confusing. The Madras Race Club celebrated its bicentenary in 1978, which means its foundation predates the inaugural Epsom Derby in 1780, yet the earliest records of organised racing in India mention a race meeting in Madras in 1795, when army officers raced each other on the long flat beach. There are suggestions of a rudimentary racecourse much earlier in the Calcutta suburbs at Akra, as far back as 1769. It is probable there were many others. According to historical information supplied by Indian representatives to the Asian Racing Conference, almost every cantonment – in effect, villages of British troops – had a racecourse.

Calcutta, the centre of British power, became the leading turf centre, and during the Victorian era the native Maharajahs became patrons of the turf, some of them even extending their interests to ownership in England. In the mid-20th century, this exodus was reversed when thoroughbreds were imported on a large scale and a series of Classics, restricted to home-breds, were established at Bombay's racecourse Mahalaxmi in the 1942-43 season. These were based on the English model of two Guineas, Derby/Oaks and St Leger.

The latter half of the last century proved an exercise in extremes for Indian racing. The sport's very existence was threatened during the early years of independence, but by the mid-1950s it was once again on a sound footing. The likes of the Aga Khan and Sir Victor Sassoon, among the leading racehorse owners in Europe, raced horses in the country, while Britain's top jockeys also found India a winter home from home. In the 1960s and 1970s, Lester Piggott and Willie Carson headed the list of regulars.

With vastly more lucrative opportunities elsewhere for the winter in places like Dubai plus the advent of all-weather racing at home, there aren't so many foreign visitors these days, but Indian racing has stabilised as an industry serviced by 4,000 racehorses and 3,000 races. The country houses nine racecourses split between various racing clubs, each with their own set of racing programmes and regional Classics. "Indian courses love Derbys," says the *Complete Encyclopaedia of Horse Racing*, and the list includes a Monsoon Derby at Calcutta as well as the track's Derby 'proper', another pair of Derbys in Bangalore and various others at racetracks like Delhi, Pune and Udhagamandalum, at varying trips.

While the Royal Calcutta Turf Club was once a byword for racing elegance, the racecourse has fallen from its pedestal as the city in which it sits, now called Kolkata, has become painfully synonymous with sickening images of third-world poverty. Mumbai is unchallenged as the nation's most prestigious venue, the former Bombay still being home to India's national Classics including the Derby early in the new year. The Turf Invitation Cup, run at a different track each year, is another prestigious event.

By common consent, India's most progressive racecourse is Hyderabad, a relative infant among Indian turf clubs yet still well over 100 years old. I visited the right-handed turf track on the national holiday commemorating Gandhi's birthday for an eight-race card featuring the Grade 1 Deccan Derby, highlight of the Hyderabad monsoon season and a recognised trial for the real Classic programme later in the season.

A bustling, predominately Islamic metropolis, Hyderabad is the biggest city in the state of Andhra Pradesh, a large slice of the country about three-quarters of the way down the map. While the racecourse is located in the fairly central district of Malakpet, it was still about five miles from my hotel. With no conventional taxis in the city, this meant taking one of Hyderabad's private wasp squad, the yellow-and-black three-wheeler auto-rickshaws that buzz around providing a cheap and effective mode of transport.

After a thrilling 20-minute journey costing a handful of rupees past mosques, minarets and bazaars, Hyderabad racecourse announced itself via its pale-green monolith of a grandstand, completed in 1993 with an eye to function rather than style. A bank of seating opposite the weighing-room complex offered a prime view over a neat paddock, caged in and ringed with billboards, which lent it the air of a minor continental football stadium – albeit one with beautifully tended lawns and brightly coloured garlands of carnations all over the place.

Patrons of the main stand were fenced off from the track, suggesting the locals could get pretty rowdy if the mood took them. The undercover betting ring beneath the stand was a free-for-all once the action started, punters pushing and shoving their way to take prices from more than 30 boards bookmakers, who operated from a series of cages arranged in a circle. A racecourse tote operated alongside.

I spent most of the afternoon in the members' enclosure, smart dress required among local bigwigs invited for lunch and tea, this particular meeting being a showpiece occasion on the Hyderabad calendar and attracting plenty of TV crews and photographers. The VIPs looked like they figured among the 'haves' of a nation infamous for its inequitable distribution of wealth, Hyderabad being a relatively affluent city in Indian terms, known colloquially as 'Cyberabad', reflecting its status as one of the nation's foremost technological centres, home to Bill Gates's Hi-Tech City.

Today's meeting featured several competitive contests, with generally open betting and decent-sized fields. Before every race, an upright-looking bay partnered by a rider in ceremonial costume fashioned in green and gold led the runners into the immaculate paddock, fences garlanded with chains of bright-orange marigolds and shocking-pink roses.

The racehorses were a uniformly impressive collection, an attractive satiny-flanked bunch generally figuring from among the nation's upper strata, either led or ridden in by attendants, many in turbans. While they were all home-breds, protected under Indian rules by weight concessions from any rare imports, the influence of Britain and Ireland was obvious. Their bloodlines, printed in the cute little racecard, featured several also-rans from recent European Classics who were based in India as stallions, horses like Razeen, Warrshan, Storm Trooper and Burden Of Proof, as well as Guineas winners Don't Forget Me and Tirol.

The list of riders had its quirks. Deep Shanker sounded like a heavy version of the sort of sitar music favoured by addled potheads in the 1960s, while another was described simply as 'Christopher'. Evidently this was the rider's surname.

Among India's top jockeys was the expatriate Mark Gallagher, cousin of jump jockey Dean Gallagher from a County Kildare racing family.

Although other British-based riders still dropped in for the Classics on day trips from Dubai, Gallagher, who was in his mid-30s, was the only one based there permanently. He lived in Bangalore with his wife and daughter.

Three times Bangalore champion jockey, Gallagher had partnered around 600 winners, including 40 victories in Classic or Graded races, among them six regional Derbys. "I wouldn't have got anywhere near that figure at home," the jockey told me as we chatted in the weighing room. "I had weight problems at home so I thought I'd take a chance and I've definitely no regrets about coming here. I'm lighter now than I've ever been, I ride four days a week and I'm very grateful to Indian racing. It is hard at home unless you get a real good horse; unless you're one of the top ten boys, it is a struggle."

With quarantine restrictions lifted in Dubai, he predicted a bright future for Indian horses. "It is difficult to say how good our horses are," said Gallagher. "I think our best horses here are probably Group 3 standard at home and it can only improve now we're able to race in Dubai."

Because foreigners are now limited to riding in just 50 per cent of races on a given card, Gallagher had just three rides, none of whom covered themselves in glory, including his mount in the Deccan Derby, a race he had won in 2004, thereby adding his name to a roll of honour featuring Sandy Barclay and Paul Eddery.

The big race featured several leading three-year-olds, among them the favourite Star Millionaire, saddled by Mumbai's leading trainer Dallas Todywalla and evidently a comfortable winner at Pune on his previous outing. According to the tip sheet, where comments were published in a twee first-person style, the colt had a good chance. "I will give anxious moments to the winner," it said.

Star Millionaire carried the colours of Muttiah Ramaswamy, India's leading owner with 350 mares and 900 horses spread across the country. The owner did win the race – but it was the 7-1 chance Candy Man ("I will be in the thick of it") who led home a locally trained 1-2-3, sparking jubilant scenes. The VIPs were excited enough to stand up, while elsewhere the crowd rushed towards the fence for a closer view and kids perched on to rails for a better look.

Horse and rider were cheered into the winner's enclosure at the climax of an exhilarating day. Or almost the climax, for there was still time for me to sing for my supper, which led me to another of those embarrassing episodes that seemed to make frequent appearances on the racing road.

Hyderabad racecourse was an impressive operation, and my hosts could not have been more accommodating, so it would have been rude to decline the chairman's request that I allow myself to be interviewed on TV. That was how I found myself in front of a camera extolling the virtues of Indian racing in general and Hyderabad in particular, subjects about which I have never claimed to be an expert. Still, suggestions that the best horse won and Indian racing was brilliant seemed unlikely to offend. Indeed, perhaps I made rather too competent a job of it as I was immediately lined up for a second bash with another channel, this time with a presenter whose accent was totally indecipherable. He must have been asking something, but I had absolutely no clue what he was saying, which isn't ideal when you're live on the national news.

Reddening sharply, I launched into a stream of consciousness about anything with any possible relevance, like why I was in Hyderabad, how wonderful the Deccan Derby was and what a fantastic horse Candy Man must have been – plus how proud I was, of course, to come from Britain, home of the original Derby.

Everyone smiled politely. Bollywood was surely beckoning. It was only a matter of time.

*

A POLITICALLY motivated trend in the 1990s prompted the renaming of a number of major Indian cities to eradicate traces of Britain's colonial involvement so Calcutta, showpiece capital of the Raj, is now Kolkata after the Bengali pronunciation.

Few such changes have been universally embraced, however, and even the official rebranding of British street names in Kolkata, a process that started as long ago as the 1960s, is still yet to be fully integrated with locals. Many of them still refer to the city's commercial centre by its old name Dalhousie Square rather than using its official title BBD Bagh, which

A study of horse and trainer at ramshackle Colonia racecourse, one of Uruguay's many regional tracks (© Jane Godfrey)

The numbers board reveals result and distances at Uruguay's premier racecourse Maronas in Montevideo (© Jane Godfrey)

How to make a grand entrance: Palermo racecourse in Buenos Aires (© Jane Godfrey)

Where the surf meets the turf: jockey David Flores enjoys a lolly with his daughter at laidback Del Mar (© Jane Godfrey)

A legend at Saratoga – Jerry Bailey (© Jane Godfrey)

The field leaves the starting gate for the Whitney Handicap at Saratoga: the winner Commentator is fourth right (noseband) while Saint Liam has the pink silks (© Jane Godfrey)

Racehorse as political protest: note the slogan on this poor fellow's flanks at Riccarton in Christchurch, New Zealand (© Jane Godfrey)

Above: *Hello, hello, hello, what have we got here? The long arm of the law studies the form at Caulfield in Melbourne (© Jane Godfrey)*

Right: *Sartorial elegance is the key at Cluden Park in Townsville, northern Queensland (Jane Godfrey)*

Birdsville, the place where someone stuck some rails around a patch of desert and called it a racecourse (© Jane Godfrey)

Abandon hope all ye who enter here: front gate at the notorious Birdsville Race Club, in the middle of the Outback (© Jane Godfrey)

Candy Man, winner of the Hindu Deccan Derby at Hyderabad; note the ladies replacing divots to the horse's left (© Jane Godfrey)

Racing at the Royal Calcutta Turf Club with the Victoria Monument in the background (© Jane Godfrey)

You couldn't say racing was black and white in Kolkata. Orange and maroon perhaps, but not black and white (© Jane Godfrey)

An impressive maple-leaf blanket of flowers for Relaxed Gesture, winner of the Canadian International at Woodbine in Toronto (© Jane Godfrey)

Time for a blind eye: a bookmaker accepts bets at the Breeders' Cup Chase in New Jersey (© Jane Godfrey)

The mother of all point-to-points: a timber race at the Breeders' Cup Chase (© Jane Godfrey)

Saint Liam (Jerry Bailey) gets the better of Flower Alley in the Breeders' Cup Classic at Belmont (© Racing Post/Edward Whitaker)

Jockeys are frisked for illegal aids before the start of a race in the Dominican Republic (© Jane Godfrey)

A typically large crowd avidly follows the sport at Kranji in Singapore (© Jane Godfrey)

Pay attention, there could be an exam: Manila Jockey Club officials explain the fine points of racing in the Philippines (© Jane Godfrey)

A great place to finish: Frankie Dettori drives home Alkaased to short-head Heart's Cry in the Japan Cup (© Japan Racing Association)

commemorates three revolutionaries hanged for trying to kill – you guessed it – Lieutenant-Governor General Lord Dalhousie. "A fine piece of official rhetoric," says the *Rough Guide*.

Whatever you want to call it, this teeming metropolis was a vivid jolt to the senses. It is possible that not every member of the country's 1.1 billion population had been crammed into its jumble of bewildering, polluted streets, but personally I wouldn't believe it. Kolkata's topography was startling, unforgettable and incomprehensible. Rare snatches of pavement were lined by merchants displaying their wares. Extra hazards were offered by touts, street kids and beggars, often mutilated: "Mother Teresa, Mother Teresa," hand stretched out, was a popular entreaty.

The roads themselves were often little more than cratered passages littered with mounds of rubbish and stray bricks, where rickshaws, pedestrians, mopeds, taxis, stray dogs and even the odd wandering cow fused themselves into near-perpetual gridlock. Vestiges of Britain's influence remained amid this cacophonous street symphony conducted in unforgiving heat. My guest house, an eccentric place close to the maelstrom, displayed portraits of the Queen and Prince Charles on its walls. Strangely, the Queen Mother was missing, but on the plus side there was Felicity Kendal.

Looking a couple of storeys above the melee revealed colossal buildings dating back to the 19th century. Once they would have been grandiose; now their formerly brightly coloured façades were caked in the grime of tough years in a city that embodies India's sharpest problems.

Towards the south, where the street scene was generally less frenetic, there were more obvious examples of the city's imperialist past, like the racecourse, where the Royal Calcutta (definitely not Kolkata) Turf Club hosts regular race meetings on the Maidan, the huge greensward without which the city would surely suffocate.

From a distance it was easy to visualise the racecourse's salad days attended by huge crowds peopling five stands situated directly opposite the grandeur of the white-domed Victoria Memorial, Kolkata's main tourist attraction with its formal gardens and fountains. But look closely and the reality of the racetrack was somewhat different. The stands were decaying and grimy, while even the track's biggest apologists would have been forced to admit that in terms of quality it had fallen well behind more successful venues like Mumbai and Hyderabad.

Still, it was testament to an enduring popularity that a crowd of at least 3,000 was attracted to the course on the day I visited for an uncompetitive eight-race card at the end of the track's monsoon meeting, which featured 15 days spread across a three-month period between July and October. The entire monsoon meeting used an inner turf track, a mile-and-a-half oval that must have drained as if its irrigation system worked on magic. The day before the meeting, a huge electrical storm had left much of the city under water – a regular occurrence, it seemed – yet, if anything, the racing surface was fast.

After a typically hair-raising taxi journey involving a terrifying driver who attempted to engage my help to "shoot the bloody bastard Al-Qaeda men", I was deposited in front of the Club Stand – admission 200 rupees (£2.60) if accompanied by a member – the entrance to which was situated under an ugly grey flyover and accessed through garbage heaps. Clustered outside were vendors selling tip sheets, racecards and form guides. Next to them were other traders. "Watches, watches," shouted one. This was strange, as his merchandise consisted solely of fake leather belts.

Inside was a tranquil scene redolent of a bygone era, an immaculately polite anachronism that cried out the track's colonial past, though it was a small coterie of well-heeled nationals who sat in private boxes served by turbaned attendants in bright white outfits.

Healthy-looking thoroughbreds, possibly better cared for than many of the city's inhabitants, paraded around the well-manicured paddock watched by well-manicured patrons standing on neat lawns. Yet while this elegantly dated tableau lent the members' enclosure a Raffles-like feel, the other four stands were either derelict, or filthy and unkempt.

As soon as I entered, a tiny man with mischievous twinkling eyes galloped over to me, promising to find a good seat. I didn't need his services, the racecourse having secured me a billet in the stand, but it wasn't the last I was to see of this devilish imp, who was at least 90. It must be close to impossible to spend more than five minutes in a public arena in any

Indian city without attracting some form of attention, and the racecourse proved no different, even in this upmarket stand. Within a minute of sitting down, three others had proffered their services, a tote runner with a sash, a representative of the espresso-machine franchise ("Very nice coffee, sir") and another espousing the virtues of a chicken sandwich. They were crestfallen when I declined their blandishments.

A pattern was established in the first three races, the opener over six furlongs followed by two over seven, all with fields of seven or eight, and all of them featuring winning odds-on favourites who were in the front rank throughout. It seemed riders here favoured the approach of the city's drivers, doing virtually anything to get ahead of their rivals as soon as possible, eschewing more subtle tactics.

Before the second race, I took the plunge into the main enclosure. It cost only 14 rupees (18p) to enter this separate universe, much grittier with an exclusively male crowd focusing on an undercover betting ring that could have served as a latter-day Black Hole of Calcutta. Punters fought to get a price inside a circle of bookmakers housed in a series of cages; each advertised two sets of odds, one list about the winner and one betting without the seemingly inevitable odds-on favourite. The prices were fairly prohibitive, and some of them looked alien indeed. Aleksei, the winning favourite in the second, oscillated at fractions between 23-100 and 45-100. I backed him with Manali & Co for 400 rupees, tax paid on at 15 per cent, or 60 rupees. After he made all, I received 560 rupees for a profit of 100 rupees on a total stake of 460. It was about £1.30.

Though there were plenty of fans whirring above the cages, you needed to be desperate for a bet to withstand the sweltering heat for long, but at least there were plenty of food-and-drink sellers around, like the Krishna Juice Corner, Anand Snacks and Junior Brothers, as well as Bata Boutique, which does a roaring trade in paan, the popular digestive that, depending on the variety, usually resulted in men launching gobs of red spit around the place.

Back in the posh enclosure, my impish nonagenarian friend, not unlike a subcontinental leprechaun, appeared unbidden at my elbow. "Drink?" he said, in insinuating fashion. "One glass?" Pleased with an answer in the affirmative, he allowed himself a mischievous grin, revealing less-than-perfect teeth. Though many were missing, only white was needed for a snooker set. Having pocketed his small amount of baksheesh, the national currency, for supplying the liquor, he decided to push his luck. "Chicken sandwich? Samosa? Very nice samosa, sir."

We were on to the fourth race by now, and dementia was clearly setting in as I looked down the list of runners. "Do you think Azinger will be below par?" I asked my photographer, who was drenched by heavy afternoon showers. "Will the jockey get a tune out of La Scala? I would back Schumacher but it looks like he hasn't got the engine."

How I laughed. Yet for some unfathomable reason, these witticisms did not go down well with my sodden photographer. "Haven't you got anything better to do than sit here drinking, gambling and writing down little jokes to yourself while I'm running around taking all these pictures?"

"No, not really," I answered. Honesty is the best policy in such circumstances.

The favourite won, completing a treble for jockey Christopher Alford and trainer Vijay Singh, just as the skies clouded over again and a swarm of huge dragonflies paid us a visit, buzzing over the heads of the women in brightly coloured sarees repairing the track and replacing divots between races.

I knew I was back at an Asian racecourse as timpani versions of *Light My Fire* and *Up Where We Belong* were piped through the stands. Then my Indian leprechaun appeared yet again at my side, Mr Benn-style, as if by magic. "Number four, 100 rupees, quick," he said, conspiratorially. With little time to establish his tipping *bona fides*, much less his sanity, I handed over the money. He hurtled away, returning five minutes later with a tote receipt. I passed him another small note. It occurred that even if his horse won, by the time I had tipped him again for picking up the winnings, I would have been out of pocket. Such astute economic analysis proved somewhat academic: number four was the first losing favourite of the day.

That racing in Kolkata was struggling was evident from cursory examination of the racecard that revealed, in effect, a duopoly. From 61 runners, 30 represented just two trainers, the aforementioned Singh and Daniel David, who trained for a pair of dominant owners who ended up sharing the first six winners, three apiece. Just to complicate matters, their colours were almost identical: gold, red belt, armband and cap ranged against an indistinguishable gold, brown belt and cap. This gold, by the way, was the 'old gold' strain. Perhaps they were both Wolves fans. Sitting next to each other under a parasol in the paddock, their jockeys certainly resembled a football team.

Before the big race, a man in a starched white shirt sidled up to me in the betting ring. "What is your good name?" he demanded. "Where are you from? I know England. I have a tailor's in Hong Kong and an office in Liverpool. Look at my shirt," he added, pulling up his collar to show me the label. "See, it says Hong Kong."

He made great play of opening his racecard and surreptitiously showing me a piece of paper contained therein with the numbers seven and two written on them. "Bet this one, it will be the better for you," he suggested. He meant number two in race seven, the Derby trial. The horse in question was called Rasalas, and he had the right colours, gold and brown.

Then again, so did three of the other four. The fifth one, a filly named Sanskara, beat them all, the 3-1 chance breaking the hegemony for a brief spell under leading rider Suraj Narredu. This one's silks were the vastly different claret with gold epaulettes.

I left before the last, hotly pursued across the lawn by my rotten-toothed friend. I put on a spurt to get away. Truth was, I wouldn't have minded a beer, and I might even have chanced a chicken sandwich or a samosa. But the last thing I needed was another tip.

*

INDIAN racing made a major breakthrough on the international stage in early 2007 when the four-year-old gelding Mystical, a multiple Group-race winner at home and runner-up in the 2006 Indian Derby, became its first winner at the Dubai International Racing Carnival. Although Indian-bred horses had won races overseas before, such as the Singapore horse of the year Saddle Up and US winner Adler, Mystical was the first Indian-trained horse to win abroad.

He represented the Poonawalla family, a driving force behind Indian racing. "This is the greatest moment for Indian racing," said breeder Zavaray Poonawalla. "His win was huge news in Indian and sparked a lot of national coverage. I had *about 50 to 70 calls that night – I needed smelling salts afterwards. But it was a huge relief and the result of a lot of hard work. There has never been any call for international competition in India, so about 15 years back we set out to change that mentality and make it happen. We built a quarantine facility and this is the result. The whole process has cost $1 million but it has been worth every cent. Whatever happens, we've achieved our goal and this is the first step to more Indian-trained horses competing on the world stage. We need champions to travel: they have to be champions, the very best we have, just like Mystical."*

The winning jockey aboard Mystical was British champion Ryan Moore. "I have never heard such tremendous applause for a horse here outside the World Cup," he said. "That was the level of excitement and pride."

It wasn't a one-off, either. Three weeks later, Mystical won again in Dubai, scoring his tenth successive victory. "I have won nine Indian Derbys but this means more than anything else," said Zavaray Poonawalla.

Mystical couldn't quite manage win number 11, however. He finished 14th of 16 in the $5 million Dubai Duty Free.

Mark Gallagher left India to ride on a permanent basis in Singapore in 2007. "I thought it was time in my career I stepped up a bit," he said. "I'm not knocking India – their horses are underrated but I needed a new challenge and Singapore is a world-renowned set-up."

He jetted to Britain in June 2007 to ride the rank outsider Leander to finish 14th of 17 in the Epsom Derby.

CANADA

VITAL STATISTICS

RACING

Racetracks	7
Fixtures	576
Races	5,238
Racehorses	7,750

BREEDING

Stallions	290
Mares	3,664
Foals	2,580

FINANCE

Total prize-money	$113.40m
Betting turnover	$568.05m

All figures for 2005

BEFORE this next chapter, jiggery-pokery must be admitted. After India, I flew back to Heathrow again before switching to Gatwick and setting off around the world for the third and final time with a flight to Philadelphia, two days before the Breeders' Cup Chase meeting in New Jersey, itself a week before the Cup 'proper', which was back at Belmont Park in 2005.

Those two meetings will be dealt with together in a few pages' time, but first we're moving out of sequence briefly by diving into Canada, where I spent the three days following the Breeders' Cup Chase. Having gone to the latter on the Saturday, I flew up to Toronto the following morning, picked up a car at Pearson International Airport and drove straight to Woodbine racecourse for the Canadian International card. Although the track was virtually next door, about 15 miles west of the city centre out in the suburbs in Mississauga, I still managed to miss the first two races at Canada's most prestigious meeting of the year. And it wasn't as if the track was easy to miss, even in heavy showers, given that the entrance to the Woodbine car park was illuminated by a huge sign advertising its colossal slot-machine emporium.

On this overcast Sunday in late October, horse racing held sway – and thoroughbred racing at that, the sport for one afternoon at least offering the star attraction in a nation where harness racing is much more popular. There are 65 trotting tracks in Canada compared to just seven for thoroughbreds, and about five times as many races. Harness racing also attracts twice as much betting turnover.

The status of Canada's horse-racing community provides an unfortunate parallel with the nation as a whole. Despite having much to recommend it, it is easily overlooked in comparison to its dominant southern neighbour. Canadian racing has its own governing bodies and racing programme, including Classics and Graded races – but it cannot avoid being seen as a mere adjunct to the US scene. The majority of Canadian racedays are broadcast in the States, and Woodbine figures among the top 15 tracks in prestige terms in the whole of North America. Its wide, galloping turf circuit, unconventionally situated outside the dirt oval, is generally regarded as the best on the continent. In 1996, the track received the ultimate seal of approval when it was chosen to become the first track outside the States to host the Breeders' Cup series.

Woodbine originally opened in 1874 in an area of Toronto that is now virtually downtown. After a couple of name changes in the following century – first Old Woodbine in 1956, then Greenwood in 1963 – live racing ceased in 1993. The current Woodbine, opened in 1956, has undergone many facelifts, including the installation of a 56,000-square-foot gaming area housing around 1,700 slot machines. It is now home to two legs of the Triple Crown, which is restricted to horses foaled in Canada and starts with the sexually confused Queen's Plate. Run over a mile and a quarter on the Woodbine dirt track in July and worth Can$1 million (£440,000), this Classic becomes the King's Plate dependent on the gender of the monarch. Dating back to 1860, the Queen's Plate, restricted to Canadian-bred horses, is the oldest continually run stakes race in North America. The final two legs of the Canadian Triple Crown are the Prince of Wales Stakes, run at picturesque Fort Erie just over the border from the US city of Buffalo, and the Breeders' Stakes back at Woodbine, which also hosts the North America Cup, the top prize in harness racing.

However, all three legs of the Triple Crown pale into insignificance alongside the mile-and-a-half Canadian International, worth about Can$2 million (£880,000). In 2006, actual prize-money crept over the £1m mark, one of only about 40 races in the world to do so, although the vagaries of currency make it impossible to be dogmatic on the subject. What's certain, though, is that in Britain and Ireland, only the Epsom Derby was worth a greater sum.

Such riches were not enough to turn the Canadian public on to horse racing, it seemed. Despite an 11-race card also featuring a couple more Graded races with high-class international runners, only about 15,000 people turned up at Woodbine the day I was there. More might have been expected given that entry was absolutely free to all-comers, allowing access almost everywhere in the six-storey grandstand that overlooked a racetrack wide indeed by North American standards.

Outside, just before the third race, the place was almost deserted on a desolate, cold grey day. Busier within, and ethnically diverse, it was still far from packed. An air of calm, quiet order pervaded a well-organised track. It was tempting to see Woodbine as a looking glass to Canadian society. Plenty of room to move, polite. At times too polite, as if the entire crowd had taken a sedative. The commentary was so unobtrusive as to be virtually inaudible, a mumble that scarcely rose even when the race reached its denouement.

There was a bit more noise during the fourth, when leading Ontario rider Emma-Jayne Wilson rode the well-backed winner. She was enjoying a magnificent season, topping the riders' table at Woodbine; she stayed there as well, becoming the first woman in the track's history to win the jockeys' championship with 175 wins. If this wasn't enough of an achievement in itself, the 23-year-old went on to a notable double, being awarded both Canada's Sovereign award and the US Eclipse award as leading apprentice for 2005.

Wilson, known as EJ, was plainly a prodigious talent, and a possible successor to Julie Krone, the best female jockey in North American history and still the only one of her gender to have ridden the winner of a Triple Crown race. Nevertheless, prejudice against female jockeys is not a figment of the imagination, though the riders themselves will seldom admit to any such unfair treatment.

"The guys at Woodbine are great," Wilson told the *Blood-Horse*. "They treat me no different than they would any other apprentice, with respect and the guidance young riders need. Yes, it is tough to be a jockey, and not because I am a girl. I think it is all about perspective. If I am thinking about it being harder for a girl to be a jockey, then it will be.

Instead, I am concentrating on being the best rider I can be by being a student of this game. I haven't noticed any adverse treatment on the backstretch or the track.

"This title is important to me because it is a symbol of how far the industry has come," she added. "I am not one to dwell on being a female jockey; I feel that this is a sign that any rider, male or female, has the opportunity to compete and excel in this game.

"Men and women are made differently. What each is able to do naturally, may take the other time, practice, and hard work to master. Some people are given talent in different areas; what one person is a natural at, others have to work for, be it strength in riding or communication with the horse. What makes a top rider is to appreciate your strengths and improve your weaknesses."

Although Wilson could hardly have started out any better, she still had some way to go before she could hope to join the national racing legends featured in an on-site Hall of Fame dedicated to those who had made a major contribution to Canadian racing. Among the biggest names there were the jockeys John Longden, the one-time world-record holder born in Yorkshire before moving to Calgary at the age of five, and Sandy Hawley, a national hero who was the first rider in North America to partner 500 winners in a season. Others featured included trainer Lucien Laurin and jockey Ron Turcotte, the all-Canadian team behind Secretariat, and EP Taylor, the chief architect of the evolution of modern Canadian racing and breeding. He was the owner-breeder behind the nation's most famous thoroughbred, Northern Dancer, commemorated in not one, but two statues at Woodbine, one of them by the British jump jockey-turned-sculptor Philip Blacker.

Taylor, who also bred Britain's most recent Triple Crown winner Nijinsky, was commemorated in the Grade 1 that immediately preceded the Canadian International, namely the EP Taylor Stakes (full of surprises, these Canucks). Standing in the parade ring before the race, I saw a familiar face for the first time in months in Frankie Dettori, over to ride the favourite Punctilious for his retainers, Sheikh Mohammed's Godolphin operation.

To digress for a second, this organisation had done much to foster my own interest in international racing. I was fortunate enough to visit Godolphin's Dubai base many times in its formative years, and reported for the *Racing Post* on some of its greatest triumphs, like Lammtarra's Derby, Dubai Millennium's Dubai World Cup and Sakhee's Arc. The sheikh's hand-picked team was never anything other than global in its scope, partly owing to the Maktoums' competitive nature, partly through the drive to advertise Dubai, which has turned into an improbable business and holiday centre in recent years. In order to follow Godolphin's horses properly, you simply had to learn about foreign racing. Otherwise, the point had been missed.

Back to Woodbine, where Dettori arrived, slightly late, in the parade ring to partner Punctilious. "Don't worry baby, it's only me, you know who I am," he said to his filly. The jockey's soothing words might have appeared cute to an eavesdropper like me, but they didn't help much. Punctilious missed the break and looked unhappy on the soft ground in labouring through a mediocre performance behind Honey Ryder, a tenacious grey representing the American champions Todd Pletcher and John Velazquez. "The ground is on the slow side of good and she just ran very flat," explained a disappointed Dettori. Without a mount in the main event, he had come a long way for such a dismal ride.

The Canadian International, inaugurated in 1938 as the Long Branch Championship at a now-defunct venue, was originally a dirt race for Canadian-bred three-year-olds. Several changes of guise, distance, surface and venue later, it became the race it is today, though it has lost much of its lustre since the beginning of the Breeders' Cup in 1984 – a series that, ironically, it helped to inspire, having fostered growing interest in equine competition on a transatlantic scale as one of the most successful international races in the world in the 1970s and early '80s. The Breeders' Cup soon established a dominant position in the North American programme that could only hurt races like the International and its siblings, the Arlington Million and the older Washington DC International.

Canada's premier race had plenty of lustre to lose, having held championship-defining status for a period in its heyday in the 1970s, when no fewer than five winners of the International ended up being voted North

American turf champions at the Eclipse awards. Just look at the three horses who won between 1973 and 1975, for example. First of them was Secretariat, showing uncanny ability on grass to match his dirt prowess with victory by a record margin of six and a half lengths on his farewell to racing. After 'Big Red' came Lester Piggott and the brilliantly tough French racemare Dahlia, revered on both sides of the Atlantic after a string of top-level successes including a pair in Ascot's midsummer weight-for-age championship, the King George VI and Queen Elizabeth Stakes. Then, in 1975, the previous year's Epsom Derby winner Snow Knight held the late rally of Comtesse de Loir. Exceller, who famously gatecrashed the party of two Triple Crown winners in 1978 when he numbered Seattle Slew and Affirmed among his victims in the Jockey Club Gold Cup, won in Canada in 1977. Despite such an exalted list of winners, there was no appreciable decline for a while – the Arc winner All Along, one of the most esteemed globetrotters in racing history, took the race in 1983 amid her gluttonous spree of the best turf events on two continents.

In recent years, though, the Canadian International has developed a second-division feel compared to the Breeders' Cup Turf. Although theoretically horses can run in both events, in practice their proximity means they seldom do, lending the Canadian race the air of a massively lucrative consolation event. Fortunately, the 2005 renewal looked one of the best of recent years on paper, featuring a number of European contenders who certainly would not have been out of place at Belmont Park six days later.

In retrospect, the race looks even stronger, featuring a couple of horses whose best days were yet to come, headed by the Italian-trained Electrocutionist, a top-class colt with a name straight out of William Burroughs' *Naked Lunch*, where it would have designated those indulging in some obscenely deviant sexual practice in the Interzone. Here, though, it was a three-year-old colt ridden by the multiple Irish champion Mick Kinane who had been beaten just once in his life – and then by a nose – and came to Canada on the back of hard-fought victory in the Juddmonte International at York. Unsurprisingly, he was sent off 6-5 favourite, despite facing a talent-laden field also featuring two immensely powerful Irish rivals in the former Irish Derby winner Grey Swallow, representing international pioneer Dermot Weld, and Yeats, handled by Ballydoyle maestro Aidan O'Brien for Coolmore, the world's most powerful breeding operation, and ridden by Europe's best, Kieren Fallon.

I was sure one of the three would win and bet accordingly, yet on ground softened by heavy overnight rain and persistent drizzle during a bitterly cold, miserably grey afternoon, the Europeans were all upstaged by an American-trained horse, Relaxed Gesture, a convincing 11-1 winner who bided his time behind a generous pace before being produced to win going away in the home stretch. The victory was a tactical masterstroke by jockey Corey Nakatani, who settled his mount well towards the rear, an energy-saving strategy that proved decisive. As the leaders capitulated turning for home, Relaxed Gesture was still back in eighth, yet Nakatani was confident enough to challenge six horses wide around the home turn when Meteor Storm kicked on. He swept past that leader a furlong out to win easily by four and a half lengths.

"I was very patient, I was turning for home and I was still waiting," said Nakatani. "He was going so well underneath me – I went by everybody and I made sure I put them all away. He was much the best."

Grey Swallow stayed on at one pace to finish third after a brave effort in front of Electrocutionist, who didn't enjoy the soft ground, while Yeats faded after chasing the front-runners early on to finish a sorry sixth. "It didn't work out the way I hoped as this horse likes to dominate," said Fallon. "He wasn't really enjoying himself when he couldn't get into the lead but I know he's better than that."

Woody Allen once said that if you want to make God laugh, you should tell Him your plans. Grey Swallow's trainer Dermot Weld probably has the proverb embossed on his psyche after the Canadian International. Weld had been the original trainer of Relaxed Gesture, a talented racehorse who had him eyeing virtually every middle-distance Classic he could find in the early part of 2004 before injury intervened. Yet when Relaxed Gesture finally came good, not before time, with such an emphatic victory, he was under the tutelage of New York-based Christophe Clément, his owners Moyglare Stud having switched him in search of easier opportunities in the US.

So impressive was the winner that it was put to Clément that perhaps he should have been a bit more ambitious and waited a week for the Breeders' Cup Turf. His rationale for taking the easier option was succinct. "I like to be cold and I like to be wet," he said. He couldn't have chosen a better racecourse for that.

For Weld, though, insult was soon added to injury when the stewards disqualified Grey Swallow, his rider Pat Smullen adjudged to have hit Electrocutionist with his whip in the straight. While it was certainly wet at Woodbine, Weld might have reflected that it never rains there but it pours.

*

ALTHOUGH many of the principal equine players in the Canadian International continued to straddle the globe in 2006, their fortunes varied dramatically. Events failed to conspire the way they had in Toronto for Relaxed Gesture, who did not display a similar level of form when well beaten in a number of top North American turf races, including a return trip to Woodbine, where he was last of ten behind Britain's veteran gelding Collier Hill. He should have done better there: for the first time all year, it was cold and wet again. Relaxed Gesture was later sold as a stallion to stand in the Czech Republic.

Electrocutionist, on the other hand, proved himself one of the best horses on the planet. After being sold out of Valfredo Valiani's stable to join Godolphin, he recorded a stirring home victory on the sand under Frankie Dettori in the world's richest race, the Dubai World Cup, in March 2006, when he outduelled top American Brass Hat. That came before a couple of fine runs in a pair of stirring races on his return to Europe, when he finished second to Ouija Board at Royal Ascot and filled the same position behind Hurricane Run in the King George. Sadly, that was Electrocutionist's final run, as he suffered a fatal heart attack at Godolphin's Newmarket base.

Yeats became Europe's top stayer in 2006 by virtue of spectacular successes in the Ascot Gold Cup and the Goodwood Cup before travelling to Australia for the Melbourne Cup, where he finished seventh under a huge weight behind the Japanese one-two in Delta Blues and Pop Rock. Grey Swallow won a Grade 2 race in California for Dermot Weld before being sold to Australian interests as a stallion prospect, though first he ran, without much credit, in the 2006 Cox Plate.

Emma-Jayne Wilson also continued to win admirers as a fully fledged rider in 2006, when she again topped the lists at Woodbine with 144 winners. She also *appeared in Britain, joining our joint-champion apprentice Hayley Turner in the Shergar Cup jockeys' competition at Ascot. Many British racing enthusiasts are disdainful of this concept, but it represented a huge honour for Wilson – and it was fully deserved. In June 2007, she made history when she rode Mike Fox to become the first female to win the Queen's Plate.*

USA (3)

IF the Kentucky Derby is probably my favourite day's racing by a short head over the first day of the Cheltenham Festival, then the Breeders' Cup cannot be far behind. A visit to Belmont Park for the 22nd running of the annual series was one of the principal targets of the trip and, given its history of momentous clashes and era-defining performances, it seemed likely to provide a natural climax before a gentle jaunt back home via a final couple of weeks in Asia.

However, my Breeders' Cup started seven days before the central event of eight Grade 1 Flat races worth at least $1 million with a visit to Far Hills racecourse in New Jersey, about 25 miles west from the city of Newark. There, at a venue situated in a tiny rural town, the 2005 Breeders' Cup kicked off with its less-revered country-hick cousin, the Breeders' Cup Steeplechase.

Sometimes forgotten and often ignored, this glorified hurdle was the highlight of a seven-race jumps card attended by a crowd of around 25,000, scores of them New Yorkers who arrived on a special racetrain that took about an hour out of Grand Central station. Crowd numbers were down, thanks to the foul, inhospitable weather, driving rain and bitter cold. Around 50,000 usually paid up to $100 a head for their annual pilgrimage to a meeting many described simply as 'The Hunt'.

The roads around Moorlands Farm estate housing the racecourse were still completely clogged even an hour after the first race, a huge tailback stretching to the nearest highway and ensuring maximum disruption for the locals in the nearby Bedminster township, dominated by big trees and big houses.

"We're absolutely great neighbours – 364 days a year," said Far Hills co-chairman Guy Torsilieri as he considered the impact of the track's sole race meeting of the year on local residents, several of whom were clearly possessed with an entrepreneurial spirit. Nearly every parking lot carried a sign offering raceday parking, among them the local fire service and the Grace Fellowship Chapel, senior pastor Ed Shuck, where for just $15 you could dump your vehicle, presumably in the hope that the Almighty would be watching over it for the afternoon. Such was the prevalence of these *ad hoc* parking lots that some residents were moved to erect placards saying "no raceparking" in case some blithe visitor fancied abandoning their jalopy on the front porch. After all, everybody else was doing it.

The annual Far Hills meeting offered the richest jumps card in North America with $525,000 in prize-money on offer in total, including $200,000 for the Breeders' Cup Chase itself. A visit to the track revealed the mother of all point-to-points: heaving car parks, the odd coach, portable toilets and charity raffles. Though there were no proper stands, corporate patrons entertained clients in a multitude of striped marquees, while a brigade of SUVs were parked in rows of 50 up the hill that overlooked the racetrack, trunks open for what the locals call 'tailgate parties', featuring ornate displays of food, booze and the odd cigar. Huntsmen acting as outriders accompanied runners and riders to the start of each race from the roped-off section of track that acted as parade ring, adjacent to a two-storey wooden tower housing race officials beside the winning line.

Much of the estate resembled the Glastonbury moshpit after a thunderstorm, but the Far Hills crowd was nothing if not game. A mass of humanity squelched through the mud, clad in waterproof wax jackets, fleeces and rubber boots, populating both the hill and the infield inside the sharp, undulating, anti-clockwise circuit, where viewing opportunities were limited, though there were a couple of big screens.

The grass circuit itself was idiosyncratic, featuring a strip that ran parallel and snugly inside the home straight itself, from which it was separated by a section of crowd before rejoining the outer loop, like Sandown Park's sprint track. From a distance, the effect of watching horses run down this alley was akin to the sadly defunct Great Metropolitan course at Epsom, where horses used to look as if they were running straight through the crowd.

There are a handful of jumping professionals in the US, but the whole thing still had the air of a vast charity fete. My press tickets, for example, had to be picked up in Willy's Tavern, a bar that was acting as event HQ ahead of the meeting, which every year raises thousands for good causes. So much, in fact, that the local hospital was due to open a new wing in 2006, to be called the Steeplechase Cancer Center.

For all that, steeplechasing is regarded as close to an irrelevance in serious American racing circles, an odd historical throwback that involves turf racing and a few enthusiasts close to the eastern seaboard in its heartland states of Maryland, Virginia and Pennsylvania. Even the code's biggest US fans conceded it was small beer. Sean Clancy, a former champion jockey, was painfully aware of the status of a sport he and his brother Joe had done much to promote, not least via their publication *The Steeplechase Times*. "There's usually 50,000 people here," said Clancy. "I bet at least 49,000 of them will come to only this one meet, I'm afraid – and this is by far the biggest day."

Famous historic races like the Colonial Cup and the Maryland Hunt Cup also attract huge crowds – but it is a social scene, a one-off day trip, rather than any more lasting attachment.

American steeplechasing was born out of the early colonists' love of foxhunting, one of many English customs they took with them over the Atlantic. It dates back at least as far as the 1830s, when records exist of a jump race in Washington DC, and now consists of a mixture of hurdle races and timber races. The Maryland Hunt Cup, a four-mile race featuring solid upright obstacles of posts and rails, remains the most prestigious event in the world in the latter category. First run in 1894, this gruelling event takes place at Glyndon, in the heart of American foxhunting country.

Jump racing survives in 12 states, its backbone being such one-day meetings in rural communities, over 30 of which are scheduled every year at regular venues like Camden in South Carolina and Fair Hill, Maryland. The former is home to the Colonial Cup, which used to attract regular British visitors; the latter houses the sport's administration, the National Steeplechase Association, which has 1,000 dues-paying members and licensees – and only four staff.

Prestigious racecourses like Saratoga and Belmont also offer the odd rare steeplechase on Flat-dominated cards, though these are generally few and far between and shunted to the outer parameters of the day owing to their being unpopular with punters and affecting the betting handle.

I wasn't surprised. As I have stated elsewhere, everywhere I came across jump racing outside Europe, it was treated as little more than a curiosity. At least in the States it seemed to be a well-attended curiosity, but that jumping had suffered a fall from grace there was unarguable.

It wasn't so long ago that American-based jumpers were much sought after in Britain. Various Maryland Hunt Cup winners tried their luck on the other side of the pond, among them Jay Trump, American-bred, -owned and -ridden when saddled by the legendary Fred Winter in his rookie season as a trainer to win the Grand National after just eight months in Britain in 1965, and L'Escargot, US steeplechase champion in 1969 before winning a pair of Cheltenham Gold Cups and a Grand National. Several other big US names left their mark in the 1970s and 80s, either after a permanent move or on a temporary visit, such as Fort Devon, sent off 2-1 favourite for the Cheltenham Gold Cup in 1976, or that tough, wiry chestnut Ben Nevis, who also won the National, ridden by US amateur Charlie Fenwick, in 1980. Flatterer finished second to See You Then in the 1987 Champion Hurdle, while Lonesome Glory performed creditably in Britain in the 1990s.

The best import of all, though, was the spectacular Tingle Creek, the breathtaking two-mile specialist who set the chasing world alight when he came to Britain from the States in 1972. In full flow, this swashbuckling front-runner could leave onlookers spellbound with spine-tingling displays of jumping, particularly at Sandown Park, the track that most played to his strengths and remembers his name in the title of a top-class two-mile event every year. The sadness was that he was never as good at Cheltenham.

Sean Clancy, who adores racing in Britain, reckoned American jumpers could still hold their own on a more accomplished stage. "I have no doubt that our best horses and jockeys could be competitive in England but there's no real comparison between the sport in the two countries," he said. "Here it is dominated by just the same handful of people all the time – sadly, there just isn't that much interest."

Although the afternoon's main event was called the Breeders' Cup Chase, it was really a hurdle, with a roll of honour featuring many names well known in Britain, among them dual winner Morley Street, whose two victories sandwiched his memorable success in the Champion Hurdle at Cheltenham in 1991. Well-known British-based riders like Richard Dunwoody, Graham McCourt and Jimmy Frost had also won the race in its early years before it was prorogued after the 1993 running at Belmont. When the Breeders' Cup Chase returned in 2000 after a seven-year hiatus, Far Hills became its permanent venue – but there were no longer any visitors, the $200,000 purse no longer enough of a carrot compared to what was on offer in Britain and Ireland.

The two-mile-five-furlong event featured 14 temporary obstacles that were halfway between a conventional hurdle and a chase fence, a synthetic construct with a steel frame and a plastic brush, just over four feet in height. As there are no conventional chase fences, most US jump races feature these hurdles, though rather more of a jumping test was provided by one of the other races on the card, the New Jersey Hunt Cup, run over three miles, four times under the wire and more than three laps over logs and rails. To excited roars, a bay son of Silver Hawk named Thari got the better of a driving finish in this timber race for trainer Sanna Hendriks, who also saddled the esteemed McDynamo in the Breeders' Cup Chase.

This eight-year-old was seeking an unprecedented Breeders' Cup hat-trick after winning the previous two renewals, but the evidence of four straight defeats before returning to his favourite venue suggested he had lost a step. He also faced a huge rival in the shape of Hirapour, who had beaten him soundly in the Colonial Cup, after which the latter claimed the Eclipse award as the nation's top steeplechaser, despite having been defeated into second at Far Hills. Hirapour had come a long way since his days in Britain as a moderate novice chaser – and he was not alone in making that journey, as the five-strong field also featured former Nicky Henderson-trained Mon Villez. Other expatriates in action included the riders Bob Massey and Xavier Aizpuru, both of whom partnered a winner, and Carl Rafter, while the recently retired David Bentley acted as clerk of the scales. None of these, horses or riders, had been remotely near the best in Britain, but they earned their keep in the States.

After the timber race it was time for a bet, which was more easily said than done, as there was no pari-mutuel operation – and fixed-odds bookmakers were illegal. As a result, many of the tailgaters were running their own sweepstakes, the truly organised having brought along their own blackboards for the purpose of keeping track of who had chosen which horse.

It was surprising to come across two separate operations, both peopled by ancient bookies, taking bets from racegoers in plain sight, in front of boards displaying prices. Attempts to take a photograph of one of them, betting right in front of the main viewing area, provoked a hostile response. "What do you think you're doing?" demanded a 70-year-old with a fistful of dollars and horn-rimmed glasses.

He softened his tone on learning that I was visiting from England, becoming positively friendly when I suggested his efforts amounted to a public service given the absence of alternatives. "Over where you live, bookmakers are considered as gentlemen but here we're frowned upon," he said.

"So, are you legal?" I inquired, disingenuously.

"Kinda," he said. "The track asks us to come in. We wouldn't be right here taking these bets if we weren't allowed to."

Certainly, a blind eye was shown to these layers, who, in any event, were doing scant business. "It's terrible," said my bookie pal. "No-one here knows what they're doing and they all bet among themselves."

Mind you, this was hardly surprising when their prices were taken into account for the Breeders' Cup Chase, on paper the most obvious of two-horse races. It was 1-4 Hirapour, 1-2 McDynamo, 2-1 Three Carat and Understood, and 3-1 Mon Villez, said to be a rank outsider by the *Steeplechase Times*. Now those prices truly were criminal, regardless of the layers' dubious legality. Still, it could have been worse – look at this list of prices for the previous race: 1-2, evens, 6-4, 2-1, 2-1, 5-2, 3-1, 3-1, 4-1.

With the ground riding heavy for the big race, McDynamo galloped off in front at a decent clip, dictating matters throughout. Although Hirapour habitually came with a late run, he had to be cajoled into second, still five lengths off the leader, and didn't seem to be enjoying himself. McDynamo, in his element in the mud, kept pouring on the pressure on the final circuit until Hirapour cracked, leaving McDynamo to jump the last well clear to complete his Breeders' Cup treble. Overall, it was his fifth successive victory at this remarkable once-a-year meeting after a couple of victories elsewhere on the card in earlier years.

Talk about horses for courses.

*

IT was a pity betting wasn't banned a week later at Belmont Park as well. I made a vow after the 2005 Breeders' Cup. Never again would I try to convince myself that I knew my arse from my elbow when it came to gambling on American racing. It made a pleasant change. Usually I give up betting on British racing. Approximately once a year.

The Breeders' Cup as a whole, and Belmont Park Breeders' Cups in particular, have a history of producing scenes of almost unbearable drama. Plans for a year-end US championship multi-million-dollar series were unveiled in April 1982 during Kentucky Derby week. The brainchild of leading Kentucky owner-breeder John Gaines, the world's richest raceday was to include five races on dirt, the traditional surface of US horse racing, plus two turf events as a sop to European visitors, to be hosted by various top American venues. From the outset, a degree of international competition was a vital component as the Breeders' Cup doffed its cap to predecessors like the Washington DC International, the Canadian International and the Arlington Million.

The name 'Breeders' Cup' is derived from its funding mechanism. Breeders pay a nomination fee to make the offspring of their stallions eligible for the series, while a fee is also paid for every foal that is born. Although there are sponsors, the event was designed to pay for itself to a degree, and it duly came into being in 1984 in front of 64,254 racegoers at Hollywood Park with prizes totalling $13m. The centrepiece, the $3m Breeders' Cup Classic, immediately became the world's richest race, won after a fierce battle in the stretch by outsider Wild Again under Pat Day, destined to become a legend at the event.

It didn't take long for the Breeders' Cup to establish itself as the most important day's racing on the global calendar, the place where US championships were decided and European horses were sent to earn their spurs, British contenders almost invariably failing in the early years. Yet by the time its promoters added a subclause to its title describing the extravaganza as the 'World Racing Championships', they had been outgunned in certain respects. The Breeders' Cup remains a fantastic meeting, but it is more of a Ryder Cup, America versus Europe. Though its prize fund is far from shabby with every one of eight races (a new turf race was added in 1999 at Gulfstream Park) worth at least $1m, the Dubai World Cup topped the charts in financial terms in 2006 at the $6m mark. Races in Dubai and Hong Kong and the Japan Cup are more truly international, habitually featuring runners from farther afield.

However, what the Breeders' Cup retains, alongside the undiluted quality of the racing from start to finish across five hours, is an aura of theatre. Nowhere has this been more evinced than Belmont Park, where the Breeders' Cup has produced some remarkable scenes. Take 1990, for example, and the first Cup held at Belmont where a thrilling afternoon – or night, if you watched it on the television in Britain, as I did – went down as one of the most unforgettable days in racing history with a range of emotional highs and lows that can seldom, if ever, have been experienced at a single meeting. Who could forget the opener, an utterly extraordinary Breeders' Cup Sprint? After years of having the dirt kicked in our European faces, the blistering Dayjur, the best sprinter in Europe for 30 years, matched strides throughout with gallant US rival Safely Kept before finally putting her away in the last furlong. Disaster struck yards from the line when he fly-jumped over a shadow in the grandstand, throwing away certain victory by a neck. "We definitely had the best horse but sadly we don't get the money," said Dayjur's crestfallen rider Willie Carson.

Just over an hour later, an all-American Distaff reduced hardened racegoers to tears as an eagerly awaited clash between Bayakoa and Go For Wand ended in tragedy when the latter shattered her foreleg in front of the stands after going stride for stride for more than a mile. Then came the Breeders' Cup Mile, and a victory that still seems scarcely credible. Lester Piggott rolled back the years to drive Royal Academy home for his old sparring partner Vincent O'Brien. Only 12 days after coming back from five years in retirement including a spell detained at Her Majesty's pleasure, the

54-year-old maestro provoked a rapturous reception with a vintage machine-gun finish. Many people consider it the greatest thing they've ever seen on a racetrack.

You would have to go a long way to match that, but successive Belmont Cups also had their moments, such as wild Cheltenham-style celebrations from the all-Irish team behind Mile winner Ridgewood Pearl in 1995, when the Classic was won in record time by Cigar. That's "the unconquerable, the invincible, the unbeatable Cigar!" according to race-caller Tom Durkin.

The 2001 Breeders' Cup at Belmont was the first major international sporting event held in an eerily quiet New York six weeks after the 9/11 attacks. This was probably the greatest race meeting I have ever seen in the flesh. After watching so many top European horses beaten over the years, it didn't hurt that there were winners from Britain, France and Ireland, including the brilliant juvenile Johannesburg on the dirt in the Juvenile, in which he floored the odds-on American favourite Officer. "He's the general, the others are officers!" said winning rider Mick Kinane. A rout was prevented only when Tiznow, the toughest horse in the world at the time, repeated his victory of 2000 in the Classic, inching out Godolphin's Sakhee by a nose after a brutal battle.

After all this, my expectations were sky-high back at Belmont for the 2005 renewal, but this meeting probably won't go down as one of the greatest Breeders' Cups in history. Not from where I was standing, anyway. From an objective perspective, the action on the track was rarely startling; on a personal level, financial disaster beckoned. Somehow I managed to select three out of the eight winners – and ended up backing none of them.

Although I fancied the winner Folklore in the first Breeders' Cup race, the Juvenile Fillies, I left her alone to concentrate on others I liked better later on, smugly congratulating myself on finally having developed the sort of bubble-gum ass that enables a punter to sit out races. My strongest selection of the day came in the Juvenile with the unbeaten First Samurai, whom I had seen win at Saratoga earlier in the summer. Although he was soundly beaten into third after going wide enough round the bend, it was perhaps unnecessary to back three European runners with far-from-obvious chances as well in a bid to take advantage of potential stamina doubts in the US contingent.

Stamina was one thing, but pretty useless when allied to being slow. It could have been a two-mile race and it was doubtful any of these Europeans would have got in a blow, but at least the winner Stevie Wonderboy looked good on a day that just failed to capture the imagination as one potential superstar after another failed to deliver, notably sprinter Lost In The Fog (couldn't win after a four-horse tear-up, dismal) and brilliant ex-Brazilian miler Lesroidesanimaux (bad draw, foot problem, fine effort really to finish second but not much if you've lumped on the horse to win).

The Breeders' Cup raised some important personal questions. Such as: after I had been suggesting all week to anybody who would listen that the European contingent was up against it, how did I manage to allow myself to be suckered yet again by big prices about horses who were unlikely to win?

The Filly & Mare Turf was notable for the presence of the wonderful Ouija Board, well on her way to becoming one of the most popular fillies in British turf history. Owned by Lord Derby, she was in grave danger of giving the aristocracy a good name after a string of top-level victories as a three-year-old in 2004 culminating in victory at that year's Breeders' Cup in Texas. Although injury threatened to curtail Ouija Board's career in the summer of 2005, she had courageously fought her way back to the track and, even though there was a doubt over whether she was as good as she had been, the British superstar was still favourite at Belmont Park. However, even if she retained all her ability, there were significant factors working against her chances, most notably a wide draw in stall 13 of 14, plus the race being slightly shorter compared to 2004. On the plus side, Jerry Bailey was riding her, and she was nearly 4-1 according to the indicative odds on the pari-mutuel screen. So I backed her, only to watch her price tumble, and then watch Intercontinental, a talented rival with stamina doubts, dictate matters from the front.

I knew all about Intercontinental. This filly wouldn't get home unless the rest of the field ignored her, which is why I was left railing against the unjust nature of the world as she bowled along in front with no-one else seeming unduly concerned to trouble her. Such a scenario virtually ensured Ouija Board couldn't win, although Bailey didn't really get serious as soon as I would have liked. She finished a gallant second as Intercontinental stole the race.

Although a small syndicate Pick 6 bet with a few friends I hadn't seen for six months was scuppered at the first possibility thanks to this result, it could have been worse. According to the *Daily Racing Form*, a panel of three punters who put together a $93,312 ticket for account holders on the Americatab online wagering service used nine horses in the Filly & Mare Turf, none of whom were Intercontinental. "Longshots the order of the day," read the *Form* headline after the meeting. No-one found all six winners in the Pick 6; 40 $2 tickets with five winners won $90,324 apiece.

With five races still to go, I suffered ridicule at the on-course cashpoint at the hands of a pair of Brits in the queue, a car dealer from Knightsbridge and an advertising exec now based in New York. "Christ, what chance have we got?" said one of them. "We're only halfway through the card and the bloke from the *Racing Post* has already run out of money!"

At least they gave me a snort of whisky to warm the cockles, and in return I put them on Funfair and Sand Springs at big prices in the Mile. One broke down; the other finished last. There were a couple more losers in races won by further outsiders, and as I had become convinced by the victory of fast-ground lover Artie Schiller that the ground could not be as soft as advertised, I jumped off an ever-accelerating Shirocco bandwagon, despite having bored to death a group of people the previous evening over copious beers at Max Fish on the Lower East Side that the Arc fourth was a stone-cold certainty. If I was so sure about that, exactly why did I back the runner-up Ace? Wasn't nearly 8-1 good enough for me now? Shirocco, trained by the French master André Fabre, was a decisive winner, much to the joy of many Europeans present who weren't me.

By now I had lost all will to live, which was hardly ideal ahead of America's most valuable race, the Breeders' Cup Classic. Having comprehensively turned the tables on his Saratoga conqueror Commentator in a subsequent outing in the Woodward Stakes, Saint Liam and Jerry Bailey were sent off a worthy 9-4 favourite for the Classic, a race worth nearly $4.7m without the field to match the immense prize. Apart from Saint Liam and impressive Jockey Club Gold Cup winner Borrego, there were few who looked to hold a serious chance, albeit in a race that has produced its share of surprises over the years.

Three visitors from Europe, headed by Queen Elizabeth II Stakes winner Starcraft, a former Australian star now trained in England by Luca Cumani and supplemented for $800,000, failed to land a significant blow, while Borrego finished tenth after what his rider described as a "clunker". Though some were worried about the trip and others the draw, Saint Liam did not clunk, despite breaking awkwardly from his box inside Starcraft, who was widest of all, and losing ground as he stepped out to the right. Bailey bided his time before moving Saint Liam up to a solid stalking position down the back stretch alongside Travers Stakes winner Flower Alley, a few lengths off Sun King and Suave in front. Flower Alley and Saint Liam, the latter out wide as usual, moved closer in tandem rounding the turn.

Flower Alley hit the front at the top of the stretch as the front-runners gave in but Saint Liam immediately offered an intimidating presence on his outside, and he took command about a furlong out with a relentless gallop. Though his tenacious rival refused to buckle under, Saint Liam scored by a length, a winning margin that didn't quite do justice to his superiority.

Before the race, Saint Liam looked an obvious winner to anyone with a brain, and 9-4 was an attractive price. But as I was close to potless, instead of backing a horse I had nominated for the race way back at Saratoga in August, I went for a needy-and-greedy and frankly desperate bet on the Irish raider Oratorio, a big price making his debut on dirt. Such horses seldom win, and neither did he. Can I blame the booze and a convivial atmosphere amid people I hadn't seen for six months for such a stupid wager?

The 2005 Breeders' Cup at Belmont concluded with my looking over a haggard punter's shoulder trying to work out form at Golden Gate, still being simulcast in the Belmont handicapping centre. An ignominious end to a shocking day ensued. Some horse I had never heard of and can't remember missed the break and came sixth of seven.

Still, at least the rains had stayed away and Saint Liam was the most worthy of winners, overcoming a stiff draw to cement his status as America's top horse on his final outing before retirement.

Standing at the top of the stand and watching his bright-pink blinkers and silks powering down the outside in front of a backdrop of greens and browns at an autumnal Belmont really did go a long way to alleviating the financial distress. It was the sort of memory I wanted to take home. And that wasn't far away any more.

*

THE amazing McDynamo went back to Far Hills in 2006 and won the Breeders' Cup Chase for the fourth year in a row. By then the race had been rebranded as the Breeders' Cup Grand National, despite the irrelevant nature of the race's obstacles.

The main Breeders' Cup series returned to Churchill Downs in Kentucky in November 2006, when Ouija Board cemented her association with the event with a stunning victory in the Filly & Mare Turf under Frankie Dettori. Early in 2007, it was announced that year's Breeders' Cup at Monmouth Park in New Jersey would become a two-day affair featuring three new races, taking the total to 11 (or 12, if you include the Chase).

Saint Liam, retired soon after the Classic, was named US Horse of the Year for 2005 at the Eclipse awards. After completing his first season at stud in 2006, he fractured his near-hind leg while being led to a paddock at William S Farish's Lane's End Farm in Kentucky, and was put down. "He was in great hands and was being led to his paddock by a man with 25 years' experience," Farish told Blood-Horse magazine. "He didn't rear up. On the path on the way to the paddock, he got a little stirred up and pulled backwards, and in the process lost his footing and fell. His leg went under him in such a way that he ended up falling with all that weight coming down on the top part of the leg. It just shattered everything."

DOMINICAN REPUBLIC

VITAL STATISTICS

RACING

Racetracks	1
Fixtures	156
Races	940
Racehorses	500

BREEDING

Stallions	*unknown*
Mares	*unknown*
Foals	150

FINANCE

Figures unavailable

All figures for 2005

WHAT is it they say about the best-laid plans? Occasionally, things didn't go entirely to plan on the travel front. Like after the Breeders' Cup, when I found myself marooned in a moderately attractive lounge at Fort Lauderdale airport in Florida, an area that had just been hit by Hurricane Wilma. Hit quite hard, it seemed, for while there were no reported fatalities, much of the area was still in darkness – including my intended hotel, shut for business, like most of the others.

Mind you, if I had believed certain scaremongers, I was better off there than my next intended destination, the Dominican Republic. Why was everybody out to scare me? Every time a new country beckoned, it seemed, people were falling over themselves to inform me that I was undoubtedly risking both life and limb by going there.

The Dominican Republic offered the prospect of a wonderful historic capital in Santo Domingo, first city of Christopher Columbus's New World, plus some of the most attractive all-inclusive resorts on the planet and merengue-filled nights mixing with locals whose reputation for friendliness was well-established. Even guidebooks that could usually be relied upon to offer excessive safety warnings refrained from mentioning anything specific to worry about. So why was it that more than one concerned citizen was seemingly hell-bent on ensuring that every second of my stay was spent looking over my shoulder?

"The Dominican Republic? You don't want to go there, it's one of the most dangerous places on earth," suggested a friend who had never been within 3,000 miles of the place. "And isn't it a bit close to Haiti?" he added. "That's even worse."

Then there was the restaurant owner in Fort Lauderdale, a native Dominican. "I don't want to frighten you," he said, before doing his best to frighten me. "Tourists must be very careful. It is embarrassing for me to say it but there are many bad men in Santo Domingo who will hassle you and some will rob you. They will pick your pockets and cut your backpacks."

"I'm not too worried about that," I told him. "I've been to a few places now. It's guns I don't like."

"Everybody carries a gun," he added, helpfully.

Determined in future to stay at home, live in fear and buy things and never take such silly risks again, I boldly set fear aside to venture forth on this dread half-isle, where baseball is a national obsession and both prostitution and cockfighting are legal. All three were more popular than horse racing. Or at least, two of them certainly were and, while no figures were available about the third, I'm willing to hazard an educated guess.

Race meetings take place three times a week to decent crowds at the Hipodromo V Centenario, a sand track about 15 miles east of the city overlooking the Caribbean on the way to the main airport.

While the Dominican Republic never quite managed to scare the living daylights out of me, much of an afternoon at the racetrack proved little other than an exercise in bewilderment. Let me explain.

Having encountered the odd linguistic difficulty at tracks in Spanish-speaking countries, the groundwork was fully prepared ahead of my visit to a six-race card on a Saturday thanks to a helpful member of staff at my hotel. On arrival, I was to be met by one Nicolas Calderon, who spoke English.

There was a snag. After a 25-minute taxi journey driven by a black Shakin' Stevens, denim jacket and denim jeans, my photographer and I arrived at the main stand, a large terracotta building approached via a circular ramp leading to a gaping maw on the second floor. Upon entering, you knew how Jonah must have felt when the whale opened its mouth.

A man with a mobile offered help. I produced a slip of paper with Calderon's name on it, and 2pm, the appointed time of our meeting. But it wasn't to be. Señor Calderon was absent, and it seemed his English wasn't all it was cracked up to be anyway, so my helper knocked on a door, interrupting a dapper gent midway through his lunch. "El Presidente," he said, by way of introduction, and scuttled off.

While 'El Presidente' spoke no English, he did have a smattering of Italian. I didn't, and attempts to convey that perhaps we might try French or German succeeded only as far as making him think I was, in fact, German. He launched into an elaborate animated mime, pointing to his heart and saying words like *"corazon"* and *"tristessa"* as he gestured one whole being split into two with his fists. Though I was far from certain, it was possible he was speaking about families being separated by the Berlin Wall. Either that or he had a severe coronary problem that had been operated on by a German surgeon.

I could not allow this imposture to continue, so I repeated that I was, in fact, *Ingles*, which prompted him to say, "Ah, Margaret Thatcher," with a little too much gusto for my liking. Then he offered, "Tony Blair", pointing to his head in a gesture possibly not designed to imply great intelligence, a suspicion confirmed almost immediately when he said "George Bush" with a similar gesture.

Enthralling as it was, this line of conversation seemed destined to run dry fairly quickly. Fortunately, before any further embarrassment could ensue, a man named Tomas was detailed to show me around, amid promises that a French speaker would soon arrive to answer any questions I could manage in my halting version of the language.

It promised to be entertaining but first Tomas provided a tour of the facilities, including the stables adjacent to the track, where horses at the Estadio Quiquito, third in the owners' list, were cooled by individual fans in every box, a necessity in the intense heat. Most of the horses looked happy enough, although one in particular had eyes pinned so far back that they were virtually touching his tail. I also noticed a dropped syringe in the wood-chip walkway next to the boxes, while there can't have been many flies elsewhere in the Dominican Republic, since most of them were congregating around a wheelbarrow of rubbish left sitting idly near the boxes. Access was denied into one particular yard, El Principado, but it looked a smarter set-up, not entirely dissimilar from a palm-fringed resort.

Tomas took me to the stewards' room, the closed-circuit TV van and the on-site studio in which three grinning presenters were gleefully dissecting the afternoon's action for local Channel 27.

With racing about to begin, we returned to the cavernous public enclosures, which were virtually empty. Racing from nearby Puerto Rico was simulcast on a handful of screens above tote counters, though it was hard to find out up-to-date prices. The screens moved laboriously through each and every exacta combination, while the tote board next to the winning post wasn't working.

Still, the latter offered an opportunity to tell you about a brutally clever marketing strategy by the Presidente beer company, whose logo adorned the board. The company had established a near-monopoly by virtue of having given away modern fridges to bar owners across the country with one stipulation: they sell only Presidente beer.

Two hours had now passed, and while it was impossible to fault the hospitality of the racecourse officials, I knew little more about racing in the Dominican Republic than when I had got there. The cavalry arrived in the shape of a young woman named Miradja, who had been summoned in a taxi from central Santo Domingo to act as interpreter for the day. A Haitian medical student, she actually had nothing to do with the track, but she did speak the odd word of English alongside a better grasp of French. On the downside, Miradja knew nothing whatsoever about horse racing, though it appeared my friend Tomas, who was finally revealed as the track's press director, was keen to teach her to judge from his attentions during the afternoon.

Soon, bits and pieces of possibly misleading or misinterpreted information were forthcoming. This was a very moderate card, but the previous weekend was the Clasico Kalil Hache, the nation's most prestigious race worth 424,000 pesos (£6,430), which drew a crowd of 8,000. No more than 500 were present when I was there.

Although there was scope for around 900 horses at the training centre, numbers were down to around 500, a result of the economic downturn in recent years and presumably responsible for the prevalence of small fields, all of which were in single figures. Dominican horses sometimes raced abroad elsewhere in the Caribbean, among them the unbeaten Triple Crown winner Excelencia, who had just left for Puerto Rico to compete against horses from Mexico, Panama and Venezuela in the following month's Clasico del Caribe. Although Excelencia was beaten by domestic hope Borrascoso, he ran extremely well, finishing second, a length behind the winner, although he was disqualified for interference.

While these bare facts may seem straightforward enough, rest assured they were the result of lengthy, convoluted exchanges in a plethora of half-understood languages. Although the interpreter did her utmost, at times it was an unequal struggle. Suspecting that Puerto Rican racing was the best in the area, I said: "Could you ask Tomas please how the standard of racing in the Dominican Republic compares to places like Puerto Rico, which was being shown on the TV screens?"

"Twenty-five," came the answer.

Perhaps they thought I was asking about life, the universe and everything. "Since 1980," Tomas added, unfathomably.

There was no obvious improvement when I tried a question about the number of foals – baby horses was how I described them – in the Dominican Republic.

"One a year," Tomas said, via Miradja.

Later I learned that while homegrown numbers were down, about 300 of the existing equine population were horses imported from the USA, low-grade animals populating a programme consisting mainly of cheap claimers.

My attention was drawn to an intriguing scene behind the stalls for the second race, where all the jockeys dismounted to be frisked. They were looking for electronic devices and the like, it emerged, though the scene is bizarre, jockeys being asked to remove their helmets in a line as they were searched by a team of security guards. This happened before every race.

Next came a visit to the Jockey Club rooms, where open-necked shirts and polos were the norm. As I examined posters of former national equine greats, like Felo Flores, a US import who won 37 races between 1967 and 1970, 'El Presidente' reappeared – and it emerged that he wasn't the president at all, but the vice-president. The head honcho was the errant Calderon, who never did show.

Anyway, the vice-president greeted the owner of the All-Star stable, who were topping the owners' list. The latter was a tall fellow in blue-checked shirt and jeans, with trainers and a big flashy silver watch. The interpreter and the vice-president said something in Spanish, which this new figure interrupted with a smile, in perfect English, to introduce himself. "He is telling her to introduce me," he laughed. His English ought to have been quite good, because he was Moisés Alou, a baseball player with the San Francisco Giants home for the winter indulging his passion for horse racing.

"I go a lot in the States, to Golden Gate and Bay Meadows," said Alou. "I always try to go when we are on the road – Del Mar is my favourite. It's not as pretty here," he added, gesturing across the track, "but it's all we've got and at least the view is nice."

Alou played a role in one of the most ridiculous stories in recent US sporting history in his days as a Chicago Cub. Everybody's second-favourite team, the Cubs have been perennial losers since winning the World Series in 1945. They were one game away from getting back to the finals in 2003 when a mishit ball from their opponents the Florida Marlins flew towards Alou in the outfield. If he had made the catch, the Cubs were as good as back to the World Series – but life-long fan Steve Bartman knocked the ball from his grasp as he tried to catch the ball himself. Alou chucked down his glove in disgust, and the Marlins went on to progress at the Cubs' expense. Bartman left the Cubs' famous Wrigley Field stadium under police protection.

Thinking it best not to remind him of the incident, I asked Alou instead if many of his baseball colleagues were keen on horse racing. "Not really but they like the betting," he said. "But the other Dominican players prefer cockfighting."

Alou had a runner named Teresito in the best race of the day, a five-and-a-half-furlong two-year-old event worth 67,000 pesos (£1,120). I ignored it and risked 100 pesos (£1.50) on Bonnita, who had beaten Teresito on their previous outing, but neither of them landed a blow behind the winner El Campeon, the 1-2 favourite who nailed a runaway leader on the line to much shouting from the stand, where the crowd makes up for in enthusiasm what it lacks in numbers.

Runners for the fifth race soon entered the charming little parade ring. As had been the case for much of the day, the majority of them were blinkered, in a variety of colours, while some had flowers and paper bows embroidered into their tails.

The day ended with a couple of competitive heats. One of Alou's horses was touched off in a photo, while the last featured a thrilling finale, four horses in a line stretched right across the track. With a tanker on the horizon miles out into the Caribbean as the day turned to dusk, it made for an exciting climax to an interesting, if occasionally confusing, afternoon.

Shakin' Stevens was waiting to take me back to my old house in the capital ahead of my departure in the morning bound for Asia, which was a shame as everyone couldn't have been more welcoming.

Admittedly I didn't make a habit of testing out dark, uninhabited streets at night and doubtless, like any city of one million-plus inhabitants, Santo Domingo possessed its less-than-savoury parts. But there were more tourist police than tourists in the central Zona Colonial district of Santo Domingo and, frankly, I've been more frightened at Fakenham.

You know what some of those backwoodsmen are like after a barrel-load of scrumpy.

SINGAPORE

VITAL STATISTICS

RACING

Racetracks	1
Fixtures	69
Races	657
Racehorses	916

FINANCE

Total prize-money	$23.6m
Betting turnover	$936.21m

All figures for 2005

BREEDING
None

THE final leg of the tour focused on three weeks back in Asia and three race meetings, culminating in the Japan Cup, one of the continent's showpiece international events.

First, though, came one of the continent's showpiece international racecourses, the sumptuous Kranji, without question one of the best things about Singapore. Not that it is overwhelmed with competition. Clean and safe, middle class and middle-aged, this hermetically sealed island nation might not be the place to visit if you are after a little sex, drugs and rock 'n' roll. I was happy enough with the racing.

Singapore is one of the most prosperous nations in the world outside western Europe, which it matches in terms of *per capita* GDP. Less attractively, its detractors might also point to a long-held reputation as a virtual police state since independence from neighbouring Malaysia in 1965. While such an exaggerated view was slowly becoming outdated, the affluent city state of about 3.3 million inhabitants on a land mass about the size of the Isle of Wight retained a distinctly sanitised air. Apart from in its prisons, perhaps, where both capital and corporal punishment were still extant. Not, however, for such serious outrages as jaywalking, chewing gum on the subway or littering. Such serious outrages merely carried fines.

Stepping into the bottom level of the giant four-storey state-of-the-art grandstand at the ultra-modern Kranji racecourse was like entering another country. A smoky betting hall full of pari-mutuel counters, LED odds boards and TV screens (34 plasmas among a total of 274) was well populated with locals who thought nothing of dropping used betting slips on the floor, just as they do at racetracks everywhere else.

On leaving the MRT (Mass Rapid Transit) station to enter the track via a covered walkway past palm trees and banks of lockers designed for the deposit of mobile phones – banned on the ground floor, silent or vibrating mode in the more upmarket enclosures – I was greeted by a familiar hawking sound. A local punter cleared his windpipe with an expansive full-throated rasp before propelling a sizeable greenie on the floor. Welcome back to south-east Asia. It was a surprise he wasn't fined.

Singapore was colonised by the British in 1819 when Sir Stamford Raffles established a port on the island and signed a treaty with the East India Company to develop its commercial potential as a significant trading post. Horse racing, introduced to the Malayan peninsula in 1802, soon crossed the strait in Raffles' wake. The Singapore Sporting Club was founded in 1842 by a group of enthusiasts on a piece of swampy land that is now a sports complex. Records are suspiciously precise concerning the date of their first race, said to have taken place on February 23, 1843, for a prize of S$150, although ponies from Java and China dominated until horses were imported from Australia in the late 1880s. The Straits Racing Association, later the Malayan Racing Association, was formed in 1896 to govern the sport in Singapore and three Malaysian turf clubs, Penang, Perak and Selangor.

During a colourful century of existence, the original racecourse grounds were used for varied activities, including the landing of the first aircraft on the island, before the Turf Club moved its home in 1933 to Bukit Timah, a rubber estate in central Singapore and the home of Singaporean racing until 1999. Japanese occupation during the Second World War curtailed racing until 1947, after which the sport remained an exclusive pursuit among the social elite for another decade and more. Race meetings were confined to owners and members until 1960, when the public was finally allowed to attend. Yet although Bukit Timah boasted a 50,000-capacity stand, as Singapore's economy continued to expand in the modern era, the racecourse faced massive problems with traffic congestion and noise pollution. The government offered the Turf Club a suitable site with excellent transport links for a new venue in return for Bukit Timah's 140 hectares. The latter is now a highly desirable residential area.

Kranji, one of the most modern racecourses and training centres in the world, was officially opened in 2000 in the northern part of the island, 20 minutes from the city centre, with the inaugural running of the Singapore Airlines International Cup, worth S$3 millon (£1.03m). The nation's foremost race regularly attracts runners from around the world. In 2005, it was won by Australia's Mummify, who beat Britain's Phoenix Reach and Alexander Goldrun from Ireland; a year later, it went to Cosmo Bulk of Japan from locally trained King And King and Bowman's Crossing from Hong Kong.

While there used to be much interchange between Singapore and Malaysia, an outbreak of the Nipah virus in 1999 that affected both livestock and humans instigated a cross-border ban on equines rescinded only in 2005, once proper quarantine procedures were in place. Jockeys, though, like multiple champion Saimee Jumaat, who once rode in the Shergar Cup jockeys' competition at Ascot, regularly make the short hop north over the causeway, and a simulcast service covered both countries, adding Hong Kong and certain meetings in Western Australia for good measure.

Kranji was an extremely impressive set-up featuring no fewer than seven circuits: both a turf and an artificial Fibresand all-weather surface for racing, the outer left-handed oval measuring 2,000 metres, plus five more training tracks. The huge glass-fronted grandstand clad in stainless steel overlooked a big screen and massive electronic pari-mutuel board behind the winning post. Tall floodlight pylons illuminated the circuit, situated beside the island's wildlife-abundant central rainforests of the Central Catchment Area, featuring the MacRitchie Reservoir.

A crowd of around 10,000 populated a stand capable of housing three times as many as when I was there for a moderate nine-race Friday-night meeting. There had been at least 20,000 in attendance five days previously for the Singapore Gold Cup, the nation's second-richest contest worth S$1.25 million (£430,000).

A rigid class system of sorts appeared to be in operation at the racecourse, where the bottom non-air-conditioned floor cost S$3 (about a pound) to enter, compared to S$7 (£2.40) for the next floor up, fully air-conditioned with a fine view behind the huge glass frontage. Although the rank and file could enter the third floor for S$20 (£6.80), owners and invited guests populated the top two floors. Here it must be admitted that I spent a sizeable proportion of the evening up there with the corporate prawn-sandwich brigade being wined and dined by the Singapore Turf Club. And very pleasant it was too.

There were few white faces discernible on the ground floor, where an eclectic range of food options is available. Besides the usual fast-food outlets offering chicken pie and pizza, local delicacies on offer included 'glutinous meatball with gingko nut' and 'grass jelly ice', the choice reflecting Singapore's schizoid persona, hugely westernised and rampantly commercial, with pockets of Chinese and Indian culture surviving alongside.

With no homegrown breeding system, Singapore's racing structure is populated purely by imports, mainly low-level older geldings from Australia and New Zealand, with a few from other places like South Africa and India thrown in. Former European horses, more expensive, tend to figure only towards the upper end of a structure based on a system of five classes.

Although the card was mediocre – in an unguarded moment, one expatriate employed at the track described it as "crap races for crap horses" – the prize-money was startling. Comprising poor six- and seven-furlong events plus a couple of maidens for younger horses, these races carried a minimum purse of $38,000 (£13,000), while the evening's best event, featuring some better-class animals, was worth $100,000 (£34,300). Unlike nearly everywhere else, there were full fields of 14 for the majority of races.

A visit to the parade ring before one early race was well worth the effort. Overlooked by yet another colossal odds board, the public had access from one side only from a banked semi-circular viewing area, all under cover but airy nonetheless. The effect was not unlike an open-air theatre. It would have been no surprise to see an actor in doublet and hose with a donkey's head take centre stage ahead of a performance of *A Midsummer Night's Dream*.

All the racehorse attendants were uniformed, apart from one individual who made a bid for free expression with a loud Hawaiian-style shirt. With hindsight, he may have reflected that he should have stuck to the regulation green polo shirts.

Back upstairs in the posh enclosure, I was introduced to Larry Foley, an Australian who ran the racecourse's ownership syndicates. Though he had a vested interest, he made having a horse in Singapore sound like an ownership dream. With appearance money of S$750 (£255) for almost every runner, it was possible to have a horse in training for only S$1,000 (£340) a month, supposing it ran twice, which was likely if the horse was sound. "There are so many races for a good horse," said Foley. "And we're second only behind Macau in terms of number of runs per horse."

With three syndicates, Foley had 150 owners and 13 horses under his wing. "It's been good but it's a while between drinks," he laughed. "We've not had a winner for a couple of months – and we fancied Sapphire Gold, our runner in the first, but he didn't run very well so I've got about 50 people chasing after me at the moment."

Ownership had recently become a more attractive proposition when laws on off-track gambling were loosened so that bets could be placed at lottery outlets and the like. A new cable TV channel covering live racing was another boon. "In the past, you couldn't see a result from here for an hour," said Foley.

To an extent, the move was necessitated by a dramatic downturn in betting turnover, which dropped by a quarter from £646m in 2000/01 to £490m five years later. Like Hong Kong, the slump could be traced back to competition from football betting; like Hong Kong, money raised from betting was used by the state for charitable causes.

Otherwise, however, Foley baulked at the comparison. "It is not really valid in ownership terms," he said. "It is just stupid there because everyone wants a horse but here we are still short on owners and we're not at capacity for horses – we have room for 1,000 but there's only about 900 here."

The next visitor was a stocky, smiling Irishman, who turned out to be the trainer Danny Murphy, one of many expatriates operating in Singapore alongside former Melbourne Cup-winning trainer Laurie Laxon and Englishman Tim Pinfield, at one time a conditional jockey for trainers Josh Gifford and Philip Mitchell. Pinfield trained successfully in the States before moving to Asia, being best known for the top sprinter Big Jag, who won the Dubai Golden Shaheen and was placed in both the Breeders' Cup Sprint and the Hong Kong Sprint.

Murphy, sporting a perpetual smile, had every right to look pleased with himself, as he was somewhat richer than he had been the week before. Only a few days previously, he saddled Terfel, bought out of Michael Bell's Newmarket yard, to win the Singapore Gold Cup. And what's more, after an owner dropped out, Murphy owned the horse as well – which meant he collected a fair few dollars for the victory.

In this context, his one-word answer when I asked him to quantify the attractions of training in south-east Asia compared to home was less than surprising. "Money," he said, eyes twinkling. "This is the only place in the world where there's appearance money for every runner. The facilities are the best in the world and the people are so nice, it's a great environment to work in."

Murphy's father John trained for 30 years on the Curragh in Ireland before his son, a former jockey, took over in 1990. The latter arrived in Singapore via Macau. "I love Asia and the standard of racing has improved here," he said, clearly not obviously afflicted with homesickness. Perhaps the conversation should have ended there, but the dreaded happened before Murphy moved on. He gave me a tip in a six-furlong event. "He's called Welcome Back – he's very consistent, never runs a bad race, and we've got KB Soo, who's the leading jockey at the moment," said Murphy. Eyeing the torrential downpour that had just started outside, Murphy added: "He likes the soft as well. What more do you need?"

Soo dutifully partnered a winning favourite in the event that immediately preceded Welcome Back's race, ahead of which a team of racetrack employees in yellow waterproofs and galoshes braved the heavy rain to repair divots. The ground was now soft, having been officially described as yielding earlier on.

Welcome Back's last six runs featured three on soft ground: one win and two seconds. It looked good – but he was the 6-5 favourite. My photographer asked Murphy for a mugshot. "Get my picture after the race when we've won," he said. You know the rest. It is boring to listen to other people's hard-luck stories *ad nauseam* so I will spare you the grim details, but Welcome Back ran a shocker, not even placed after folding dramatically two furlongs out in a contest won by a horse trained by Tim Pinfield. However, any financial damage was rectified by a winning tiercé (trifecta) featuring the first three favourites in the next race, boxed each and every way for a total of six bets. It paid 20-1, in reality just over 3-1 given my permutations, but enough to get me smiling like a Murphy.

Downstairs in the cheap seats, the punters were really warming to the occasion, cheering in animated fashion for the last couple of furlongs of every race in a manner that belied the cliché about Singaporean reserve.

Although the first half of the card was marked by a succession of favourites smashed out of sight, results appeared easier to predict later on, and the volume was turned up a couple of notches during one particular race in which Saimee's mount Fast Tycoon, sent off 2-1 favourite after a huge plunge, just held on from a stablemate in a crunching finish. Frenetic stuff, it prompted desperate shouting from the ground floor of the stand as the locals clambered on benches to get a better view.

In his ground-breaking book *Picking Winners*, published in 1975, revered US journalist Andrew Beyer considered the life of a punter. "A gambler may have as many periods of pain and frustration as he does of exhilaration," he says. "But at least he knows he's alive."

It seemed to be the same everywhere. Even in Singapore, where they can probably do with a shot of adrenalin now and again.

*

TRAINER Danny Murphy may have enjoyed himself in Singapore, but that did not stop his accepting a job in the summer of 2007 to train in Bawtry, South Yorkshire, with 50 horses owned mainly by the Scottish football agent Willie McKay. "It's a chance in a lifetime," said Murphy. "It's too good an opportunity to turn down."

PHILIPPINES

VITAL STATISTICS

RACING		FINANCE	
Racetracks	2	Total prize-money	$5.35m
Fixtures	129	Betting turnover	$58.67m
Races	1,368		
Racehorses	1,576		

All figures for 2005; aside from racetracks and breeding, they refer to Manila Turf Club only

BREEDING	
Stallions	72
Mares	1,250
Foals	520

CONTRARY to the impression given by this book, I did manage to do a few things unconnected to horse racing during eight months on the road. You have been spared the gory details of a 24-hour return journey from Australia back to Europe to act as best man at a wedding on the Greek island of Syros, or the week-long drive from Arizona to Boulder, Colorado, and back via the Rockies. Rest assured, though, that if they had been racing in Athens or Monument Valley in Utah, you would have heard all about it.

Yet far from becoming tedious in its regularity, even when the racing was short of intoxicating, it provided a welcome focus to the journey for someone to whom the notion of hippy-style drifting is not far off anathema. Going to the racetrack never became a bit of a chore, as several people asked after I returned, although perhaps it should be remembered that it would be a struggle to find a more obsessive individual. Jane, too, maintained her enthusiasm for the racing. Or said she did, anyway.

Thankfully, there was seldom any shortage of variety. The least interesting days were those that felt overly familiar, those closest to the British model, and even they had their moments. By the time I reached my penultimate destination, however, the thought of returning to everyday life was hanging heavy. Before then I was hoping to encounter an equine thriller in Manila.

*

AS they raced six days a week, 52 weeks a year, it was straightforward enough to find a race meeting in the Philippines, where racing started in the mid-19th century and remains a popular sport, servicing hundreds of off-course betting shops.

The Manila Jockey Club was formed in 1867 by a group of sportsmen led by the Spanish general of the Philippines. Initial members were descendants of the most affluent sectors of society, leading lights in government and business, who raced Philippine ponies once a year over a quarter-mile track between a pair of churches in the Quiapo district. When this site became a commercial centre, the track was moved to a rice field in Santa Mesa, at the end of what is now Hippodromo Street in modern Manila. More meetings were held every year, and when racing was suspended temporarily for the conflict that brought Spanish rule to an end, it started again just a few months after the capital's occupation by American forces in 1899.

Racing was popularised by the introduction of betting as early as 1903, three years after the Manila Jockey Club found a permanent home at the original San Lazaro. Two more tracks were founded in the 1930s: a short-lived enterprise at Cebu and the Philippine Racing Club, run by Filipino and American businessmen. The latter claims to have been responsible for ushering in the thoroughbred era in Philippine racing with the import of Australian horses after being founded in 1937.

Apart from another extended break for the Pacific War, when Manila fell to Japanese forces, the two remaining Filipino tracks have continued to exist side by side, both contributing large sums to charitable causes and taxes to government. Now they each operate their own dirt track from Tuesday to Sunday on alternate weeks, with 13- or 14-race cards at the weekend.

Santa Ana racecourse, operated by the Philippine Racing Club, is situated right in the middle of Manila in the district of Makati City, commercial centre of a chaotic capital, a metropolis full of shopping malls, skyscrapers and noxious fumes, and seemingly in a state of near-perpetual gridlock. While I could have walked to Santa Ana from my hotel – roadblock, armed guards, bodyscan on entry plus bag search – it wouldn't have made much sense, as my visit to the friendly south-east Asian island chain coincided with the other racetrack's turn at the plate. Although San

Lazaro was still operated by the Manila Jockey Club, the racecourse is situated about 40 kilometres north of the capital in a leisure park adjacent to the town of Carmona, the operation having been moved in 2002 from its former, much more accessible location.

With no public transport worth the name going that way, a $40 taxi was the only option. "You will need to allow at least two hours because of the traffic," said the concierge at my hotel. Just to be on the safe side, I left at 3.30pm ahead of an eight-race card scheduled to start at 6pm. Barely 30 minutes later, the taxi zipped through ugly Carmona to a much leafier area of residential developments and parkland. "Less pollution here," said the awestruck taxi driver. There could hardly have been any more.

I entered the grandstand at 4.10pm, somewhat ahead of schedule, though this was just as well, as your correspondent was soon embarking on the mother of all meet and greets. Foreign visitors to San Lazaro Leisure Park were few and far between and the employees of the Manila Jockey Club were falling over themselves to make me feel at home. As a series of barrier trials took place out on the left-handed oval track beneath us, I was introduced to deputy chief executive, racecourse manager, senior handicapper, racing-channel broadcaster and leading trainer. Uncle Tom Cobley was absent, but unlike the racecourse chairman, he didn't phone one of his underlings to apologise for not being there to welcome me in person.

A young whippersnapper was dispatched to collect a mounted map of the racecourse facilities. Blackboard pointer in hand, the deputy CEO, Rear-Admiral Juan de Leon, proceeded to enlighten me on the various buildings, stable blocks and paddocks. It felt a little like being back in the classroom; perhaps they were planning an exam.

Racecourse manager Jose Alfredo Valdes then took me on what his boss described as a "windshield tour" of the premises. Bizarrely, this involved an extended visit to a show home overlooking the track in the Canyon Ranch development, prior to a quick spin around the on-site training centre. Unlike Canyon Ranch, the latter was by no means at the luxury end of the market, a ramshackle affair peopled by youths displaying their chests amid the oppressive heat, still sweat-inducing despite darkness having fallen half an hour previously. In the circumstances, it was tempting to dive into the equine swimming pool, which my guide told me was already extremely popular with trainers.

Following the US model, workouts at the track were officially timed and made available to the public. "Some horses go straight from here to the races without posting any trials," said Valdes. "Without the timing, people can win big bets at big prices."

Returning to the grandstand, I was treated to a routine from broadcaster Jay-R Cabansag, a Filipino version of Derek Thompson sporting larger-than-life shades and a personality to match. Much to the delight of the Rear-Admiral, Jay-R entertained us with a variety of mock racecalls in various languages, from English to Japanese and Korean. He really should have been on a bigger stage somewhere else. Or just somewhere else would have done.

A few tables away, trainers were drawing lots for post position ahead of Sunday's stakes race, a championship race for imported horses. "Although we have studs in the provinces, most of the stock comes from abroad," explained trainer Jose Panhilio, who had previously owned horses at the Meadowlands in New Jersey.

"I liked it so much I came home and tried to train myself here," he said. "Our racing is improving. I think it's ready to explode – we've had a big increase in prize-money. In the last five years it has gone up by 15 per cent per year, and the quality of breeding and horses is getting up there."

There was still a long way to go. While around 1,500 people were employed in an industry serviced by nearly 2,000 racehorses, a leading Filipino performer had only recently made a rare foray abroad, to race in Singapore. He could finish only fifth in a relatively minor event.

The locals clearly liked a bet, the average turnover for a moderate night meeting standing at around 25 million pesos (£260,000), and going up to around 40 million (£420,000) for top stakes races, like the three legs of the domestic Triple Crown, held in May, June and July and alternating between the Manila tracks. A multitude of exotic wagers were on offer, among them daily Pick 6s, daily doubles, pentafectas and the super six. The last two, unfathomably popular, required you to name either the first five or the first six home in the correct order.

There was, however, a huge problem with illegal gambling, according to Panhilio. "If our handle is 50 million, then there must be the same amount in illegal gambling," he said. "If we could control it, the handle would go through the roof. Basically, though, the racing is pretty honest. There used to be problems – you would find people pulling their mounts – but I would say 80 per cent are out to win now after the increases in prize-money."

That still left 20 per cent unaccounted for, and headlines had been made shortly before my visit over an investigation into a racehorse owner who had allegedly threatened to shoot a jockey who did not follow instructions to lose a particular race at Santa Ana. "I can buy your life, I will kill you," the owner was reported to have said. "Hotheads have no place in sports," concluded the *Philippine Daily Inquirer*, which suggested racing officials should "wield the big stick".

Stick or not, the vigilance of the local stewards at San Lazaro was demonstrated later in the evening when one particular horse, sent off favourite for a sprint, was banned for an indefinite period for posting a time more than three seconds slower than its previous start over course and distance. Such a performance was deemed below the required standard, rather like a professional foul in snooker.

One of the racecourse stewards was a greying gent by the name of Francisco Fernando, who was employed on the Curragh for a spell in the 1970s, when he worked for trainer Stephen Quirke and even rode work in the morning on the stable's star performer, Parnell, runner-up to Brigadier Gerard in the 1972 King George at Ascot. He also rode in a number of races in Ireland. "One time I was following Lester," Fernando told me. "All I could see was his backside it was so high."

San Lazaro's bijoux stand was modelled on Singapore's Kranji, only smaller and nowhere near as smart. Then again, any more space would have been wasted, as only around 300 people turned up at the meeting, the majority preferring to do their betting in the nation's 330-plus betting shops. Even a big day, such as the Presidential Gold Cup in early December, attracted only around 4,000 to the track.

Security guards with rifles slung over their shoulders joked around next to a confectionary stand decorated with fairy lights. A recorded version of the national anthem was played over the PA system. Although the laid-back, unfussy locals stood up, there was still much laughing and joking to be heard. Try that in America.

Although the scheduled off-time of the first race was 6pm, it was nearly half an hour late. As had been the case in Thailand at the very start of the racing road, a couple of horses were in the stalls for 20 minutes more than their rivals, which probably explained why one of them lost about ten lengths when someone finally bothered to open the gate. The horse in question was soon nearly a furlong adrift, which wasn't bad going in a five-furlong event, in which the field was strung out like Pete Doherty after a night on the tiles. The horse who trailed in last looked about as healthy as the rock star as well, barely cantering as he passed the post miles behind the 1-10 winner.

Later races proved more competitive, very much akin to US-style racing, but there was still a shock in the second race, which took place on an inner circuit I had assumed was a training track. Forget Chester; this was more like the Palio in Siena, though thankfully they didn't race on pavement in the Philippines.

Following a few more races, the Rear-Admiral grabbed me for a stint on Philippines TV, Jay-R moving aside for a few seconds as I was asked what I made of their set-up based on the briefing he had given me a couple of hours earlier. This was worrying, for Royal Ascot it wasn't. Looking at large, unsightly mounds of displaced earth, the track looked more like a building site than a racecourse. It was a mess.

Then again, as the lights of the city twinkled in the distance and the occasional bat divebombed the crowd from the roof of the stand, it was still a unique place to watch horse racing.

Or at least, that's what I told the Rear-Admiral. Even if the content wasn't up to much, surely I deserved an A+ for tact and diplomacy.

JAPAN (2)

THE Japanese make a point of looking after their guests ahead of the country's flagship international event, the Japan Cup. Three days before the 2005 running in Tokyo, visitors were treated to a lavish banquet at the Century Hyatt hotel featuring crab and caviar terrine, foie gras, scallops and Japanese steak, washed down with more than the odd glass of fine wine. It sounded nice, particularly after weeks of dining on less rich fare. While I am no expert on caviar, I would have been prepared to give it a go. So it was a shame that I arrived back in Tokyo, my final destination, the day after the feast, having spent the previous night in a featureless airport hotel in Osaka after contriving to miss the necessary connecting flight. Bet your heart bleeds.

Had I been there with the other journalistic freeloaders, I would have heard Masayuki Takahashi, president and CEO of the Japan Racing Association, tell his guests about Haseiko, the horse who popularised horse racing in Japan in the 1970s, when he became a national hero.

Deep Impact had already attained even greater iconic status in Japan in 2005. While I had been fighting off the horrors of flies, dust and bus trips into the Outback at Birdsville, losing more than I had at the Breeders' Cup and suffering acute linguistic embarrassment in the Dominican Republic, this fantastic colt was busy recording a spectacular sequence of victories in his nation's Triple Crown, starting with that memorable performance in the Satsuki Sho in April. He was still unbeaten in seven starts, never having started at a price longer than 1-3.

Having been mesmerised once by Deep Impact, I had returned to Japan specifically to round everything off with another glimpse of him in action. Yet while I eventually made it to the Japan Cup, Deep Impact did not, his connections preferring to wait for Japan's biggest domestic race, the Arima Kinen on Christmas Day.

Even without Deep Impact, the Japan Cup weekend proved no sort of anticlimax, producing two of the most rousing Group 1 finishes of 2005 or any other year. Also commonly known as Fuchu after the district in which it stands, Tokyo racecourse and its wide, sweeping left-handed circuit is situated to the north west of the city centre. It is readily accessible via a frighteningly efficient public-transport network, the best options including a special train that takes 30 minutes on the Keio line from Shinjuku station, in the heart of the neon-drenched skyscraper district, or a five-minute walk from Fuchu-honmachi station on the JR Musashino line.

The Japan Cup meeting covered both days of the last weekend in November, starting on the Saturday with the younger, and less-celebrated dirt version of the race. Less celebrated, and worth considerably more than £1 million, that is. A crowd of 53,000 turned up, and we were treated to a classic as the three-year-old Kane Hekili just held on in a blistering three-way battle to the wire from two of his compatriots. The winner was ridden by Deep Impact's jockey Yutaka Take.

Three foreign visitors were routed, two US dirt specialists finishing down the pan and Eccentric, Britain's all-weather horse of the season, doing worst of all. The Lingfield Winter Derby winner's audacious bid for one of the world's top dirt prizes was akin to Accrington Stanley winning a few minor matches and then thinking they can take on Manchester United at Old Trafford. It ended with a predictable result. Eccentric was stone last of 16 runners, well adrift of the 15th-placed horse.

After the race, the 11th of a 12-race card, I could scarcely believe the scene as I walked back to the station, more akin to Wimbledon tennis than a racecourse. The walkway was lined by racing enthusiasts queuing ahead of the following day's big race. They already had tickets; they were just keen to secure a prime position on the rails.

*

ALTHOUGH a massive crowd of 95,635 was reported the following day, this figure was well below the record of 187,524 achieved eight years previously. Such is the popularity of the Japan Cup.

Those who did show up were hardly short in the fervour department. Packed ten deep around the parade ring from early on, they draped banners over the rails in support of their favourite jockeys and horses, all of whom had official fan clubs. "I wish a victory," read one to pin-up boy Yutaka Take, written in that strangely charming, formally polite version of English often employed by bilingual Japanese. Take might have been the crowd's favourite, but it seemed Frankie Dettori's popularity had not been lost in translation. He received plenty of rides from Japanese trainers over the weekend, most of them ending up among the favourites.

Beset by a lower profile in comparison to the Breeders' Cup, the Japan Cup is a vastly more international event. Since the inaugural running went to the American mare Mairzy Doates in 1981, winners of the mile-and-a-half race have come from Britain, France, Ireland, Italy, Germany, Australia and New Zealand, as well as Japan. Six of the last seven winners had been domestically trained, a significant pointer to the rapidly improving nature of Japanese stock.

The 18-strong field assembled for the 2005 running looked one of the strongest in history, with an Arc winner in top-class French colt Bago plus two horses with victories at the Breeders' Cup in Ouija Board and US-trained Better Talk Now. The visiting team also included Warrsan, a multiple Group 1 winner for Clive Brittain, and Alkaased, ridden by Dettori for his mentor Luca Cumani. Although the latter had broken through at the top level with a Group 1 victory in France in the summer, Cumani and owner Mike Charlton were on a recovery mission after an ambitious global campaign had threatened to blow up in their faces. After being rested ahead of the autumn's big international races, Alkaased had already been forced to miss both the Arc and the Breeders' Cup in annoying circumstances for his connections. A small cut became infected just before the former; an unsatisfactory blood count scuppered plans to run in the US. At least these setbacks ensured he arrived a fresh horse in Tokyo for the Japan Cup, where conditions were certain to suit him, rock-hard ground and a guaranteed fast pace being tailor-made.

The home defence looked formidable, however, headed by the 2004 winner Zenno Rob Roy, a short-priced favourite to become the first horse to win back-to-back runnings of the Japan Cup. His compatriots included Heart's Cry, a regular at the top level, plus another previous winner in Tap Dance City, who had scored in 2003.

Such a stellar field produced one of the races of the season. Tap Dance City set a scorching pace, and it looked for a moment after he turned for home with a five-length lead as if he had stolen the race. Kieren Fallon kicked the gallant Ouija Board hard in pursuit and Zenno Rob Roy arrived on the scene in menacing fashion on the outside. Tap Dance City folded two furlongs out, while Ouija Board soon flattened out, leaving Alkaased to grab the favourite a furlong out under the strongest of drives from Dettori, who had ridden a peach, biding his time after angling his mount across to the rails from a wide draw at the start. Alkaased was immediately attacked by domestic hope Heart's Cry, who sneaked up the British horse's inner with a desperate late lunge, drifting across Ouija Board in the process. With the near-100,000 crowd going mad in the stands, Alkaased and Heart's Cry crossed the line seemingly in unison ahead of the vanquished Zenno Rob Roy.

Given the hosts' reputation for promptness in declaring results, it was an agonising few minutes until Alkaased's number appeared on the screens to indicate that he had become the first British-trained winner since Pilsudski in 1997 – by a nose. Even then, there was a stewards' inquiry before it was confirmed that Dettori had landed his third success following Singspiel (1996) and Falbrav (2002). "My gut feeling was that I had won, but the JRA is very professional and usually puts the numbers up within seconds," said the rider. "To my disbelief, it took about 20 minutes; they made me suffer and sweat. It's like a dream to be able to win the Japan Cup for the third time. It was a close win but a win is a win. Japan, arigato [thank you]!"

Dettori appeared more emotional than usual after winning such an important race for his fellow countryman Cumani, to whom he was apprenticed at the very start of his brilliant riding career. "I cannot believe it," said the irrepressible rider. "It really is unbelievable. I spent eight years with Mr Cumani and it was the best time of my life. If I am stood here talking to you, then he is mainly responsible for it. He taught me, moulded me, everything I do now is mainly down to him, so to win this great race like this in this fashion means a lot."

Dettori's affection for his old boss was obviously fully reciprocated, though Cumani could not resist a joke at the former's expense. "Obviously I hate the little bastard!" he said. "When he came to England he was basically a pest and he still is a pest. But he is probably the best rider we've seen in the world for a very, very long time.

"I have known him since he was a little kid, and his father was jockey for my father. In fact, I probably knew him before he was born. It's great to have a horse win the Japan Cup, especially with Frankie riding him. Our association goes back a long, long time – we have won many Group 1s together and hopefully this won't be the last."

The pair's mutual affection was obvious at the post-race press conference when the subject of race tactics was brought up. Cumani claimed to have allowed his rider a free hand. "I left the strategy to Frankie," he said.

Dettori grabbed the microphone. "That's a lie," he said. "We were drawn 14 and Luca said, 'You must get over to the rail'. I said, 'Who do you think I am, Houdini?' But he is very, very slow at the gates – and as it was a very quick pace at the start, I was able to get across."

Alkaased's owner Mike Charlton, who had bought the horse as a prospective handicapper, was understandably delighted. Then again, who wouldn't be, after claiming a first prize of around £1.25 million? "Not a bad day out, is it?" he joked.

The Monaco-based businessman, who had just seven horses in training at the time of the Japan Cup, had shelled out 42,000gns to buy Alkaased at the end of his three-year-old season. Then, the colt could boast just a lowly Ripon maiden-race success from six starts, though admittedly he had shown a degree of promise, and the figure was rather less than the $325,000 that Sheikh Hamdan Al Maktoum had paid for Alkaased as a yearling. But he came with a distinct risk attached, a history of minor ailments that screamed out *caveat emptor*. "We were told he had never scoped clean and would never be given a clean bill of health by the vet," Charlton told me. "I bought him knowing the risk. In fact, if someone had gone to 50,000, they'd have got him."

In winning the race, Alkaased shaved a tenth off the previous track best, his time of 2min 22.1sec bettering a mark set by New Zealand's Horlicks in 1989. It was to be his final outing as he was sold as a stallion to stand at Sheikh Mohammed's Japanese stud, Hokkai Farm.

Charlton couldn't help but admit how lucky he had been over his allegedly risky purchase. "While I thought he might improve as a four-year-old, this is a million-to-one shot," he said. "When I bought him, I thought he might be the type of older horse Luca does so well with – I hoped we might try to win a nice handicap at Royal Ascot."

The formidably gritty Alkaased never did quite manage that. Not that his owner was complaining. Neither was I. Thanks to Alkaased's victory by the snot of a nostril, the Japan Cup was probably the most exciting race I had seen anywhere on the racing road. It was also the last, and a most appropriate place to end.

You can always rely on Frankie Dettori when it comes to the biggest stage.

CONCLUSION

AND so to bed. After more than 100,000 miles, 80 flights, three times around the world and more than £50,000 between the pair of us visiting racecourses in 21 separate countries, the time came to say goodbye to the racing road. Long and winding it may have been but yellow bricks were notable for their absence.

While I was doing little more than guessing in many minor racing nations, I almost fulfilled my pledge to have a bet everywhere I went, with the exception of China, where gambling was prohibited, and the Breeders' Cup Chase, where I couldn't bring myself to patronise the 'legal illegals'. Not out of any moral objection, you understand – perish the thought – just that their prices were so outrageously unrewarding. Any ideas of part-financing an expensive eight-month trip through gambling would have been fanciful indeed as the final stats suggested a tale of financial idiocy, with 38 days' racing producing a gambling deficit well into four figures in pounds sterling.

Although a ratio of 12 winning days to 23 losing days doesn't sound too shabby in itself, my poorest efforts had come in the States, where the stakes were increased. Oh Baltimore, so much to answer for; a Breeders' Cup that wasn't even half-empty, let alone half-full; and as for Del Mar, don't go there. Well, do go there, because it's wonderful, but you get the picture.

I broke even at La Gavea in Rio, by the way.

*

WHAT, then, did I learn in eight months of chasing racehorses around the world? Not to walk down dark streets in Mexico City was one thing, while being careful with the *bhang lassis* in India was another. Next time I might be more wary of mysterious Thai-based owners as well, though nothing untoward happened in his armoured car flanked by those pistol-packing heavies. The rum-based hooch distilled somewhere up the Amazon in Peru is heartily recommended, but I would think twice in the future about enjoying a quick post-racing drink with expatriate trainers somewhere outside Beijing, though perhaps only because of a dominant karaoke fetish.

Soon, though, that was the past and literally another country. After my return in December 2005, it was disturbing how quickly I fell back into the routine of commuting an hour both ways every day to the *Racing Post* office in Canary Wharf. The concept of 'work/life balance' is a buzz phrase much beloved of life coaches, whatever they are. I have never been any good at it, and it did not take long before I allowed myself to become preoccupied with work issues.

While at times it felt as if I had never been away, rehabilitation wasn't straightforward. The dreaded 'R' word – redundancies – had been mentioned, despite the *Racing Post*'s continuing, multi-million-pound success, so it was not a contented ship I rejoined at racing's daily. My promised role as a writer pure and simple did not materialise. It wasn't anyone's fault: the job just wasn't there.

That I was fortunate to still have a well-paid job was beyond question. Rather than simply getting on with it, however, I made the situation more difficult than was strictly necessary, struggling with a confidence crisis that stretched beyond the confines of my working life. Evidently such feelings are far from rare when travellers return from extended trips abroad, and they are not really deserving of much sympathy. Although it is one thing to struggle with the return to normality, few people have the opportunity to escape it in the first place.

As usual, Jane slotted in seamlessly with a new post with the racing authorities, while I descended into the most unappealing sort of navel-gazing self-absorption. Ridiculously, though, having managed to work my passage away for a period of time, it felt that life in Britain was temporary and unreal. And certainly disagreeable.

Yet what cannot be cured must be endured, as some optimistic soul once pointed out, and as the bank account was not exactly overflowing, it was time for a bit of enduring. That's probably why I turned to Satan. Not really. I didn't move into PR. After a time, even without the help of the horned one, matters improved. I started writing this book – even as I consider this section, any interior observation feels much less comfortable than the exteriors – and, more importantly, used the knowledge I had accrued to develop a new concept for the *Racing Post* and its coverage of worldwide racing, eventually taking on the role of international editor.

This was less glamorous than it sounded, being entirely office-based once more, but it suited me. While I attended the Dubai World Cup, the Kentucky Derby, the Jockey Club Gold Cup, the Arc and the Breeders' Cup in 2006, working at three of them, I paid my own way apart from three nights in a Louisville motel. In fact, the bulk of any disposable income went on such trips, but that was my own choice – no-one was forcing me to go. I was being paid to write about horse racing, and international horse racing at that. It could have been worse, as anybody forced to work for a pittance doing something they don't enjoy can probably testify. I have been slightly more fortunate.

By the end of 2006, both US and Australian racing were being shown regularly in daily broadcasts in Britain, and every edition of the *Racing Post* carried a page of international racing at the minimum, and often more. Ignore the Little Englanders who have failed to recognise the increasingly global nature of horse racing. Top horses now travel regularly between continents, let alone between nations. They have to do so if their owners and trainers want them to compete in the most lucrative races, which explains why horses from the United States, the most insular major racing country in the world, travel to Dubai and Japan.

While money isn't everything, prestige usually follows when it comes to horse racing. Like it or not, all but the very top races at home are in danger of being left behind by the more cosmopolitan, more richly endowed contests abroad. To use a footballing analogy, in status terms they are the FA Cup compared to the Champions League; worth winning, but no longer the primary objective. A *de facto* grand-prix series of what are, in effect, 'Super Group 1s' already exists, rather like those mountain climbs in the Tour de France that are so steep they are designated as *hors categorie* (without category), above and beyond the usual grading system employed. If all Group and Grade 1s are equal, some are more equal than others.

Whether the much-trumpeted British virtues of tradition and variety can sustain the domestic industry's standing in the face of this global tide remains to be seen. In 2006, the Epsom Derby was the only British race in the world's top 20 in prize-money terms. Only one more Flat race, Ascot's

King George, and the Grand National joined the premier Classic in the top 100. It is worrying. International racing, if not the present, is certainly the future. Britain could be left in the past.

On a personal level, people often ask me on a regular basis if the trip got something out of my system, as if it were an itch that needed scratching. I don't think so. While I am pretty sure the opportunity to embark on a similar journey will never come again, that doesn't mean I wouldn't like to do it. Birdsville and Emerald Downs; Deep Impact and Lost In The Fog; Jerry Bailey and Jorge Ricardo: I will never forget encountering any of them. Nor, for that matter, Chichen Itza and Machu Picchu, or magical Kyoto and the pink city of Jaipur, the blue city of Jodhpur and the golden city of Jaisalmer. As mentioned in the previous chapter, it wasn't *all* racing.

I don't know if I will ever set out on the racing road again, though I suspect the odd flying visit will always be somewhere on the agenda. Once you step out of your everyday environment, it can be hard to sit still, even when circumstances dictate that you must.

This book started with a quotation, so let's end it with another, courtesy of Byron's great roister-doisterer Don Juan, constantly on the move across thousands of stanzas. "The great end of travel," suggested the poet, "is driving."

I couldn't have put it better myself – and, as far as I know, he never went to the races. He never knew what he was missing.

APPENDICES

i) INTERNATIONAL RACING AND BREEDING WORLDWIDE 2005

COUNTRY	RACES	PURSES	BETTING HANDLE	MARES	REG. FOALS	STARTS	STARTERS
Australia	19,968	280.08	8,564.58	27,882	17,178	196,683	31,037
Austria	150	1.52	***	65	37	1,271	370
Bahrain	152	0.61	†	102	51	1,439	287
Belgium	198	0.87	39.89	94	47	1,856	425
Brazil	5,105	13.94	137.19	4,267	3,034	35,062	7,017
Canada	5,238	113.4	568.05	3,664	2,580*	41,596	7,750
Chile	6,270	22.56	214.18	2,451	1,761	68,030	4,169
Colombia	656	0.64	3.75	239	125	4,787	417
Croatia	13	0.02	***	65	17	64	44
Cyprus	1,020	11.73	114.5	799	429	9,808	1,418
Denmark	300	2.37	***	203	140	4,108	595
France	6,687	244.68	9,689.36	8,787	5,252	70,568	13,625
Germany	1,907	25.08	222.22	2,210	1,185	17,630	3,260
Great Britain	8,588	174.45	18,397.48	11,947	6,003	94,659	18,768
Greece	1,212	20.49	380.66	476	309	10,515	1,345
Hong Kong	708	87.21	7,727.55	0	0	9,018	1,151
Hungary	317	0.8	6.29	980	217	2,864	427
India	2,981	13.72	250.43	2,518	1,429	27,957	4,141
Ireland	2,241	60.63	3,383.52	18,817	11,748	31,410	7,774
Israel	***	***	***	94	0	***	***
Italy	5,897	108.36	3,257.37	2,973	2,184	48,948	7,529
Japan	18,213	953.51	27,701.71	10,623	7,930	196,268	26,420
Lebanon	359	***	***	0	0	2,662	390
Macau	960	32.15	507.73	0	0	10,890	950
Madagascar	105	0.04	3.41	5	2	657	82
Malaysia/ Singapore	1,346	32	1,214.05	68	38	15,292	2,025
Mauritius	240	2.55	85.63	0	0	1,986	322
Mexico	***	9.22	20.98	599	421	10,989	1,353
Morocco	455	2.41	234.01	401	99	5,444	730
Netherlands	115	0.37	38.99	40	28	864	209
New Zealand	2,807	***	***	8,871	4,600	31,363	5,975
Norway	264	3.64	410.41	79	50	2,423	548
Peru	***	3.67	20.43	710	386	***	1,526
Poland	351	0.72	4.24	902	462	2,318	479
Qatar	210	4.06	†	40	12	1,793	303
Saudi Arabia	422	5.91	†	1,295	747	5,541	1,294
Slovakia	161	0.62	0.11	223	121	1,470	508
South Africa	4,113	40.14	685.25	3,521	2,974	43,848	6,876
South Korea	1,238	78.9	4,573.54	1,612	1,094	13,186	2,437

Spain	437	4.11	***	340	232	3,533	807
Sweden	645	7.67	1,375.10	421	299	6,294	1,373
Switzerland	230	2.17	83.14	111	37	2,004	421
Tunisia	360	2.07	***	133	64	3,500	600
Turkey	3,165	89.74	968.24	3,166	995	35,282	4,073
United Arab Emirates	288	35.77	†	63	36	3,600	1,038
United States	52,257	1,085.01	14,561.23	58,996	34,070*	428,048	66,903
Uruguay	1,035	4.38	12.87	2,855	1,686	9,378	1,635
Venezuela	2,835	23.75	776.23	1,936	1,132	25,587	3,284
Total	**169,487**	**3,633.89**	**106,366.61**	**197,143**	**118,024**	**1,596,093**	**256,872**

Notes: In some cases, Betting Handle includes harness racing.
Wagering statistics include bookmaking in countries where such activities are legal.
US $ Conversions of the Euro at 1 Euro = US $1.1806
* Estimated figures
*** Not reported
† No wagering
~ Dollars in millions
Source: International Statistical Survey of Horse Racing and 2005 Statistics, compiled by the International Federation of Horseracing Authorities and presented at the 40th International Conference of Racing Authorities, Paris, France, October 2, 2006.
Reproduced by permission of the IFHA and Jockey Club

ii) JUMP RACING WORLDWIDE 2005

COUNTRY	JUMP RACES	HORSES	STARTS	AVERAGE HORSE PER RACE	AVERAGE STARTS PER HORSE
Australia	140	446	1,234	8.8	2.8
Austria	2	12	14	7.0	1.2
Belgium	4	29	29	7.3	1.0
France	2,155	3,654	21,325	9.9	5.8
Germany	67	89	466	7.0	5.2
Great Britain	3,287	7,794	34,569	10.5	4.4
Hungary	5	7	46	9.2	6.6
Ireland	1,373	4,727	20,133	14.7	4.3
Italy	292	644	2,327	8.0	3.6
Japan	133	211	1,701	12.8	8.1
New Zealand	136	364	1,227	9.0	3.4
Norway	8	9	48	6.0	5.3
Poland	8	16	73	9.1	4.6
Slovakia	22	85	170	7.7	2.0
Sweden	18	64	130	7.2	2.0
Switzerland	54	62	347	6.4	5.6
United States	196	496	1,527	7.8	3.1

Reproduced by permission of IFHA

iii) THE WORLD'S 100 RICHEST RACES 2006

	RACE	HOST NATION	TRACK	WINNER	TRAINER (COUNTRY TRAINED)	JOCKEY	2005 PRIZE (£)	2006 PRIZE (£)
1	Dubai World Cup	UAE	Nad Al Sheba	Electrocutionist	S Bin Suroor (UAE)	L Dettori	3,488,372	3,750,000
2=	Dubai Duty Free	UAE	Nad Al Sheba	David Junior	B Meehan (GB)	J Spencer	1,041,667	2,906,977
2=	Dubai Sheema Classic	UAE	Nad Al Sheba	Heart's Cry	K Hashiguchi (Jap)	C-P Lemaire	1,041,667	2,906,977
4	Breeders' Cup Classic	US	Churchill Downs	Invasor	K McLaughlin (US)	F Jara	2,235,187	2,662,791
5	Japan Cup	Jap	Tokyo	Deep Impact	Y Ikee (Jap)	Y Take	2,447,618	2,365,691
6	Melbourne Cup	Aus	Flemington	Delta Blues	K Sumii (Jap)	Y Iwata	2,081,633	2,179,487
7	Arima Kinen	Jap	Nakayama	Deep Impact	Y Ikee (Jap)	Y Take	1,762,822	1,709,125
8	Tokyo Yushun (Derby)	Jap	Tokyo	Meisho Samson	T Setoguchi (Jap)	M Ishibashi	1,742,429	1,674,382
9	Breeders' Cup Turf	US	Churchill Downs	Red Rocks	B Meehan (GB)	L Dettori	1,088,937	1,597,674
10	Hong Kong Cup	HK	Sha Tin	Pride	A de Royer-Dupré (Fr)	C-P Lemaire	1,206,434	1,502,630
11	Prix de l'Arc de Triomphe	Fr	Longchamp	Rail Link	A Fabre (Fr)	S Pasquier	1,276,596	1,379,310
12	Cox Plate	Aus	Moonee Valley	Fields Of Omagh	D Hayes (Aus)	C Williams	1,234,694	1,341,880
13	Kikuka Sho (St Leger)	Jap	Kyoto	Song Of Wind	H Asami (Jap)	K Take	1,377,573	1,331,244
14	Kentucky Derby	US	Churchill Downs	Barbaro	M Matz (US)	E Prado	1,249,792	1,286,744
15	Derby	GB	Epsom	Sir Percy	M Tregoning (GB)	M Dwyer	1,250,000	1,284,672
16	Golden Slipper	Aus	Rosehill	Miss Finland	D Hayes (Aus)	C Williams	1,224,490	1,282,051
17=	Tenno Sho (Spring)	Jap	Kyoto	Deep Impact	Y Ikee (Jap)	Y Take	1,306,156	1,266,051
17=	Tenno Sho (Autumn)	Jap	Tokyo	Daiwa Major	H Uehara (Jap)	K Ando	1,304,631	1,266,051
19	Takarazuka Kinen	Jap	Kyoto	Deep Impact	Y Ikee (Jap)	Y Take	1,300,056	1,258,945
20	Japan Cup Dirt	Jap	Tokyo	Alondite	S Ishizaka (Jap)	H Goto	1,286,535	1,247,298
21	Breeders' Cup Distaff	US	Churchill Downs	Round Pond	M Matz (US)	E Prado	955,208	1,203,581
22	Hong Kong Mile	HK	Sha Tin	The Duke	C Fownes (HK)	O Doleuze	938,338	1,202,104
23	Breeders' Cup Filly & Mare Turf	US	Churchill Downs	Ouija Board	E Dunlop (GB)	L Dettori	506,260	1,171,628
24=	Dubai Golden Shaheen	UAE	Nad Al Sheba	Proud Tower Too	S Gonzalez (US)	D Cohen	1,041,667	1,162,791
24=	UAE Derby	UAE	Nad Al Sheba	Discreet Cat	S Bin Suroor (UAE)	L Dettori	1,041,667	1,162,791

	Race	Country	Course	Horse	Trainer	Jockey		
26	Breeders' Cup Mile	US	Churchill Downs	Miesque's Approval	M Wolfson (US)	E Castro	967,148	1,155,651
27	Satsuki Sho (2,000 Guineas)	Jap	Nakayama	Meisho Samson	T Setoguchi (Jap)	M Ishibashi	1,193,006	1,147,658
28	Breeders' Cup Sprint	US	Churchill Downs	Thor's Echo	D O'Neill (US)	C Nakatani	506,260	1,134,349
29	Yushun Himba (Oaks)	Jap	Tokyo	Kawakami Princess	K Nishiura (Jap)	M Honda	1,155,431	1,116,172
30	Caulfield Cup	Aus	Caulfield	Tawqeet	D Hayes (Aus)	D Dunn	1,026,531	1,074,786
31=	Breeders' Cup Juvenile	US	Churchill Downs	Street Sense	C Nafzger (US)	C Borel	759,391	1,065,116
31=	Breeders' Cup Juvenile Fillies	US	Churchill Downs	Dreaming Of Anna	W Catalano (US)	R Douglas	506,260	1,065,116
33	Singapore Airlines International Cup	Sin	Kranji	Cosmo Bulk	K Tabe (Jap)	F Igarashi	905,752	1,052,631
34=	Hong Kong Derby	HK	Sha Tin	Viva Pataca	J Moore (HK)	C Soumillon	938,338	1,051,841
34=	Hong Kong Vase	HK	Sha Tin	Collier Hill	A Swinbank (GB)	D McKeown	938,338	1,051,841
34=	Queen Elizabeth II Cup	HK	Sha Tin	Iridescence	M de Kock (SA)	W Marwing	938,338	1,051,841
37	Goffs Million	Ire	The Curragh	Miss Beatrix	K Prendergast (Ire)	D P McDonogh	—	1,041,379
38	Canadian International	Can	Woodbine	Collier Hill	A Swinbank (GB)	D McKeown	877,543	1,034,522
39=	Irish Derby	Ire	The Curragh	Dylan Thomas	A O'Brien (Ire)	K Fallon	921,986	1,034,483
39=	Prix du Jockey-Club	Fr	Chantilly	Darsi	A de Royer-Dupré (Fr)	C Soumillon	1,086,830	1,034,483
41	Oka Sho (1,000 Guineas)	Jap	Hanshin	Kiss To Heaven	H Toda (Jap)	K Ando	1,050,831	1,022,307
42	Mile Championship	Jap	Kyoto	Daiwa Major	H Uehara (Jap)	K Ando	940,273	965,800
43	Yasuda Kinen	Jap	Tokyo	Bullish Luck	A Cruz (HK)	B Prebble	939,968	964,319
44	The BMW (Tancred Stakes)	Aus	Rosehill	Eremein	A Denham (Aus)	G Boss	816,326	961,538
45	Takamatsunomiya Kinen	Jap	Chukyo	Orewa Matteruze	H Otonashi (Jap)	Y Shibata	939,358	917,436
46	Sprinters' Stakes	Jap	Nakayama	Takeover Target	J Janiak (Aus)	J Ford	936,309	915,363
47	February Stakes	Jap	Tokyo	Kane Hekili	K Sumii (Jap)	Y Take	936,919	909,638
48	Hong Kong Sprint	HK	Sha Tin	Absolute Champion	D Hall (HK)	B Prebble	670,241	901,578
49	NHK Mile	Jap	Tokyo	Logic	K Hashiguchi (Jap)	Y Take	919,534	892,760
50	Victoria Mile	Jap	Tokyo	Dance In The Mood	K Fujisawa (Jap)	H Kitamura	—	875,487
51	Queen Elizabeth II Commemorative Cup	Jap	Kyoto	Fusaichi Pandora	T Shirai (Jap)	Y Fukunaga	994,154	873,711

52	Shuka Sho	Jap	Kyoto	Kawakami Princess	K Nishiura (Jap)	M Honda	886,901	860,189
53=	AJC Australian Derby	Aus	Randwick	Headturner	J Hawkes (Aus)	D Beadman	785,714	854,701
53=	Doncaster Handicap	Aus	Randwick	Racing To Win	J O'Shea (Aus)	G Boss	775,510	854,701
55	JBC Classic	Jap	Kawasaki	Time Paradox	H Matsuda (Jap)	Y Iwata	864,129	838,968
56	Nakayama Daishogai	Jap	Nakayama (j)	Maruka Rascal	T Setoguchi (Jap)	M Nishitani	776,242	754,281
57	Nakayama Grand Jump	Jap	Nakayama (j)	Karasi	E Musgrove (Aus)	B Scott	776,191	753,837
58	King George VI & Queen Elizabeth Stakes	GB	Ascot	Hurricane Run	A Fabre (Fr)	C Soumillon	703,500	750,000
59	Grand National	GB	Aintree (j)	Numbersixvalverde	M Brassil (Ire)	N Madden	700,000	700,000
60	Irish Champion Stakes	Ire	Leopardstown	Dylan Thomas	A O'Brien (Ire)	K Fallon	709,220	689,655
61	Stayers' Stakes	Jap	Nakayama	Eye Popper	I Shimizu (Jap)	O Peslier	626,137	674,727
62=	JBC Mile	Jap	Kawasaki	Blue Concorde	T Hattori (Jap)	H Miyuki	691,302	671,174
62=	Tokyo Daishoten	Jap	Ohi	Blue Concorde	T Hattori (Jap)	H Miyuki	691,302	671,174
64	Hanshin Cup	Jap	Hanshin	Fusaichi Richard	K Matsuda (Jap)	Y Fukunaga	—	670,680
65	Sapporo Kinen	Jap	Sapporo	Admire Moon	H Matsuda (Jap)	Y Take	633,965	669,595
66	Derby Italiano	It	Capannelle	Gentlewave	A Fabre (Fr)	M Monterisi	651,064	652,468
67	Victoria Derby	Aus	Flemington	Efficient	G Rogerson (NZ)	M Rodd	616,326	645,299
68	Mainichi Okan	Jap	Tokyo	Daiwa Major	H Uehara (Jap)	K Ando	635,592	616,592
69	Kyoto Daishoten	Jap	Kyoto	Sweep Tosho	A Tsurodome (Jap)	K Ikezoe	633,152	614,124
70	Hanshin Daishoten	Jap	Hanshin	Deep Impact	Y Ikee (Jap)	Y Take	632,034	613,039
71	Sankei Sho All Comers	Jap	Nakayama	Balance Of Game	Y Munakata (Jap)	K Tanaka	625,324	609,781
72	Nikkei Sho	Jap	Nakayama	Lincoln	H Otonashi (Jap)	N Yokoyama	627,052	608,794
73	Nakayama Kinen	Jap	Nakayama	Balance Of Game	Y Munakata (Jap)	K Tanaka	627,764	608,696
74	Sankei Osaka Hai	Jap	Hanshin	Company	H Otonashi (Jap)	Y Fukunaga	625,121	608,202
75	Kinko Sho	Jap	Chukyo	Kongo Rikishio	K Yamauchi (Jap)	Y Iwata	625,527	607,807
76	Kyoto Kinen	Jap	Kyoto	Six Sense	H Nagahama (Jap)	Y Take	626,646	607,412
77=	Champions Mile	HK	Sha Tin	Bullish Luck	A Cruz (HK)	B Prebble	536,193	601,052
77=	Hong Kong Champions & Chater Cup	HK	Sha Tin	Viva Pataca	J Moore (HK)	M Kinane	536,193	601,052

	Race		Racecourse	Horse	Trainer	Jockey		
77=	Hong Kong Classic Mile	HK	Sha Tin	Sunny Sing	J Moore (HK)	E Saint-Martin	536,193	601,052
77=	Hong Kong Gold Cup	HK	Sha Tin	Super Kid	J Moore (HK)	S Dye	536,193	601,052
77=	Stewards' Cup	HK	Sha Tin	Russian Pearl	A Cruz (HK)	G Mosse	536,193	601,052
82	Haskell Invitational	US	Monmouth Park	Bluegrass Cat	T Pletcher (US)	J Velazquez	528,646	598,837
83	Teio Sho	Jap	Ohi	Adjudi Mitsuo	M Kawashima (Jap)	H Uchida	604,890	587,277
84	Delaware Handicap	US	Delaware Park	Fleet Indian	T Pletcher (US)	J Santos	521,771	582,093
85=	Arkansas Derby	US	Oaklawn Park	Lawyer Ron	R Holthus (US)	J McKee	520,833	581,395
85=	Arlington Million	US	Arlington Park	The Tin Man	R Mandella (US)	V Espinoza	520,833	581,395
85=	Belmont Stakes	US	Belmont Park	Jazil	K McLaughlin (US)	F Jara	520,833	581,395
85=	Colonial Turf Cup	US	Colonial Downs	Showing Up	B Tagg (US)	C Velasquez	260,417	581,395
85=	Delta Jackpot	US	Delta Downs	Birdbirdistheword	K McPeek (US)	R Albarado	520,833	581,395
85=	Florida Derby	US	Gulfstream Park	Barbaro	M Matz (US)	E Prado	520,833	581,395
85=	Godolphin Mile	UAE	Nad Al Sheba	Utopia	K Hashiguchi (Jap)	Y Take	520,833	581,395
85=	Pacific Classic	US	Del Mar	Lava Man	D O'Neill (US)	C Nakatani	520,833	581,395
85=	Preakness Stakes	US	Pimlico	Bernardini	T Albertrani (US)	J Castellano	520,833	581,395
85=	Travers Stakes	US	Saratoga	Bernardini	T Albertrani (US)	J Castellano	520,833	581,395
85=	Santa Anita Handicap	US	Santa Anita	Lava Man	D O'Neill (US)	C Nakatani	520,833	581,395
85=	Sunshine Millions Classic	US	Santa Anita	Lava Man	D O'Neill (US)	C Nakatani	520,833	581,395
85=	Virginia Derby	US	Colonial Downs	Go Between	W Mott (US)	G Gomez	390,625	581,395
98	Hanshin Juvenile Fillies	Jap	Hanshin	Vodka	K Sumii (Jap)	H Shii	588,929	571,978
99	Swan Stakes	Jap	Kyoto	Precise Machine	K Hagiwara (Jap)	M Matsuoka	588,726	571,781
100	Centaur Stakes	Jap	Chukyo	She Is Tosho	A Tsurodome (Jap)	K Ikezoe	395,822	571,682

(j) = jump races

Figures are total prize-money, converted to sterling at 2006 IFHA exchange rate; some differences between 2005 and 2006 may be explained purely by currency fluctuations. Prize-money figures compiled by James Fry of the International Racing Bureau and reproduced by permission.

The concept of the 'nationality' of a winner is less straightforward than might be imagined. While both breeders and owners have claims, most racing fans would recognise a horse's nationality most readily as the nation in which it is trained, hence that being identified in these tables.

For southern hemisphere nations, these results straddle two different seasons owing to the parameters of the racing calendar.

iv) MORE BIG-RACE WINNERS 2006

HOST NATION	RACE	TRACK	WINNER	TRAINER (COUNTRY TRAINED)	JOCKEY	2006 PRIZE (£)
Argentina	Derby Nacional (dirt)	Palermo	Eu Tambem	V Fornasaro (Brz)	J Moreira	99,590
Argentina	Gran Premio Jockey Club (turf Derby)	San Isidro	Gran Estreno	D Etchechoury (Arg)	R Blanco	24,450
Argentina	Gran Premio Carlos Pellegrini	San Isidro	Storm Mayor	R Desvard (Arg)	J C Mendez	105,400
Australia	Blue Diamond Stakes	Caulfield	Nadeem	D Hayes (Aus)	D Dunn	427,350
Australia	Newmarket Handicap	Flemington	Takeover Target	J Janiak (Aus)	J Ford	427,350
Australia	Queen Elizabeth Stakes	Randwick	Eremein	A Denham (Aus)	G Boss	341,880
Australia	Stradbroke Handicap	Eagle Farm	La Montagna	B Baldwin (Aus)	C Newitt	427,350
Brazil	Grande Premio Brazil	La Gavea	Dona da Raia	A Cintra (Brz)	M Goncalves	137,280
Brazil	Grande Premio Cruzeiro do Sul (Rio Derby)	La Gavea	Heroi do Bafra	V Nahid (Brz)	J Ricardo	21,750
Brazil	Grande Premio Sao Paulo	Cidade Jardim	Dona da Raia	A Cintra (Brz)	M Goncalves	69,290
Brazil	Grande Premio ABCPCC Matias Machline (Breeders' Cup)	Cidade Jardim	Top Hat	J Macedo (Brz)	N Cunha	87,020
Brazil	Derby Paulista	Cidade Jardim	Quick Road	J Macedo (Brz)	N Cunha	20,570
Canada	Queen's Plate	Woodbine	Edenwold	J Carroll (Can)	E Ramsammy	519,098
Canada	Woodbine Mile	Woodbine	Becrux	N Drysdale (US)	P Valenzuela	501,600
Canada	EP Taylor Stakes	Woodbine	Arravale	M Benson (US)	J Valdivia	517,778
Chile	Clasico El Ensayo (turf Derby)	Club Hipico (Santiago)	Eres Magica	P Baeza (Ch)	F Diaz	85,220
Chile	Clasico St Leger	Hipodromo Chile (Santiago)	Don Dominguin	C Saide (Ch)	A Vasquez	81,940
Chile	El Derby (dirt)	Valparaiso	Porfido	J I Mayer (Ch)	L Torres	61,030
Chile	Gran Premio Hipodromo Chile	Hipodromo Chile (Santiago)	Feliz de la Vida	C Conejeros (Ch)	A Rivera	51,070
France	Grand Steeple-Chase de Paris	Auteuil (j)	Princesse d'Anjou	F Cottin (Fr)	P A Carberry	494,552

Country	Race	Racecourse	Horse	Trainer	Jockey	Prize money
France	Prix de Diane	Chantilly	Confidential Lady	Sir M Prescott (GB)	S Sanders	551,724
France	Grand Prix de Paris	Longchamp	Rail Link	A Fabre (Fr)	C Soumillon	344,828
France	Prix Jacques le Marois	Deauville	Librettist	S Bin Suroor (GB)	L Dettori	413,793
Germany	Deutsches Derby	Hamburg	Schiaparelli	P Schiergen (Ger)	A Starke	275,862
Germany	Grosser Preis von Baden	Baden-Baden	Prince Fiori	S Smrczek (Ger)	F Minarik	517,241
Great Britain	Champion Hurdle (j)	Cheltenham (j)	Brave Inca	C Murphy (Ire)	A McCoy	350,057
Great Britain	Cheltenham Gold Cup (j)	Cheltenham (j)	War Of Attrition	M Morris (Ire)	C O'Dwyer	393,920
Great Britain	Oaks	Epsom	Alexandrova	A O'Brien (Ire)	K Fallon	434,687
Great Britain	Juddmonte International	York	Notnowcato	Sir M Stoute (GB)	R Moore	500,000
India	Indian Derby	Mumbai	Velvet Rope	I Sait (Ind)	P Kamlesh	98,950
Ireland	Irish Oaks	The Curragh	Alexandrova	A O'Brien (Ire)	K Fallon	275,860
Italy	Oaks d'Italia	San Siro	Dionisia	R Menichetti (It)	C Soumillon	406,620
Italy	Gran Premio del Jockey Club Italiano	San Siro	Laverock	C Laffon-Parias (Fr)	D Bonilla	272,827
New Zealand	NZ Derby	Ellerslie	Wahid	A Sharrock (NZ)	L Innes	228,571
New Zealand	Kelt Capital Stakes	Hastings	Legs	K Gray (NZ)	L Cropp	357,142
Peru	Clasico Derby Nacional	Monterrico	Muller	A Olivares (Per)	V Fernandez	29,711
Puerto Rico	Clasico del Caribe	El Comandante	Ay Papa	J Carillo (Pan)	F Jara	174,420
South Africa	J & B Met	Kenilworth	Zebra Crossing	N Bruss (SA)	J Lloyd	174,419
South Africa	SA Derby	Turffontein	Elusive Fort	G Woodruff (SA)	M Khan	91,900
South Africa	Durban July	Greyville	Eyeofthetiger	D Kannemayer (SA)	G Schlechter	161,760
USA	Kentucky Oaks	Churchill Downs	Lemons Forever	D Stewart (US)	M Guidry	439,477
USA	Whitney Handicap	Saratoga	Invasor	K McLaughlin (US)	F Jara	436,046
USA	Jockey Club Gold Cup	Belmont Park	Bernardini	T Albertrani (US)	J Castellano	412,244
USA	Breeders' Cup Grand National	Far Hills (j)	McDynamo	S Hendriks (US)	J Petty	86,298
Uruguay*	Gran Premio Latinoamericano	Maronas	Latency	J Udaondo (Arg)	J C Mendez	87,200
Uruguay	Gran Premio Jose Pedro Ramirez	Maronas	Jampro	R Cardoso (Uru)	W Maciel	48,000

*Race is run in various South American nations

Compiled by author; some prize-money figures are approximate. NB. For southern hemisphere nations, these results straddle two different seasons owing to the parameters of the racing calendar.

v) WEBSITES (and emails)

INTERNATIONAL RACING AUTHORITIES

General: International Federation of Horseracing Authorities –
www.horseracingintfed.com

Asian Racing Conference – www.asianracing.org

Argentina: Jockey Club Argentino – www.jockeyclub.com.ar

Australia: Australian Racing Board – www.australian-racing.net.au

Australian Jockey Club (Sydney) – www.ajc.org.au

Victoria Racing Club (Melbourne) – www.vrc.net.au

Austria: Direktorium für Galopprennsport & Vollblutzucht in Österreich –
www.magnaracino.at

Bahrain: Equestrian and Horse Racing Club –
www.horseracingbahrain.com

Barbados: Barbados Turf Club – www.barbadosturfclub.com

Belgium: Jockey Club Royal de Belgique –
www.galop.info/newslist/jockeyclub/link1.htm

Brazil: Jockey Club Brasileiro – www.jcb.com.br

Jockey Club de Sao Paulo – www.jockeysp.com.br

Canada: Jockey Club of Canada – www.jockeyclubcanada.com

Chile: Club Hipico de Santiago – www.clubhipico.cl

China: China Stud Book – chinastudbook@vip.sina.com

Croatia: Jockey Club of Croatia – jockey-klub@email.t-com.hr

Czech Republic: Jockey Club Ceske Republiky – www.dostihy.cz

Denmark: Danish Jockey Club – www.danskgalop.dk

Finland: Suomen Hippos – www.hippos.fi

France: France Galop – www.france-galop.com

Germany: Direktorium für Vollblutzucht und Rennen –
www.galopp-sport.de

Great Britain: British Horseracing Board – www.britishhorseracing.com

Jockey Club – www.thejockeyclub.co.uk

Greece: Jockey Club de Grece – jockey@otenet.gr

Hong Kong: Hong Kong Jockey Club – www.hkjc.com

Hungary: Nemzeti Loverseny KFT – www.kincsempark.com

India: Bangalore Turf Club – www.bangaloreraces.com

   Hyderabad Race Club – www.hydraces.com

   Royal Calcutta Turf Club – www.rctconline.com

   Royal Western India Turf Club – www.rwitc.com

Ireland: Horse Racing Ireland – www.horseracingireland.ie

   Turf Club – www.turfclub.ie

Israel: Israel National Association of Horse Racing – www.inahr.org

Italy: UNIRE – www.unire.it

Jamaica: Jamaican Racing Commission – jaracing@cwjamaica.com

Japan: Japan Racing Association – www.jra.go.jp

   National Association of Racing – www.keiba.go.jp

   Japan Association for International Racing – www.japanracing.jp

Kazakhstan: Jockey Club of Kazakhstan – www.ippodrom.kz

Kenya: Jockey Club of Kenya – mbinks@swiftkenya.com

Lebanon: SPARCA – www.beiruthorseracing.com

Macau: Macau Jockey Club – www.mjc.mo

Malaysia: Penang Turf Club – www.penangturfclub.com

Mauritius: Mauritius Turf Club – www.mauritiusturfclub.com

Mexico: Jockey Club of Mexico – jockeyclubmex@aol.com

Morocco: Société Royale d'Encouragement du Cheval – sorec@iam.net.ma

Netherlands: NDR – www.ndr.nl

New Zealand: New Zealand Thoroughbred Racing Inc. –

   www.nzracing.co.nz

Norway: Norsk Jockeyklub – www.ovrevoll.no

Oman: Royal Horse Racing Club – www.rca.gov.om

Pakistan: Jockey Club of Pakistan – jcpakistan@yahoo.com

Peru: Jockey Club del Peru – www.jcp.org.pe

Philippines: Philippines Racing Commission – www.philracom.gov.ph

Poland: Polski Klub Wyscigow Konnych – www.pkwk.pl

Qatar: Racing and Equestrian Club – www.qrec.net

Russia: Russian Jockey Club – www.jockey-club.ru

Saudi Arabia: Equestrian Club of Riyadh – www.frusiya.com

Singapore: Singapore Turf Club – www.turfclub.com.sg

Slovakia: Turf Diretorium fur die Slowakei – www.zavodisko.sk

Slovenia: Slovenian Turf Club – www.sloturf.com

South Africa: National Horseracing Authority of Southern Africa –
www.jockeyclubsa.co.za

South Korea: Korea Racing Association – www.kra.co.kr

Spain: SFCCE – www.turf-spain.com

Sweden: Swedish Jockey Club – www.galoppsport.se

Switzerland: Galopp Schweiz – www.galopp.ch

Thailand: Royal Bangkok Sports Club – sportsclub@rsbc.org

Trinidad & Tobago: T&T Racing Authority – www.ttra.net

Turkey: Jockey Club of Turkey – www.tjk.org

United Arab Emirates: Emirates Racing Authority –
www.emiratesracing.com
Dubai World Cup – www.dubaiworldcup.com

USA: National Thoroughbred Racing Association – www.ntra.com
Jockey Club – www.jockeyclub.com
National Steeplechase Association – www.nationalsteeplechase.com
New York Racing Association – www.nyra.com
Equibase – www.equibase.com

Uruguay: Hipica Rioplatense Uruguay SA – www.maronas.com.uy

Venezuela: SUNAHIP – hectordavilam@yahoo.com

RACETRACKS VISITED (where available)

Argentina: Palermo – www.palermo.com.ar

Australia: Birdsville – www.birdsvilleraces.com
Caulfield – www.melbourneracingclub.net.au
Townsville (Cluden Park) – www.cludenpark.com.au

Brazil: La Gavea – www.jcb.com.br

Canada: Woodbine – www.woodbineentertainment.com

Dominican Republic: Hipodromo V Centenario –
www.hipodromovcentenario.com.do

India: Hyderabad – www.hydraces.com
Kolkata (Royal Calcutta Turf Club) – www.rctconline.com

Japan: Nakayama – www.jair.jrao.ne.jp/courses/jra/jra002.html
Tokyo – www.tokyoracecourse.com

Mexico: Hipodromo de las Americas – www.hipodromo.com.mx

New Zealand: Riccarton – www.riccartonpark.co.nz

Peru: Monterrico – www.jcp.org.pe

Philippines: San Lazaro (Manila Jockey Club) – www.manilajockey.com

Puerto Rico: Hipodromo Camarero (El Comandante) –
www.elcomandantepr.net

Singapore: Kranji – www.turfclub.com.sg

South Korea: Seoul – www.kra.co.kr

Trinidad: Santa Rosa – www.santarosapark.com

Uruguay: Maronas – www.maronas.com.uy

USA: Belmont Park – www.nyra.com

 Del Mar – www.dmtc.com

 Emerald Downs – www.emeralddowns.com

 Golden Gate Fields – www.goldengatefields.com

 Pimlico – www.pimlico.com

 Saratoga – www.nyra.com

 Breeders' Cup – www.breederscup.com

OTHERS

General: International Racing Bureau – www.irbracing.com

 Directory of the Turf – www.directoryoftheturf.com

 jockeys – www.jockeysroom.com

Argentina: general – www.paginadeturf.com.ar

 general – www.monti.com

 history – www.argentinethoroughbreds.com

Australia: general – www.skychannel.com.au

 general – www.racingpages.com.au

 statistics – www.rsb.net.au

 Hall of Fame – www.racingmuseum.com.au

Canada: general – www.horseracingcanada.com

Caribbean: Clasico del Caribe – www.clasicocaribe.org

India: general – www.indiarace.com

New Zealand: Hall of Fame – www.racinghalloffame.co.nz

USA: *Daily Racing Form* – www.drf.com

The Blood-Horse – www.bloodhorse.com
Thoroughbred Times – www.thoroughbredtimes.com
Kentucky Derby – www.kentuckyderby.com
Hall of Fame – www.racingmuseum.org
general – www.horseracing.about.com
racecourse info – www.trackinfo.com
Venezuela: general – www.meridiano.com.ve/sitehipismo

SOURCES

It is next to impossible to identify the source of every piece of information contained in this book, much of which came from conversations held by the author with racing officials in the various featured racing nations.

Wherever possible I have identified the derivation of quotations from other sources within the text itself, while statistics, as mentioned elsewhere, come mainly from submissions made by member nations to the International Federation of Horseracing Authorities and the Asian Racing Conference. Much information about the history of racing in the various nations also comes from these submissions; the websites of both organisations, as well as the American Jockey Club, are packed with data. These, plus official websites of national governing bodies, are listed in Appendix (v).

Various travel guides and internet sites also proved invaluable for general information, in particular the *Rough Guide* series and *Time Out* city guides. Never leave home without them.

In racing terms, a number of websites other than those operated by the various national authorities were extremely useful. These are also listed in Appendix (v), but chief among them were individual racecourse websites, which often feature brief histories, and the extensive sites of the three main US racing publications, the *Daily Racing Form*, *Blood-Horse* and *Thoroughbred Times*. Articles by Michael Burns, South American correspondent for the last-named, were especially helpful. On trips to the States, the newspaper edition of the *Daily Racing Form* is always invaluable.

Although a short bibliography is included at the end of this section, I must make specific mention of *The Complete Encyclopaedia of Horse Racing*, by Bill Mooney and the late George Ennor. The international section therein provided an excellent base camp.

I cannot finish without reference to the *Racing Post*'s own website, www.racingpost.co.uk, without which it would have been quite a struggle to keep in touch with equine matters at home. The work of Newmarket's International Racing Bureau in the paper over the years was also a fecund source of material.

BOOKS

The Complete Encyclopaedia of Horse Racing, by George Ennor and Bill Mooney

The Blood-Horse: Top 100 Racehorses of the 20th Century

The Blood-Horse: Horse Racing's Top 100 Moments

Against the Odds – Riding for my Life, by Jerry Bailey with Tom Pedulla

Guinness Book of Horse Racing Records, by Tony Morris and John Randall

Horseplayers – Life at the Track, by Ted McClelland

Betting on Myself, by Steven Crist

Picking Winners, by Andrew Beyer

The Home Run Horse, by Glenye Cain

The Best and Worst of Thoroughbred Racing, by Steve Davidowitz

Del Mar: Its Life and Good Times, by William Murray

The Agua Caliente Story, by David Jimenez Beltran

Palca a la Memoria – Hipodromo Nacional de Maronas, edited by Guillermo Giucci

Jockey Club Brasileiro 130 Anos, edited by Ney O.R. Carvalho

Jorge Ricardo: O Lendario Cavaliero das Inumeraveis Vitorias, by Jessie Navajas de Camargo

Sunline, by Fiona McKee

The Track – Australian Racing's Hall of Fame, by Rod Nicholson

Tales of the Turf, by Bill Casey

ACKNOWLEDGEMENTS

AS a project such as this could never have succeeded without the help of a multitude, there is a distinct danger this piece could read like the credits of *Ben Hur*. However, there are a few individuals I must thank especially, headed by Jane Godfrey, not least for putting up with me for eight months in such close proximity. At least she gets the occasional break the rest of the time. Apart from her organisational skills, her efforts as a photographer were fantastic considering she had hardly ever picked up a camera before the trip and had no tuition whatsoever.

A special mention is also needed for *Racing Post* editor Chris Smith, without whose enthusiasm the enterprise could not have happened. If anything, though, his support since my return has been even more valuable. Others at the *Post* whose assistance was invaluable include John Hopkins and John Randall, whom I must thank for their estimable editing and proof-reading talents, plus Jon Winter, John Kettle, Vic Jones and the picture-desk team and Jonathan Taylor, Julian Brown, Adrian Morrish and Tracey Scarlett at publishers Highdown.

I would like specifically to thank the *Post*'s long-serving US correspondent Dan Farley, who has long been a friend rather than just a colleague at the end of a telephone, making life in the States much easier than it has any right to be for a visiting Limey. The team at the Newmarket-based International Racing Bureau may not have had a great deal to do with the practicalities of the trip, but their assistance at all times in international-racing matters cannot go without mention. James Crispe, Robert Carter, Alastair Donald and James Fry, who provided the prize-money rankings in Appendix (iii), are the individuals who most merit a namecheck.

In addition, several members of family and friends gave us shelter and lodging at various intervals, headed by my mother Doris Godfrey and my aunt Sally Tanner. Without their unwavering support, who knows where I would have ended up? I must also thank Richard and Maggie Pullen, Mark Tanner, Bill and Joyce Madigan, Glenys Ward, Vanessa Ramirez, Ross Mayne, Andy and Jane Bain, plus Mark and Gina Schneider.

I was extremely grateful to anyone and everyone who sent a much-needed message of support while I was away – it was a relief to know someone had been reading, or looking at the pictures. In particular, I must thank Mark Blackman for his initial burst of enthusiasm and Steve Dennis for his assistance both then and since, while the encouragement of Brough Scott, Howard Wright, Paul Haigh, James Willoughby, Stuart Baker and Peter Jones was much appreciated. The last-named kindly allowed Jane to leave work early enough for us to make the Nakayama Grand Jump.

A host of racing folk smoothed my path around the world. I have tried to mention as many as I can below; sincere apologies if I have managed to ignore anybody. A couple who went well above and beyond the call of duty were Andrew Harding at the Australian Racing Board and Bertrand Kauffmann at the Jockey Club Brasileiro, while Jim Gluckson at the Breeders' Cup, Shannon Luce at the American Jockey Club and Bridget Bimm at the Jockey Club of Canada had every right to get fed up with my constant inquiries, usually involving some obscure racing statistic. Trainers Nigel Smith and Brian Lawrence ensured an unforgettable stay in Beijing.

Here then, in no particular order, are a few others who deserve a thank-you: Hsu King Hoe, Dato Terry Lee, Takashi Ogawa, Kevin Connolly, Geoffrey Barton, Fausto Gutierrez, Patrick Kerrigan, Betty Baird, Fran La Belle, Mike Gathagan, Joe Clancy, Sean Clancy, Jerry Bailey, Russell Baze, Marco Rivera, Yaminna Morales, David Loregnard, Roy Podmore, Robin Jaisingh, Shammi Kowlessar, Margarita Calderon, Juan Martinez, Mayra Frederico, Paulo Pires do Rio, Jorge Ricardo, Dr Martin Canepa, Juan Jose Garcia Docio, Dr Antonio Turturiello, Jorge Simonetti, Antonio Bullrich, Colin Barraclough, Tim Miles, James Heddo, Dr Veerendra Kaja, Sanjav Reddy, John Siscos, Larry Foley and Rear-Admiral Juan de Leon.

INDEX